Art Director: Leanna Schroeder
Graphics Design Layout: Robbie Destocki: Creative Image Design Group
Publishing House: IMPACT Publications, Inc.

SWIMMING THROUGH LIFE

Terry Schroeder and the
USA Olympic Men's Water Polo Team

Diana Addison Lyle

IMPACT PUBLICATIONS

Impact Publications, LLC
3835-R East Thousand Oaks Blvd. Suite 153
Westlake Village, CA 91362

Printed in the United States of America

First Printing, 2016

ISBN - 13: 978-1535275491
ISBN - 10: 1535275499

DEDICATION

My story, and for that matter my life, has been pretty amazing - full of adventure, great achievement and yes, some painful experiences that were mostly from my own choices and decisions. When I read through my Swim Through Life on these pages that follow - I can only say that I am so thankful for all the people in my life that have filled it with love and support. I have been very blessed and yet I know that my journey is far from over. I am excited about what the next decades will bring.

First and foremost, I must say thank you to my lovely wife, Lori, who has always loved me and supported me in any and every way possible. She has always put my dreams and goals ahead of her own. Her perseverance, determination, commitment, faith and love are the reason that we have the family that we have today. With the miracle of IVF and the help of two very special women – Robin and Stacy – we have two beautiful daughters who have filled my life with abundant love and great joy. Lori, you are truly the love of my life.

Thank you to my girls for providing inspiration, entertainment and adventure in so many ways. Leanna's artistic and athletic abilities are tremendous. However, more than anything else, her faith has been unwavering. Sheridan is our little "tuffy" who has the world in front of her. She is gifted as an artist and as an athlete too. She has a very special gift of communicating and working with animals. I look forward to watching my daughters grow and develop. Nothing makes me prouder than watching them succeed.

I am thankful for my dad who loved me with all of his heart but who was also incredibly tough on me. He always did his best as a parent. He was my rock and there is still a hole left from when he made his early departure from this earth. I am thankful for my mom and her gentle soul. From my mom I learned to listen better and be more sensitive. These two qualities have served me well. I inherited her shyness and quietness.

My brother Lance taught me to never give up. We wrestled for many hours at a time growing up, and no matter how badly I had him pinned, he would never give up. There were times when he watched an entire football game with me holding him down. He also taught me what it meant to be a competitor. We competed in everything that we did. He was my partner and best friend through Pepperdine and Palmer College of Chiropractic. With all my world travels for water polo, I could have never made it through school without Lance and his brilliant note taking.

My sister Tammy has been trying to teach us all to live a more simple life. Having 6 kids and homeschooling them all tells you something about this woman. She was, perhaps, the best natural athlete in our family and in my opinion could have easily made it to the Olympic level in volleyball. Unfortunately, a coach tried to mold her into what he thought she needed to be - instead of allowing her to develop her talent.

I am thankful to all of my teammates in high school - especially our core group – Pat Meaney, Ken Watson, Joel Holiday, Paul Hartloff and Phil Wolf. They helped me come out of my shell a little and even though you guys called me "fat boy", I am thankful that you inspired me to be better. To my teammates at Pepperdine - Don Caskey, Dave Myers, Doug Demerelli, John Sterkel, Pat Padilla, John Wasko, Lance, and of course teammate Tarzan. We had so much fun in college and we owned the pool! Our midnight swims and crazy adventures remain some of my favorite times. You guys pushed me to become the best that I could be. Without you, I never would have become an Olympian. I am especially thankful to have shared so many incredible experiences and travels with all of my Olympic teammates. I was very fortunate to be on some very special teams. After the boycott in 1980, the team basically stayed together for another 4 years and when 1984 came, we were ready. It was a very special group - Figgy, Kev, Dougie, Varg, Willy, Jod, Sven, Drew, Dorst, John and Timmy. These guys made every day in practice a challenge and in the process we made each other better. This was the golden era of USA Water Polo. From 1980 – 1992 the USA team was consistently in the top 3-4 of the world. There are thousands of stories that come to mind when I think about you guys and many are included in this book. My teammates in 1988 and 1992 were equally awesome. I loved playing with all of you and I am so thankful that you were all a part of my life.

I am thankful for the coaches that I had the privilege to play for along my journey. A special thank you goes to Coach Mike Irwin, my high school coach, who taught me so much about being disciplined, and building good habits. To Ian McPherson, my first swim coach who actually made swimming fun. I am also very thankful to my college coach, Rick Rowland who believed in me and inspired me to follow my dream of becoming an Olympian. Also, a big thank you to each of my coaches at the Olympic level - you are some of the best in the world! Monte Nitzkowski, Bill Barnett, Steve Heaston, Ken Lindgren, Rich Corso, Pete Cutino, and John Tanner - thank you for being leaders and giving so much of your time to make us better.

I am also very thankful to USA Water Polo – more importantly the special people that have made up USA Water Polo. Many of them volunteered their time for years to give players like me an opportunity to play in the Olympic Games for our country. Barbara Kalbus is on the top of that list. A volunteer for most of her time with USA Water Polo, she was always there with the players' best interests in mind. She was an amazing lady who only just recently passed away. Terry Sayring is also near the top of the list. Sunshine, as we called Terry, was our team manager for many years. He gave so much of his time and resources to making our team successful. He truly cared about the players. Terry was also a high-level referee for many years and one of the best that this country ever had. There are many more including Burt and Becky Shaw, Andy Burke, Rich Foster and Bruce Wigo who have made this sport what it is. Also, I need to give a special thank you to Ricardo Azevedo who believed in me enough to bring me on as his assistant coach with Team USA in 2006.

I am thankful for my assistant coaches who have supported me and helped me to be the coach I am today. You have all touched my life in your own special way and rarely did you get the credit that you deserved. At Pepperdine these coaches are Dave Myers, Jim McMillan, Jack Kocur, Alex Rodriguez, Merrill Moses, Mike Tragitt. On the national team, Robert Lynn, Ryan Brown, Marco Palazzo and Rick McKee.

Pepperdine University has been a very special place in my life. In a way it has been like my home. From my days as a student, to the Olympic pool, to the chapel where I would marry Lori, to the pool deck where I spend many hours per day - I appreciate Pepperdine. I am thankful to Dr. Howard White for bringing me to Pepperdine and providing me this wonderful opportunity. There are so many good people at Pepperdine – who are a part of my family. To all of the players who have played for me at Pepperdine and with the USA Olympic team: each of you has made my life better. I have learned so much from coaching and being involved with young college-age athletes (and Olympians). It has been an honor to have the opportunity to inspire each of you and to help you accomplish more than you may ever have thought possible. There is magic when teams come together. I love meeting up with my players from years ago - for lunch or just a catch-up and chat.

From the day I was born I learned that chiropractic would change my life. It has certainly done that and it has now changed so many of my patients' lives. I am thankful to my partner of 20 years, Dr. Eran Bikovsky, who covered the office and allowed me to follow my dream as the Olympic coach from 2006 – 2012. Also, I am very thankful to Sue Baker and Jeannine Ostrander who have both been outstanding office managers -running the office for Lori and I.
I am thankful to all of my chiropractic patients for trusting me with your health. I am thankful that I have had the opportunity to connect with so many amazing people. You have enriched my life by sharing a part of yours with me.

To a few men that were huge mentors in my life: when I was down and out and hurting - Ken Bastian and David Holder picked me up and showed me the way back to God and helped me refocus and understand what was most important. Also, Dr. Charles Hollingsworth, our special family friend, who has been there for Lori and I in so many ways.

Finally, I am thankful to the woman who helped bring this story to life. Di, your vision, hard work, patience and dedication made this book possible. I am so thankful that my story can now be truthfully told. You are also responsible for helping to show my family how special Africa is. Wow – we are so blessed to have traveled to your amazing homeland and experienced the people and the animals. Thank you for capturing my story.

I have lived a full and blessed life and I know that I am a very lucky man. I also know that my Swim is far from over. I want to keep learning and growing and following God's guidance to my next adventure. Thank you for reading my story.

Terry Schroeder

CONTENTS

Terry Schroeder at the 1988 Seoul Olympics carrying the U.S. flag
at the Closing Ceremonies

Swimming Through Life

Swimming Through Life is a vast portrait of an exceptional era in USA Men's Olympic Water Polo that chronicles the lives of the players who represented the United States and other top Water Polo countries in the world. The era spans from 1980 to 2012 but also includes news on players in the 2016 Rio Olympics.

Central to the story is the multi-faceted odyssey of Terry Schroeder, who captained the USA Men's Olympic Water Polo team in 1984, 1988 and 1992 and who earned two silver medals in the process. He then went on to be Head Coach of the 2008 and 2012 USA Olympic Men's Water Polo teams – where he took his country back to the podium in the Beijing 2008 Olympics.

The book is an extensive account of Terry's life including his loves, his trials and his triumphs - all comprehensively covered in a poignantly revealing story that is swathed in elation, heartbreak, humor and candor.

Above all, **Swimming Through life** is a celebration of the remarkable strength in unity that is achieved when elite athletes come together at the Olympic Games with an exceptional vision. They form a selfless team that displays the very best aspects of our humanity. They guard each other's backs; they form deep bonds of brotherhood, and they are willing to sacrifice everything for the goal of making their country proud. No other event compares to the Olympic Games, which brings out the best in human potential.

Beyond that, the book is a comprehensive canvas of the social and economic fortunes and ills of the decades in which these men traveled and played all over the world. Interlaced with their personal lives, **Swimming Through Life** covers the journey of human growth - of Terry Schroeder and the people who have enriched his life immeasurably. It is a celebration of the experiences that etched such indelible memories in the lives of special people – all of whom contribute to the book's richness.

A

"It is not the critic who counts, not the man who points out how the strong man stumbled, or where the doer of deeds could have done them better. The credit belongs to the man who is actually in the arena; whose face is marred by dust and sweat and blood; who strives valiantly; who errs and comes short again and again; who knows the great enthusiasms, the great devotions, and spends himself in a worthy cause; who, at the best, knows in the end the triumph of high achievement; and who, at worst, if he fails, at least fails while daring greatly, so that his place shall never be with those cold and timid souls who know neither victory nor defeat."

- Teddy Roosevelt

President Jimmy Carter shakes Terry Schroeder's hand at the
White House – 1980. Terry Sayring on the right.

CHAPTER 1

A Tidal Wave of Disappointment

The important thing in life is not the triumph but the struggle; the essential thing is not to have conquered but to have fought well
- Baron Pierre de Coubertin

January 22, 1980: It was a bitterly cold winter's night in Communist Bucharest, Romania. The country's harsh economic austerity measures – imposed by their brutal leader, Nicolae Ceausescu - had left most Romanian citizens without electricity in the evenings as they drudged home from their factory work to cold, frigid apartments. Ceausescu's rule was the most rigid application of Stalinism in the Soviet bloc. His secret police, the Securitate, were part of an intensified campaign to smother dissent in the country. The snow-dusted streets of Bucharest were laden with something much more sinister than a winter wonderland as members of Ceausescu's Securitate roamed around menacingly - looking for anyone whom they could interrogate or intimidate.

Fearful of any encounter with this brutal force, most Romanians scurried indoors after work rather than expose themselves to aggressive questioning on the streets. Bucharest's evening ritual painted a picture of tired workers wrapped up in gray, somber clothes against the cold temperatures - scampering with their heads down until they were locked behind the reclusive anonymity of their tiny apartments – their cocoons.

This is the scene that the USA Men's Water Polo team witnessed as they stared – transfixed - out the bus window while traveling back to their hotel rooms after a physically-challenging day's training. The golden-tanned Californian boys could not have been more starkly contrasted to their environment. Virtually all beach boys with sun-kissed hair, they cruised into Bucharest with their All-American Levi jeans and that enviable easiness that comes from a Californian upbringing. The mood amongst them was buoyant – filled with promise – making them the most convincing embodiments of Journey's rock anthem, *Don't Stop Believin'*.

For the men who were used to perfect water polo weather in California, the training facility in Bucharest was indoors, a merciful relief as they watched the snowflakes falling from the gray skies. Right then, their thoughts turned to food – lots of it - even though Bucharestian dining was not without its risks. All their preceding meals had consisted of ominous-looking dishes with mystery meat that could have been ratatouille. The imaginative discourse on that night's meat made for jocular banter and for some, the risk of not knowing what they were consuming forced them to fall back on the peanut butter and tang they had carefully packed in their luggage, in case of emergency. The 10,000 to 15,000 calories each man burned per day meant that food was a top priority, and the ol' American staple supplements were always on hand.

Ensconced in their rooms after dinner, the team whiled away their evenings telling humorous stories, playing cards or playing 'Risk' - sometimes late into the night. In typical Californian fashion, in-between training, they started exercising their entrepreneurial skills during the day by selling Levi jeans to grateful Romanians who had no contact with non-Communist lifestyles. A pair could fetch $US 50.00 and with the advantage of the trading power on the black market, each team member could accrue three to four times the Leu (Romanian dollar) than they could harness at the bank.

But despite what appeared to be a carefree nonchalance, the athletes were anything but casual when it came to the real reason they were in Romania. At this critical stage – six months before the 1980 Moscow Olympics - they had already handily beaten some of the strongest men's water polo teams in the world - Yugoslavia, Italy, Hungary and the powerful Soviet Union. In the case of the Soviet Union, USA had beaten them convincingly the previous three times they had played them: 9-4, 7-3 and 5-2. Under the intense, loquacious direction of Head Coach Monte Nitzkowski, this was a time of abundant optimism and hope-charged expectations for the team.

But none carried that hope quite like Terry Schroeder. Not one to show his emotions outwardly, he had silently dreamed of this buildup to the 1980 Summer Olympics since his boyhood days in Santa Barbara, California. Through all the years of exhaustive training, he carried this torch-like vision with him – and it gave him a heightened sensitivity to life's possibilities. There was something peculiarly captivating about his singular determination. That night, as the bus trundled back to the hotel, Jon Svendsen, captain of the 1980 team, turned to

Terry and with an ebullient smile he said, "We can actually do this. We're beating the best teams in the world. We can do this." Those words couldn't have resonated more viscerally than they did with 21-year-old Terry.

Jon's words and hopes were especially poignant in light of the previous years' disappointments. The American team had wallowed in mediocrity, failing to qualify for the 1976 Olympic Games altogether and so they were left back in the States to watch the Games on TV. Heading into the 1980 Games, Coach Nitzkowski had injected an imperative balance of young, talented players into an experienced veteran squad that up until then did not particularly believe in itself. The revitalized concoction was producing some spectacular plays in the water. Somewhere in that mixture, the magical quality of conviction spread its powerful ripples.

Terry Schroeder, known as Schro and also the Rock of Gibraltar, was an invincible starting 2-meter man in the team – dominant against anyone in the world. The 2-meter position is similar to the center of a basketball team; the player's job is to control the frontcourt offense by setting a deep post in the opposing team's water. The biggest difference between a basketball center and a water polo 2-meter player or center is that in water polo, the center may get fouled as many as 100 times per game (since the officials don't keep track of normal fouls) so the 2-meter player or center has to take a beating and stay focused on doing his job, controlling the position, making assists and scoring goals.

Kevin Robertson, a young, left-handed playmaker, was fast and smart, both as a passer and as a scorer. Kevin was also the most selective eater on the team. Vegetables were his sworn enemy and trying anything new threw him into panic mode. Despite what might have been his lack of consumption of good nutrients, he was a formidable player. Come game time, you wanted him on your team. He was usually good for a couple of goals and a couple of assists per game.

Fig, formally known as Gary Figueroa, was a high-powered shooter and his quick release was a valuable game component. He read opposing goalkeepers well enough to know when the goalie was out of place or distracted, and his accuracy in catching goalies off guard made him a great goal scorer. He saw the game almost with a sixth sense and he was a critical part of the team.

Joe Vargas – Varg – was the team's energizer bunny and the ladies' heartbreaker. Countless times when the team was leaving a country, be it Yugoslavia, Hungary or Romania, scenes that were reminiscent of the drama from *Gone with the Wind*, played out as heart-broken ladies sobbed as they waved goodbye to Varg – devastated that they might never see their muscled knight in golden armor again. Varg only knew how to live and play at 110% and that prompted the opposition's defense to jump at him, thereby opening up his fellow team players. It was an effective strategy and oftentimes Varg didn't get the credit he deserved for creating so much opportunity in the water with his energy.

Chris Dorst – known as Dorst – was the backup goalkeeper whose humor provided levity and well-timed laughter, especially when the going was tough. On numerous occasions when the team was physically or mentally beaten up, he would be the sturdy rudder that helped calm the storm. On a training trip to Yugoslavia, he dressed up as Orange Crush man and lifted the spirits of his bruised mates.

Steve Hamann was the starting goalkeeper on the 1980 Olympic squad. Harpo, as he was called because of his similar appearance to Harpo Marx, was in his prime. He played collegiately at San Jose State University in California and was a part of the USA team that did not qualify in 1976. He came with an impressive track record, having been named the top college goalkeeper in the world at the Moscow Student Games in 1973.

Amongst the sturdy veterans there was Peter Schnugg, a disciplined force of cool-headed intelligence. Peter was another Pete Cutino player from the University at California at Berkeley. He had a high water polo IQ and could play very well at either end of the pool.

Eric Lindroth, another skilled left-hander, played center and he and Terry formed a lethal 1-2 combination, making it tricky for opposing defenders. Eric was the only member of the team that had any Olympic experience; he was a youngster on the 1972 team that had won a bronze medal.

On team USA's defense there was John Siman, Drew McDonald and Jon Svendsen. Each raised the game of everyone else in the pool with his own individual intensity. They were tough, determined and highly experienced.

Amongst the substitutes, there was Doug Burke (Dougie) who had the quickest wrist shot on the team and he was Terry's roommate for full-time training. Dave Myers (Gomer) was a fellow Pepperdine University teammate of Terry's and at 6 foot 9 inches tall, he produced a deadly shot from the perimeter. Jeff Stites hailed from University of California, Los Angeles (UCLA) and was a consistently hard worker. Driver, Doug Demerelli (Demir) - was a 6-foot-9-inch lefty and another fellow Pepperdine teammate of Terry's. With Los Angeles traffic being the ultimate nemesis of many a player, Dave's, Doug's and Terry's decision to carpool together the thousands of miles commuting in order to arrive at practices and tournaments ready for action, was an invaluable support system.

1980 Olympic Men's Water Polo team in cowboy theme

But the team was about to encounter a cruel dose of reality. Being on the world's stage in sport, they were about to become pawns on a political world stage. Back home in the USA, President Jimmy Carter was teetering on a precipice of disaster. Inflation domestically was in the double digits; oil prices ran up to triple what they should have been; unemployment was above 7% and interest rates were topping 20%. Carter's run at the White House was largely characterized by the failures of Lyndon Johnson and Richard Nixon. He believed that his role was to restore morality to the White House; that he had been elected to reestablish a government "as good and honest and decent and compassionate and filled with love as are the American people." But the American people were not quite as filled with love for Carter as he had hoped. He became so absorbed in detail that he was never really able to articulate a coherent public policy, foreign or domestic, and the American people blamed him for the out-of-control domestic inflation. However, it was two major crises that had just loomed while team USA Water Polo were in Romania that changed the course of history forever.

Three months previously, in October 1979, Iran's exiled Shah, Moham-med Reza Pahlavi, was welcomed by the United States government and admitted to New York's Hospital-Cornell Medical Center to be treated for cancer. The hosting of such a controversial figure as Pahlavi was fraught with international criticism. The Shah's human rights record in Iran was not only indefensible, but he was notorious for the use of his secret police, the SAVAK, who inflicted brutal attacks on Iranian citizens. Critics found it hypocritical that President Carter, who adamantly advocated the importance of upholding human rights, should be turning a blind eye to the Shah's travesties while granting him asylum in the USA.

Meantime, back in Iran and under the influence of Ayatollah Ruhollah Khomeini, an aging Islamic fundamentalist, a young militant Islamic group called the Muslim Student Followers decided to take revenge on the USA for hosting their unpopular, deposed Shah. In their fervor to launch an Islamic revolution throughout the Middle East, on November 4, 1979, they seized the American Embassy in Tehran and its 52 occupants while demanding that the U.S. release the Shah so that he could return to Iran and stand trial.

Jimmy Carter refused to acquiesce to this extradition request and so the American hostages continued their terrifying ordeal – an ordeal that lasted 444 days under the Carter administration – with the compounding damage of a botched rescue attempt that cost the lives of 8 American servicemen. Film Director, Ben Affleck, captured the drama in his movie ARGO. But that was not the only drama unfolding.

Just one month after the Iranian militants stormed the U.S. Embassy in Tehran, the Soviet Union invaded Afghanistan in December 1979 – merely a month before the team's arrival in Romania. The Soviet aim was to prop up the communist government of the People's Democratic Party of Afghanistan (PDPA) against a growing Afghan Mujahideen insurgency. Texan politician Charlie Wilson urged the U.S. Congress to support Operation Cyclone, the largest-ever covert Central Intelligence Agency (CIA) operation in which they supplied military equipment including Stinger anti-aircraft missiles to the Afghan Mujahideen so that they could defeat the Soviet Union. This morphed into a miscalculated decision that would come back to bite the U.S. – hard – a few years later.

The cold war was in no way diminishing and President Carter took the already icy relationship between the United States and Russia to a cryogenic low by responding to the Soviet invasion by embargoing grain sales and banning technological exports. That was just the start. He solemnly warned his Russian counterpart, Leonid Brezhnev, in his letter of ultimatum dated January 20, 1980, that unless the Soviet Union withdrew from Afghanistan within one month, the United States would boycott the upcoming 1980 Moscow Olympics. The letters that ensued in the next few weeks between Carter and

Brezhnev proved that their relationship was an incongruously mismatched cocktail that was doomed to fail.

President Carter's intransigence towards Leonid Brezhnev was in sharp contrast to the manner in which he brilliantly handled the Egypt-Israel Peace Treaty a year earlier in March 1979. Back then, the best aspects of Jimmy Carter shone through: He brought out the most sterling characteristics in Egypt's Anwar Sadat and Israel's Menchem Begin – imploring them to make peace for the sake of their grand children. That was Jimmy Carter at his best. The Russian debacle and the 1980 boycott was not the finest hour of his Presidency.

Simultaneously back in Romania, the USA Water Polo team watched the unfurling of events with some concern but many on the team thought that it was just a lot of smoke blowing, political posturing and they did not believe that Carter would proceed with the threats. Undeterred from achieving their goal of medaling at the Olympics, the robust team approached each day's training with the kind of seismic amplitude that confirmed their non-deterrence. There was no going into abeyance or any detour. In Terry's case, his laser beam focus was augmented by the notion that this was his one and only shot at the Olympic Games; that he would go to Moscow to realize his dream, and then come home to pursue the other facets of his life.

Back home in Southern California after Romania, the team resumed full-time training which meant 6 days per week - 6 hours per day. They trained mainly in Long Beach at the Belmont Plaza pool which was the site for the 1972 Olympic trials for swimming. It was a beautiful indoor facility that allowed the team to train rain or shine. There was some dry land training too: 3 times per week they would lift weights but most of the training was in the water and it was grueling. The coaches were preparing the team to be in the best shape of their lives knowing full well that going for a gold medal in Moscow demanded nothing less than that. They would swim up to 8,000 meters per day, do leg work, hold up water bottles, weights, and push down on each other until there were close drownings. They were eating, sleeping and playing water polo.

A typical day would consist of being up at 07h00: breakfast. 08h00 – 11h00: training followed by lunch and a nap. Back to training from 15h00 – 18h:30 or longer depending on whether Coach Monte was in the mood for a lengthy dissertation, which could last up to an hour and render the team's home-time departure an hour later than usual. It was difficult to plan anything after practice due to Monte's oratory penchant.

In February, the team was in the midst of the most difficult training. Rumors of the boycott would surface sporadically but they were so rigorously engaged in their fitness schedules that they averted the thought of it happening. Adding to the Olympic excitement, they had the opportunity to watch some of the Lake Placid Winter Olympics on television between and after training. The USA Ice Hockey team was a source of inspiration to all of them. Terry and Dave Myers watched at the home of the Myers while Mrs. Myers plied them with prodigious quantities of homemade hearty meals. Chanting USA, USA, USA, the two Pepperdine teammates cheered wildly as the young USA boys beat the Soviets and then went on to beat Finland and win the gold medal in ice hockey. Hopes were sky high and training seemed to ramp up another notch during the Winter Olympic weeks. It was all the team talked about.

But the political winds of change were starting to gain momentum as the frigid temperatures between the USA and Soviet Union plummeted further. The dreaded blow occurred on March 21, 1980 when President Carter announced that the USA was officially boycotting the Moscow Olympics. The team was in Canada, and Coaches Nitzkowski and Ken Lindgren called their charges into a meeting at their hotel and conveyed the searing news. It scorched like an iron prod. Stunned while processing the news, the team sat still in crushing silence for close to an hour and somewhere in the cognitive fog, Terry began to articulate their feelings as well as his own.

March 21, 1980
I will never forget this day. Tears stream down my cheeks as I write this. President Carter made it official today; the USA Olympic Team will not attend the 1980 Olympic Games; we will boycott the Games as a protest towards the Soviets who have invaded Afghanistan and did not listen to our warnings to get out. We (the athletes) are being used as political pawns . The real losers here are the athletes who have dreamed of and trained for these Games. For most of us this is our one and only chance to become an Olympian and compete for our country. I feel torn. I don't believe in the boycott. It is a bad decision and may hurt the Olympic movement forever. And yet, part of being an athlete who has the chance to represent his country means being proud of your country. I love America – it is my home – there is not a better place in the world to live but right now I feel wounded, my spirit is broken, and my heart aches because my dream has been crushed by

our President. This is a nightmare. Everything was working towards my master plan. I would compete and win a gold medal in the 1980 Olympic Games and then enter chiropractic school. Now what? I don't even want to think about it. I can't - I am in so much pain. I am mad! How could this happen? Why did this happen? Finally, I close my eyes and just try to give it to God. I have not necessarily been close to God lately. Now I come to him in pain. Isn't this what we as humans do most of the time? We wander away and then when we need God we come with our pain...

The International Olympics Federation protested that the pressure by the U.S. and other supporting countries for the boycott was an inappropriate means to achieve a political end and that the victims of this action would be the athletes. Both sides of the argument bolstered up their respective stances with unrelenting fervor. German Chancellor Helmut Schmidt stood stead-fastly behind the U.S. stating that the NATO allies "should stand together in protest against the Soviet Union". The contention between Carter, Schmidt and some of the other NATO allies was that the Soviet Union posed a signifi-cant threat to the world with their expansionist ambitions and that this would give them pause to recognize that powerful countries were prepared to take action against them.

In the meantime, albeit regrettably given the outcome, legendary boxer Muhammad Ali was dispatched by the Carter administration on a 5-nation tour of Africa in a quest to gain sizeable support for the boycott. Tanzania, Nigeria and Kenya were some of the critically important countries on the visitation list and the people in the Carter camp were optimistic of the out-come – given Ali's highly-respected stature in Africa. But the expected warm reception failed. Tanzania's Julius Nyerere pointed out to Ali that when Afri-can leaders boycotted the 1976 Summer Olympics, the U.S. had failed to support them in that initiative.

Given that President Carter's central contention in his Presidency was always his strong assertion of human rights, the leaders of some of the 5 nations in Africa found it somewhat hypocritical that the U.S. was taking this strong stance against the Soviet Union while they had failed to take a sim-ilar stance against apartheid South Africa where human rights were being severely denied on a grand scale. When African leaders had called for trade sanctions against the apartheid regime in South Africa, the U.S. declined to take any action or support the sanctions. Furthermore, it became quickly apparent that Ali was unaware that the Soviet Union was assisting many of the liberation movements in South Africa at the time. That hardly made it the grand foe in their eyes. Ali did receive a warm reception in Senegal. However, its leader, Léopold Senghor, made it clear that they had a policy of keeping politics and sport separated. Despite the fact that Kenya and Liberia did support the 1980 Olympic boycott, the general consensus amongst the other African leaders was that the tour was a clumsy diplomatic move and that Muhammad Ali was being used as a Carter puppet.

Despite Carter's resolute stand, the team still held flickers of hope in their hearts that things might change; that either the Soviet Union would withdraw from Afghanistan before the Olympics or that Carter would soften and lift the boycott. For that reason they continued to train in anticipation of there being light at the end of the tunnel. But the tunnel continued interminably and the opening ceremony of the 1980 Summer Olympics, which took place on July 19 in the Grand Arena of the Central Lenin Stadium in Moscow, was final confirmation that the dream was dead. The members of the team sat in their respective living rooms in the U.S. watching it with weighted emotions and bruised hearts.

In August 1980, a month after the Olympic closing ceremony, President Carter invited the USA Olympians to the White House in Washington D.C., a gesture that was reminiscent of a consolation prize for their trashed hopes. While many athletes across the various sports elected not to go, the collective decision amongst the men's water polo team was to stand in solidarity and show up because the action represented everything that the Olympics was about: the unification of nations – not the imposition of barriers.

Each athlete received a Congressional Medal of Honor in lieu of what might have been. But for the recipients, it was hardly a substitute for standing on a podium and receiving the real deal – something they had earned. The incomparable scenario was awash with disappointment - hidden partially by the same ironclad discipline and skills the team had always exercised in training. They walked up to shake President Carter's hand with their emotions outwardly in check even though everything about the ceremony smacked of platitudes.

Ironically, 10 years later, the name of the award was changed to simply 'Medal of Honor', a switch that amplified the confused, apologetic mood at the White House that day. Terry recalls their visit to the White House like this: "We were ushered in through the back gate rather than the front entrance and each team member wore patches on their shirts which read, 'I am here because I never want this to happen again'. When I was up on stage and shaking President Carter's hand for my picture, he asked me what sport I was in and I told him water polo. Wanting to appear as if we had something in common, he told me that he had played a little water polo at the Naval Academy. I remember thinking 'I wish that you still played because I would love to get in the water with you and show you some moves – perhaps even see how long you can hold your breath'. I do think that President Carter had to know that there was an undercurrent of discontent; he had to have seen it in our eyes. But on a lighter note, there is a great picture from the White House visit of our entire team in speedos, cowboy boots and cowboy hats – all supplied by sponsors Levi Strauss. The theme was – yes you guessed it – a western theme."

1980 Olympic Men's Water Polo team in cowboy theme

The Soviet Union Men's Water Polo team took the gold medal at the 1980 Olympics, beating Yugoslavia 8-7. Yugoslavia took the silver by beating Hungary. Given the convincing beating the U.S. team had meted out to the Soviets in their recent 3 games, the sting of exclusion and what could have been was inconceivably painful. Over 35 years later, the sense of loss is as strong today as it was back then. The boycott changed the course of these men's lives irrevocably and for some, the scar of exclusion is a stolen dream that will remain with them forever.

Terry with his parents Bob and Pat Schroeder at the White House

Terry with proud dad Bob Schroeder 1980

John Siman, Joe Vargas and Steve Hamann

Terry in action after the 1980 Olympics

Terry the aqualete

Schroeders '*National Lampoon Vacations*'

CHAPTER 2

Santa Barbara Estuary

I cannot think of any need in childhood as strong as the
need for a father's protection
- Sigmund Freud

June 15, 1965: Spanish architecturally inspired Santa Barbara, California is pretty much the ideal oasis in which to live. A typical summer's day features the morning fog breaking into almost year-round cobalt blue skies with warm sun and crystal-clear water.

However, that day was far from typical in the Schroeder home: 6-year-old Terry and his 5-year-old brother Lance were not outside playing and catching lizards in the giant field at the end of the cul de sac in which they lived - nor were they exploring the creek that ran directly behind their home. In fact, they weren't outside playing at all. Completely out of character, they were in-doors with their mother, Pat, who was 8 months pregnant and ready to give birth at any moment. Their father, Bob, had put Terry in charge of the perilous situation with strict instructions to call him at work should his mom give the urgent signal.

Waiting apprehensively in their beautiful 5-year-old home, Terry stared at the bump inside his mom's stomach and realized with an acute sense of older brother responsibility that he was navigating unchartered waters – that being on baby watch was not part of Lance's and his daily repertoire. Stationed close to the black dial-up phone anticipating that emergency moment, Terry continued his daylight vigil with his eyes opened abnormally wide. His ice blue stare canceled out any blinking – in case it robbed him of a critical observation second.

The Schroeder family home was bare – save for the fundamental essentials like beds, drapes and a couple of tables. Bob had stretched himself to the maximum to purchase this idyllic home and he wasn't about to put anything on his credit card to make it more comfortable. Later on, when he had cash in hand, he added a dining room table, a couch and some chairs for the living room. In that terrifying moment, Terry took note of the newly added crib for the about-to-be born infant Schroeder.

Bob had always held strong views on many things including a fervent conviction that hospitals and medications should be avoided if at all possible. Just as he had home-delivered Terry and Lance, Schroeder baby number 3 was about to experience the same home birth. Five agonizing hours later, at 13h15, Pat began to scream, "Call dad!" Never before had Terry dialed a phone with such speedy, deft accuracy. Bob made it home within 7 minutes of the 15-minute drive from the office and delivered his daughter, Tammy.

A 6-year-old remembers acutely impressionable incidences in his young life, and Terry was in awe of his father at that moment. Known as a 'miracle man' by his patients and by family, Bob Schroeder had earned a reputation as a top chiropractor and as a man who helped others in extensive ways. "Healing hands" is how Bob was often described, and Terry felt – particularly in that miraculous moment - that his father had this rare, magical ability.

Within an hour after the birth of their sister, Terry and Lance ran – relieved - right back to their habitat: the great outdoors with its fields, an adventure-filled creek and a deserted street that was devoid of cars and other obstacles to their fun. Their street ball game ensued and later they played hide and seek until they were called in to have dinner – their first meal with their new sister, Tammy. If most young boys could take a vote, the Schroeder family home was about as ideal as any child's home could possibly be. With his family now complete, Bob set about organizing the next phase of their lives in Santa Barbara.

Santa Barbara

Robert (Bob) Emanuel Schroeder was born in Brooklyn, New York on March 29, 1929 to Frederick and Augusta Schroeder who had immigrated from Sweden to find a better life in America.

The same year of his birth, The Wall Street Crash occurred on October 29, 1929, and on that 'Black Tuesday' the Dow Jones Industrial Average fell almost 23%, and the market lost between $8 billion and $9 billion in value. But it was just one in a series of losses during a time of extreme market volatility that exposed those who had bought stocks 'on margin' – with borrowed money. The crash changed the face of New York overnight.

Widespread unemployment spread its ugly tentacles and New Yorkers reeled as the implications of the stock market crash hit them with the voltage of a lightning streak. The ramifications spread like an infectious catastrophe and the whole world plummeted into an unimaginably devastating depression that nobody saw coming. There were near halts in industrial production and construction, and an 89% decline in stock prices. By 1932, the unemployment rate in the U.S. had soared past 20%. Thousands of banks and businesses closed their doors. Millions were homeless. Men and women returned home from fruitless job hunts to find their dwellings padlocked and their possessions and families turned out onto the streets. Brooklyn absorbed an abnormally large share of the depression's ills, and the local boys like Bob Schroeder learned to survive with very little. There were days when the family hardly ate. Life was challenging to say the least, but Bob kept his head above water and always remembered President Franklin D. Roosevelt's words when he said, "the only thing we have to fear is fear itself." Being armed with physical strength quelled many of those fears.

Frederick had worked on the docks early in his life and then he discovered a relatively new profession called chiropractic - done by hand. He was a healer and treated many patients at $5.00 per adjustment. But he had a difficult time making ends meet and balancing his family priorities. To the detriment of them all, Frederick left home with another woman when young Bob was just 12 years old, and his departure left behind an inconceivable vacuum.

Fatherless, Bob had to learn to fight for himself while growing up in the tough neighborhood of Brooklyn during the Great Depression years of the 1930s. It was unlike any other place with its unique set of challenges. Out of necessity, Bob figured that survival of the fittest meant that Neanderthal behavior was a basic coping mechanism, and feral instincts often replaced reason.

In addition to born-and-raised Americans calling Brooklyn home, a kaleidoscope of immigrant families sought refuge there after fleeing their native European roots in-between two tough world wars. Brooklyn was inhabited by throngs of different nationalities who were struggling to find their place in a melting pot that often became a pressure-cooker of conflicting attitudes.

Inevitably the simmering tension burst out on the streets where testosterone-charged teenage boys vented their frustrations and their burgeoning anger in destructive ways. Bob's strong physique worked to his advantage in the rough playing pen but he also recognized that this was not the environment in which he wanted to spend the rest of his life. From that restless era, Brooklyn became a spawning ground for some of the USA's finest entrepreneurs; young men and women who grew up there were hungry, lean and filled with dreams of upward mobility. Bob was one of those fledglings who flew the Brooklyn nest.

Bob and his brothers Al and Rich each followed their father's footsteps into the chiropractic profession. In the short period of time that their father Frederick was around, each was impressed and intrigued by chiropractic. Bob's strong desire to have a family and be a better dad than his father carried him through chiropractic school while working two jobs to pay for school. Davenport, Iowa was the home of Palmer School of Chiropractic and it was also home to WHO radio station featuring Ronald Reagan. Surrounded by farmland and corn, Bob's direction was clear: as soon as he graduated from chiropractic school, he planned to leave the corncobs behind and expand his horizons westward.

In the 1950s, fate's compass and astute planning navigated Bob to Santa Barbara, California where he met his future wife, Pat, a native of this west coast paradise. Pat's and Santa Barbara's charms seduced Bob unequivocally – producing a surprise pregnancy in 1958 that was about to change the course of their lives – seismically. Following the star-studded gravitation to Las Vegas of Frank Sinatra, Dean Martin and Bing Crosby, Bob whisked Pat away to Vegas' main strip for a 'Love Me Tender' wedding in preparation for the arrival of their first son, who didn't come into the world inconspicuously. Terry Schroeder dove into the world fluidly on October 9, 1958 and started swimming before he could walk or talk. Naturally, his priorities were in order.

It was a cool, foggy Saturday morning, typical of summer June gloom in Santa Barbara when 7-year-old Terry swam in his first competitive swimming race. It was the start of his first 50-yard backstroke – two lengths of the pool requiring a neat tumble turn on the other side. "Swimmers take your marks; get set...BANG".

That heart-racing back splash was the beginning of his aquatic sports journey. Excited, nervous and slightly unsettled in this new environment, he immediately felt the pressure to perform – externally but mostly - internally. That raw, unabated desire to push himself beyond his previous 'best' was as intrinsic to Terry's DNA as climbing a tree is to a cat. It's as if there was an electrical prod inside his brain that said, "go faster, do better, swim like your life depends on it!"

But things didn't go according to plan. So amped was he with nerves, determination and expectation that he sprang from the blocks like an overly-coiled, spring-loaded top and his foot slipped off the pool's gutter, jamming his right knee into the wall. The ensuing physical pain was nowhere near as blistering as the pain of humiliation. Making up for the costly clumsy start was imperative so he whirled his arms around like a speedy windmill but that flurrying motion only took him off course. Instead of swimming straightly, he was taking an excursion into his neighbor's lane and an over correction resulted in an unintended encounter with the other neighbor on the other side of the black line. Finally, furious, humiliated and still whirling his arms frantically, Terry's eyes began to fill up with emotional tears – the wrong kind of water – making it impossible to see.

The final spectacle of disgrace was an overly motivated 7-year-old not being able to see the 5-yard backstroke flags signaling that he was about to hit the wall. Within seconds, young Terry rammed his head against the wall with as much speed as a novice can muster – the final inauspicious coup de grâce and his first concussion. He emerged from the water carrying a boatload of injured pride and an emerging egg-sized bump on his head. Last in the race was the kind of inglorious baptism into competitive aquatics that young Terry had not planned.

Hoping that he could scurry away in his uncomfortably exposed Speedo to a secluded cave to hide in his shame, Terry soon realized that this was impossible since his dad, Bob, was approaching him like a land submarine along the perimeter of the pool. How was he going to face the father who wanted his son to achieve equally as much? How was he going to explain what a terrible race it was? Letting his father down was not an option – so he thought.

But his worst fears didn't actualize; instead, his dad wrapped a soft, dry towel around him and with his big football arms enveloping his young son, he said, "It's OK Terry, you did your best and I love you for that." This could not have been easy for Bob Schroeder to say; he had already set the bar extraordinarily high for Terry, both in sports, and in life, and so while hearing those words, Terry wondered if his dad was actually sure about what he had just said. But the continuing, warm paternal embrace he received was incalculably reassuring and he luxuriated in the consolation and surety that effort counted – it counted enormously to the man he revered. Of course winning would have been even better, but giving of one's best was an early lesson that Terry understood from his mentor – his dad.

In the next three races he attended, his confidence began to build and as that happened, his swimming stroke became more fluid, more harmonious with the water – less frantic. As that ease of motion unfolded, Terry's enjoyment of competitive swimming began to osmotically permeate into his being. As his positioning in race results improved, the sense of achievement became a catalytic necessity that converted into hungry motivation.

Bob drove Terry to his early morning workings every day at 05h30 at the local YMCA before school. There is no kid that enjoys getting up at that hour, besides which it was usually unappealingly foggy, cool and damp. But it was Terry's herculean drive that persuaded him that the hour and the repetitive nature of training - was worthwhile. His daily progress was measurable and during each consecutive practice, he could feel his strengthening lats pulling him through the water with greater speed and efficiency. For the first time he had some sense of what it must feel like to be a dolphin. Swimming was natural, soothing, peaceful and with the growing strength in his body – fluidly easy.

10-year-old Terry's unabated fascination with the Olympics began on October 12, 1968 with the opening of the Mexico City Summer Olympic Games. It was particularly tangible in that it was being held in next-door Mexico and some of the palpable energy and excitement flowed across the Tijuana border into nearby Southern California. Little did he know that the Olympics would come to consume his life for three decades; all he knew right then was that he couldn't watch enough television coverage – limited as it was.

The athletes who particularly sparked Terry's imagination were Mark Spitz, Don Schollander and Bob Beamon – all of whom won gold medals. Terry's mind was made up. The Olympics was where he was headed and nothing was going to stop him. Doing his best became synonymous with being the best. He looked at his dad and with conviction in his voice he said, "I want to be an Olympian." That was music to Bob's ears.

Visualization is one of the most powerful galvanizers towards success, and the picture in Terry's head of Mark Spitz and the world's greatest athletes – triumphing on the Olympic podium - replaced any other visual dreams that a 10-year-old might have. He didn't want a new train set or a tree house in his family's Santa Barbara garden; instead he wanted to work towards becoming one of the world's top athletes. That powerful vision paid dividends. 10-year-old Terry was ranked the second fastest backstroker in his age group – nationally - that year.

His plan was in order but his heart began to cause a sense of unease in him. Swimming did not hold the exciting ingredients he was looking for in a sport. The sense of unease was further compounded by the changing relationship he had with his dad. Bob had become fixated on winning and every weekend was spent at swim meets and traveling to get there. The part about "I love you for simply doing your best" seemed to be replaced with "winning is everything" and the consequent disappointment of letting his dad down when he didn't win began to weigh heavily on Terry who was growing increasingly unhappy with the pressure and the monotony of a routine that was no longer firing his spirit. He instinctively knew that without that passion for his chosen sport, he would never make it to the top. Passion and a love for what you are doing are vital components towards achieving. That fired-up edge had disappeared – dissipated – and there was no getting it back.

With an assured voice, Terry announced to Bob that he was quitting swimming. Yes – quitting. Bob absorbed the news in stunned silence, and to his credit, he didn't try to talk his golden son out of his decision. Terry knew that there was something else out there - another sport at which he could excel. For a while, he dabbled in baseball and football. A natural athlete, he was talented in both sports and could have excelled had he chosen either. Although, he enjoyed football, Terry sensed that this was not the best sport for his body. Even at a young age, he suffered some semi-serious soft tissue injuries. In baseball he performed impressively – becoming a good little shortstop – playing on the same Little League team as Jesse Orosco, who later became a major league pitcher. What those experiences revealed to Terry was that he was definitely a team player and enjoyed the interactive process of playing with members of a team. However, neither football nor baseball was an Olympic sport at the time and since his vision of becoming an Olympian was concretely central to the grand plan – that was a fundamental problem.

The 1972 Munich Summer Olympics was where the plan began to take shape with unbridled conviction. Californian swimmer, Mark Spitz, dominated the games in Munich by setting a record at the time of seven gold medals. But as the television coverage continued, Terry's interest began to gravitate away from swimming to a sport that encompassed great swimming skills but it had that all-important ingredient: team interaction. It solved the solitude of swimming by bringing in a dimension that Terry knew he needed: fast, exciting maneuvers while catching and throwing a ball with teammates. It involved strategizing and playmaking – a combination of all the sports he had played. Finally – he found the ideal mixture that fired his dolphin spirit. Not only did he love watching team USA Water Polo play but they ended up on the podium, winning a bronze medal. It was the first medal the USA had won in water polo in 40 years. The dye was cast. Terry knew exactly where he needed to invest his energy. Water polo was the elixir – the quintessence of what he needed to attain his dream.

In 1973 he entered San Marcos High School in Santa Barbara. As school began, Terry's classmates encouraged him to try out for the water polo team but for him, it wasn't a slam-dunk decision. Fully aware that he had never played the sport before, he realized that the disappointment of possibly not being picked for the team would be crushing. After practice that first day – a practice that entailed some of the most difficult workouts he'd ever experienced - Terry felt exhausted and apprehensive. There were many players who were much better and more experienced than he. Fortunately, there was a core group of first-year players - Pat Meaney, Ken Watson and Paul Hartloff - all swimming buddies who stuck together and supported one another and so there was a collective sense of learning the game together.

As with most things in life, the power of a superlative mentor and coach is incalculably valuable to a young person. Mike Irwin was the first coach in Terry's formative teenage years and he impacted him in the most positive way. He encouraged, motivated and gave his charges the skills they needed to succeed while always encouraging them to give of their best. His mellow personality worked for Terry. Dramatic displays of out-of-control emotions and coaches whose style was to over-talk, yell and scream – didn't resonate with him.

A fond memory Terry has of Coach Irwin is sitting on the mats in the wrestling room during one morning chat when Coach said, "The height of athletic achievement is to be at your best when it matters the most." That statement really impacted Terry and he instantly knew that to be his best entailed knowing the right moment when extra human strength was needed. Timing and recognition of that moment was key. As he practiced day after day, he asked himself that question: "How do I achieve my best when it matters the most?"

He can still recall the exact game and the words he voiced: "This is the time; this is a big game against our cross-town rival, Santa Barbara High, and I want to be at my best." Unfortunately, Terry became so over-exuberant about the game that he played with too much emotion and by the third quarter, after bodily shoving and half drowning his opponents, he found himself sitting on the bench in awfully foul trouble – literally. But by learning how to keep those emotions in check and by tempering the aggressive physicality that sometimes interfered with the winning, Terry began to develop all the accouterments that go towards making a world-class athlete. While talent and skill go a long way, reaching the top entails intelligent timing and carefully managed super-human effort – when it matters the most.

Terry fell in love with the game. This time there was no soul-searching and no indecision; this was where he was meant to be. He knew it without any reservation. Coach Mike was a bit of an innovator; he did not like the traditional front-court offense that revolved around a center (Terry's eventual position) so the team ran a 'rotating lung' offense. There was constant movement and every player was forced to play each position. This became an invaluable component in Terry's game. He was ready to take up any positional play the team required. Unlike so many water polo players, he wasn't restricted to just the center position.

Many centers in high school never learn to use their bodies properly - particularly their legs - and therefore when they arrive at college they have to unlearn some bad habits before they can advance. Since San Marcos was only a 3-year high school and this was Terry's first exposure to the sport, he was fortunate to be in this type of system that helped him develop more quickly with an array of proficient skills.

While Mike Irwin was a critical component of Terry's water polo career trajectory, there were two other linchpins that he knew he needed: his faith in God and winning his supportive father back. He probably never lost his dad's support, but he earnestly wanted to make him proud – and he knew he could do it with water polo. Just as fate had intended, Bob loved the game and rallied around Terry in every conceivable way. At last those words of "I'm so proud of you" came forth regularly and Terry bathed in its reassurance. It released the pressure and allowed him to fully sink into enjoying his time in the water – which was a considerable period of time. In fact, he became more fish than human. He looked the part too. Oftentimes he reeked of chlorine and walked around with crusty green hair and blood-shot red eyes.

Bob often impressed upon Terry how important it was to use the gifts that God gave him. It was about fully utilizing his talents - a message he understood well. For the first time, Terry's faith began to really grow and actualize. He turned more to prayer and while reading the Bible he discovered that the lessons applied directly to his life. It seemed to give him an inner peace – a more settled feeling that replaced his anxiety. The pieces were coming together harmoniously and Terry relied on his faith to stay focused and treat his teammates like he would want to be treated. That foundation, coupled with Coach Irwin's steady encouragement and the support of his dad, became the powerful triumvirate that allowed him to progress exponentially.

Inspiration for Terry during his high school years presented itself a fourth way in the form of a friend and teammate named Paul Hartloff. He had competed with Paul during his YMCA swimming days and they shared a common goal – to make it to the Olympics. Paul worked hard and he excelled at one of the most grueling swimming events that existed: the 1,500-meter freestyle. He soon became one of the best in the country at that distance and in 1975, while

Lance, Tammy and Terry

still in high school, he earned the right to represent the USA at the Pan American Games (Pan Ams). Terry was excited for his friend, but truthfully, he was also a bit envious. Witnessing Paul make the team and then winning a silver medal in the competition made him realize more than ever that his Olympic goal was attainable. If Paul could do it, so could he. The boys had grown up swimming age-group meets together and Terry had beaten him in many of the events. Paul made the dream more realistic and it augmented Terry's confidence.

However, this was Santa Barbara in the 1970s. Think Beach Boys and their anthems, *I Wish they All could be Californian Girls*, and *Wouldn't it be Nice* – and you'll understand the flavor of the time and the place. Beautiful people and beautiful bodies strutted on Southern Californian beaches; the girls' bikinis became more micro than ever, and the boys began to muscle up in the gymnasiums in their quests to win the girls' attention. This was the era of sun, surf and bodily perfection that quite naturally accentuated body conscious-ness – particularly for young people - to a crescendo of competitiveness. Peer pressure and conformity only added to the exaggerated awareness.

Surprisingly, the teenage Terry Schroeder did not fall into the body per-fect category. Cruelly nicknamed 'fat boy' by his peers at high school, he

San Marcos High School Swim Team

admits, when looking back at pictures from that era, that he was on the pudgy side – but 'fat boy' was an unnecessary stab that hurt him to the core. It detracted from his need to be accepted and admired – particularly by the pretty high school girls that he was starting to notice and discover. But more than that, how was any 'fat boy' supposed to make it to the Olympics? Oftentimes teenagers don't fully comprehend the wounds they inflict with their jocular words – but from there forward, Terry armed himself with the single-minded determination to shape the course of his life and his body. He tucked into his inner strength, which was supported by his strong faith, and found the courage to move forward proactively. Whenever those bow-and-arrow words stung, he handed the teasing over to God and asked for guidance and peace. Very soon, he could see the conversion process take form: the mocking became a challenge. Each time 'fat boy' rang out behind him on the school corridors, he said to himself, "I'll show you".

Bob Schroeder assisted Terry with his getting-into-shape goal by reassuring him that he would soon experience a massive growth spurt and when that happened, the fat would dissipate. He bought his son a jump rope and encouraged him to continue to work hard. Terry's DNA also came to the fore. Over the next two years, he wore out three jump ropes, and worked his way up from 100 sit-ups at a time to 2,000 sit-ups each day. He never skipped a day. Then, just as Bob had predicted, Terry's Jack-and-the-beanstalk transition began. Growing weekly, the puppy fat melted away and the strong athletic physique Terry had always hoped for – took form. With six-pack abs of steel, Terry entered his senior year in the kind of shape that would take him to the next level. His peers developed a new respect for him – probably because he didn't retaliate from all the years they called him 'fat boy'. There was a silent satisfaction he felt – knowing that he had done the right thing and achieved the desired result.

High school water polo training, however, didn't always fire Terry's imagination. There were the endless workouts where he never touched a ball or played a game. It was just a monotonous cycle with the hundred of lengths swimming and drills that at the time made no sense. While some players fell by the wayside, Terry made the necessary mental shift towards a strong conviction that all of this seeming monotony was preparation for the big day: the day when he could become one of the world's best water polo players. He knew that the strengthening in his body and the cardiovascular fitness were pivotal components towards the Olympic stage. Performing each drill with renewed vigor, Terry kept his eye on the prize and his strong visual imagination kept him inspired and it reeled in his mind in when it began to wander.

Science and Math were two of Terry's strong subjects in high school. He excelled in those and did well enough to get by in the other courses. It was during a history course that Terry first learned about Dr. Victor Frankl who, during World War II and thereafter, put the spotlight on the imperative need to visualize and find meaning and purpose to one's life – in order to surmount life's most cruel and challenging obstacles. In his case, obstacle is a vast under-statement. On October 19, 1944, Victor Frankl and his wife, Tilly, were transported by the Nazis to Auschwitz Concentration Camp simply because they were Jewish. From there they separated Frankl from his wife and transferred him to Dachau Concentration Camp, where he spent five months working as a slave laborer and later as a physician.

Dr. Frankl saved countless Jewish lives by showing his fellow prisoners that the power of the mind is infinitely more powerful than the body. Using the techniques of visualization, he inspired the desperate people around him to hold on – to visualize that they would one day see their loved ones again. He encouraged them not to let go; he kept reminding them that love was the most powerful and most beautiful reason to live…that they had to find the strength to go on…to surge through the hunger, the illness and the sense of absolute desperation. To many people, he was an angel amongst them and he saved so many precious lives.

Tragically, his wife perished after being separated from him and sent to Bergen-Belsen Concentration Camp. He lost his mother, Elsa and his brother, Walter in Auschwitz. The only member of the Frankl family – aside from Victor – who survived was his sister Stella who escaped from Austria by immigrating to Australia. Dr. Frankl continued to achieve immense success in his career and received prodigious awards for his life-affirming research. He spent his last days in the U.S. and is famous for this phrase: "To give light one must endure burning."

While Dr. Frankl's experience of hell in a Nazi-run Jewish concentration camp is in no way comparable to the training of an Olympic athlete, the power of the mind and the art of visualization that Frankl taught became a central application in Terry's daily routine. In 1974 in the middle of what is commonly known as 'hell week' – a week wherein the athletes' limits are pushed to the maximum – Terry sometimes asked himself the question, "is this worth it?" and "why am I doing this?" It was not unusual for at least two or three players to be vomiting each day due to the intensity of the workouts. But that's when that power of visualization kicked in. When his body told him to quit, he closed his eyes, took a few deep breaths, and went to that place in his mind where he saw himself at the Olympic Games, competing for the USA. At that palpable moment, quitting was not an option.

On one particular day, Terry decided that he was going to work harder than anyone else in the pool. He was going to push himself, and in so doing, challenge his teammates around him to work harder and take it up a notch. It worked. Pushing himself beyond what he thought were his limits stimulated everyone around him to go to another level – to reach deep inside of themselves and find a strength they never knew they had. Before long, a new behavioral pattern had been established in the water polo team; one where they were challenging each other to be the best athletes they could be – as a habitual choice. Mediocrity was no longer part of their training lexicon and by his senior year, Terry led the charge in his high school water polo team – consistently setting that standard.

Edward Robinson, who would play with Terry years later in the USA National Water Polo team, remembers him vividly during these high school years: "I met Terry when he was playing for San Marcos High in Santa Barbara. He dominated high school water polo with his formidable strength, and by college level, he elevated everyone's game with his dominant presence. His raw strength was unmatched and he had that uncanny ability to produce those moments of brilliance when it counted. He will go down in history as an iconic player because he was highly skilled, smart, powerful, competitive and supremely focused. It was impossible to break him mentally."

Just as understanding the fundamentals of the game and applying them were crucial, so too was leading a healthy lifestyle, if making it to the top was a priority. Sleep was imperative for Terry. Oftentimes he would stay awake late, studying for a test in the hopes that his youth would see him through the math test and the water polo game the next day. But that never worked. Playing while fatigued meant that he was unfocused and unable to give of his best. Living on junk food also didn't give his engine the nutrients he needed for top performance. Terry laments the fact that mom Pat, although very capable, did not enjoy cooking, so fish sticks and chicken pot pies were common items on the Schroeder family menu. In reality, most of America had adopted the unhealthy habit of eating fast, nutrient-deficient food in front of the television screen. Bob's root beer floats were the equivalent of today's protein shakes and smoothies. He assured his son after serving him each root beer float that they would help him to have a strong and powerful body one day. That was, perhaps, the only misinformation that Bob ever fed him.

Those years between Terry's first water polo games in high school and the Olympics were a journey filled with more depth and more richness than he could ever imagine. Though he made it onto the 1980 USA Men's Olympic Water Polo team, it would take him another four agonizingly long years before he would actually make his Olympic debut – and experience the realization of a dream that made his body and his soul tingle with each privileged moment.

Pepperdine University

CHAPTER 3

Leaving the Family Pond

Desire is the key to motivation, but it's determination and commitment to an unrelenting pursuit of your goal - a commitment to excellence - that will enable you to attain the success you seek
- Mario Andretti

August 20, 1976: Considerably transformed physically, 17-year-old, 6-foot-4-inch Terry drove out of the safe, cul-de-sac enclave of the Schroeder family home in Santa Barbara to begin carving out his adult journey at Pepperdine University in Malibu, California. He had just left behind the sanctuary of a life-time home that always promised him the unconditional support and love of his parents, Bob and Pat. He was also bidding farewell to a boyhood with his little brother Lance that was awash with memories of adventures with lizards, snakes and frogs in wide-open fields. There were also many friends whom he'd miss – friends who challenged him every day to be better and to try harder – whether that was in ping pong, street ball, hide and seek, swimming or water polo. The safe haven was behind him and he knew that the next day, his two formative mentors, his dad and Mike Irwin, would no longer shape his daily path.

During the lump-in-the-throat, one-hour-and-15-minute-drive to Malibu, Terry absorbed his new reality: that he was crossing the Rubicon to fend for himself in a new water pond with a new shoal of unknown variables. While Lance was always the more outgoing, ebullient of the two brothers, Terry inherited his mother's gentle shyness and a preference for a quieter modus operandi. Since it's usually the more gregarious, fun-loving students who gain all the attention at university, Terry carried more than a hint of apprehension during his drive, wondering how he was going to be received by his new world. More importantly, he wondered how he was going to survive without the familiarity and protection of the safe bubble in which he had grown up.

As Terry's white Ford Mustang with its cool red seats hugged the corners of California's Pacific Coast Highway towards his alma mater for the next 4 years, the geography of his new home began to impact him. While having the opportunity to live in Malibu carries its own cache of privileges, few resident movie stars are able to purchase, even with their copious millions, the piece of majestic property that Pepperdine University occupies. There are plenty of celebrity mansions across Malibu that stand on beautiful, hill-top perches, but few can rival Pepperdine's geographic positioning. Moreover, it's not just a group of drab school buildings spread over a flat campus on dry grass in some lame part of Malibu; instead it's a palm-tree-fringed green oasis on top of a mountain overlooking the blue Pacific Ocean – similar in its scope to a Greek acropolis overlooking the Aegean Sea – a fitting analogy for Terry's aspirations when one considers that Greece is the birth place of the Olympic Games. The pioneers behind Pepperdine's land purchase were brilliant strategists.

Pepperdine University Pool, Malibu California

The road to Pepperdine was paved with an incisive amount of thought as Terry and his dad spent months weighing up the options and the advantages of the opportunities. In Terry's senior year at San Marcos, they finished third at CIF (California Interscholastic Federation) in all of Southern California, losing to eventual champion and powerhouse Newport Harbor High School – a team led by Terry's future Olympic team mate, Kevin Robertson. This was a resounding accomplishment for a small Santa Barbara team that was competing in the same division as the larger Orange County, California teams. Stanford University and California State Long Beach offered Terry the same type of scholarship that Pepperdine offered, but in the end, he chose Pepperdine because it was small, and it had the kind of family atmosphere in which he knew he'd thrive.

He also shrewdly deduced that he would be a big fish in a smaller pond. Knowing Coach Rowland gave him an extra level of confidence. He had swum for Coach Rowland while training at the La Cumbre Country Club in Santa Barbara years before. Rowland had recruited some other Santa Barbara athletes, namely Pat Meaney and Terry Erwin, but most importantly, he had often expressed confidence in Terry and believed he had what it took to achieve his Olympic dream. Since the Olympic quest had become Terry's obsessional focus, he planned all his choices around the attainment of that goal.

Accepting Pepperdine University's combination swimming and academic scholarship made all the sense in the world to Terry. He'd carefully concluded that the opportunity to excel in swimming fitness – despite its lackluster appeal – would create an exceptional advantage for him in water polo. Beyond that, Pepperdine was a logical choice for other priorities: it was a Christian-based university that Terry knew would assist his growth in faith. Also important was the curriculum it offered – a great program in Sports Medicine that proved to be perfect for his eventual career as a chiropractor.

The chiropractic profession fulfilled every tenement that Terry knew to be true about the human body: that if it is in alignment with regular physical adjustments, plenty of exercise and a healthy eating plan, the body learns to heal itself and perform miraculously. From an athlete's perspective, this is critical. Beyond that, becoming an elite athlete is a fine line between being good and being great – and that fine line is dependent on all those acutely important consistencies.

Little did Terry know in August 1976 that Pepperdine was – from that day forward – about to become a core part of his life and his destiny. But what the USA water polo fraternity did know on that day was that there was a burgeoning star arriving at Pepperdine University and they were watching every aquatic maneuver he made.

Despite the childhood rough-housing and antics that often made Terry and Lance adversaries as they duked it out on the playing fields of Santa Barbara, they were close brothers who relied upon each other for many of the unspoken comforts of family and home. As such, Terry was determined to make sure that his younger brother had the opportunity to join him at Pepperdine the following year – by using his influence in the water polo team. He set about firmly encouraging the coaching staff that Lance was part of the family package deal or he may have to consider leaving for other options.

When Lance's bid to attend was successful, Terry welcomed his brother on campus and relished the assuredness of having him in close proximity.

Family was critical to Terry. On the weekends when he was able, he drove his Mustang straight back to Santa Barbara to visit with family and friends. Enjoying home-cooked meals and spending quality time with the people he loved was the essential balance he needed against the high-level water polo training and the Sports Medicine curriculum. An extra special dimension was that Bob and Pat loved to welcome Terry's Pepperdine teammates over to their home for barbecues and team dinners. In this way, the whole family became intertwined with the Pepperdine family.

Like most college freshmen, Terry was assigned a roommate on day one. His was Don Caskey, a 6-foot-6-inch junior college transfer who was also a center on the incoming water polo team. While he had the size to play the game, Don was a bit soft around the middle, which ultimately may have helped to keep him afloat better - at least in Don's mind! Don had an arresting smile that was a powerful lady magnet, and a personality that reflected his abundant passion for life. Everything he embarked upon was infused with boatloads of enthusiasm and an unreserved zest for living.

Always the character, Don would often eat an entire onion or garlic glove prior to practice or a game. The intended effect after each pungent exhalation was mixed: either it worked like a charm and his opponents would avoid guarding him closely, or they'd retaliate by pummeling him. Don and Lance Schroeder were somewhat similar: fun, outgoing and occasionally crazy, and perhaps this is why Terry liked Don so much.

Terry's energies were not as widespread as Don's, and in any case, they were wholly different in temperament. Don was gregarious and outgoing; Terry was a quiet introvert who usually channeled his energies into staying on task: training, studying and keeping his body healthy by making sure he was sleeping enough. Their contrasting natures and schedules could have resulted in an imminent roommate fallout situation: over the 2 years that they shared a room, Terry had a more rigorous schedule; he was committed to both the Pepperdine swimming and water polo seasons while Don could sleep in until lunch time once the water polo season was over – and he did. His nocturnal party-time antics necessitated these morning-long siestas.

Oftentimes Don rolled in at 03h00 and clunked his way into bed noisily – waking Terry who knew he had to be at swimming training at 06h00. The sleeping giant was not amused. Always the congenial friend, though, Don tried to remedy the situation by inviting Terry to an array of parties, insisting that it would be prodigiously beneficial for him to partake in his festive night-life calendar.

On one conspicuously rare occasion, when Don finally convinced Terry to go out with him, they spent a few hours out on the town. When they returned to campus that night, the two roommates decided to extinguish a streetlight that was shining into their dorm room and interfering with their exotic nighttime ocean view.

They strategized that the best way to eliminate the light for perpetuity was to hit it with a rock. After about 10 attempts they both hit and smashed it with bull's eye accuracy. The celebration of that achievement was thwarted almost immediately as the Pepperdine security team converged on the sinners and apprehended them for their misconduct. They were summarily punished with a game suspension – a relevant lesson that taught them the consequences of impulsive actions.

Much as oil and water don't mix, it was a testament to both Don's and Terry's good natures that they managed to maintain such an amicable and congenial friendship whilst also tempering each other slightly; Don needed more structure, and Terry needed to loosen up a bit and have more fun at college. They achieved that measured balance and the loyal friendship endured. In the end, Don took the medal for increasing Terry's fun times quotient at college.

Terry's daily schedule elicited his strong disciplinary habits – without which – it simply wouldn't have been manageable. During the swimming season, he clambered out of bed at 05h30 every day and propelled his way down to the pool for 5 – 8,000 meters of lap swimming. The monotony of the routine diminished any enjoyment for him. It was a daily struggle but he viewed it as a necessary component to his ultimate goal. Although there were moments when he had doubts, the fighting fit form that the swimming commitment produced made each one of the tough morning workouts worth every single stroke.

Much of water polo is about immense swimming fitness and when USA's water polo squad began their training schedule in January, Terry could swim with the best of his teammates - courtesy of his swimming scholarship. The fact that he was a center – and centers typically are not the best swimmers - made it that much more important for him to show up in the best possible swimming shape. It was an invaluable base upon which to build.

At last – that Mikasa water polo ball that brought on the irrepressible smile – landed in Terry's solid hands. It turned on a light inside him that nothing else could, and every fiber inside every muscle of his body was involuntarily triggered to the challenge of that yellow ball - especially when it had the insignia USA written on it.

In December of 1977 at the end of his sophomore season at Pepperdine,

Terry was called into Coach Rowland's office. Upon entering, he immediately felt the positively-charged ions suspended in the air: Coach Rowland was beaming as he shook Terry's large hand and congratulated him for being asked to join the USA national team training camp in January. With pride and emotion on his face, he said, "I am so proud of you and I have no doubt that you will make the USA Olympic team in 1980."

Terry shut his eyes so as to soak in the moment more intensely while thanking God for the opportunity ahead. It was the confidence booster that would ignite his engine to reach the next level, and Coach Rowland's words were powerfully affirming.

The next 5 weeks turned into a physical fitness regime like no other as Terry resolved to get into the best shape of his life. This was the moment and everything hinged on his fighting form. He swam hundreds of lengths of the pool, did jump ropes, sit ups; he ran the stairs at Pepperdine to give his legs a more vigorous workout, and he enlisted players to throw a ball with him. A typical day consisted of swimming 6,000 meters, various egg beater drills in the water to strengthen his legs, 2,000 sit ups, 2,000 jump jumps, 10 -15 sets of stairs, and passing and shooting with teammates in the water.

When he arrived at the National team training camp at the Belmont Plaza pool in Long Beach, California in January 1978, Terry was willing to do whatever was asked of him. He was excited, confident and nervous as this was a level he had never experienced before. Making the team was "the dream" and realizing it meant as much to him as life itself; he was ready to give everything he had to prove to the coaches that he deserved a berth on the National team. There were 30 players present and 4 of them were centers. Only 11 players would eventually make the Olympic team in 1980 and only two of those would be centers.

Despite being in such great physical shape, Terry began the camp ranked 4th out of 4 centers. The obstacles were compounded by what seemed to be an apparent pact amongst the veteran players – in particular Jim Kruse and the captain, Jon Svendsen – to play extra physically aggressively with the younger players – as if to test them and see if they had the chops to handle the pressure.

Terry's emotional control and his resilience were tested maximally: determined not to let the punching, kicking or pushing phase him, he endured whatever pain the veterans meted out. That spot on the Olympic team was so important that he was prepared to tolerate any form of physical and mental torture. Breaking was not an option.

The 6-week training camp was tough. As this was Terry's first exposure to the National team, there was much to learn. There were physical and mental challenges as players were required to acquire enhanced skills. New and challenging drills were introduced and each day felt like a test. At the end of the camp, the first tournament of the season was scheduled for March 1978. Terry was shattered to find his name not on the National "A" or "B" team but on the USA Junior National Team. Although making any team was a crucial stroke forward – it was not where he had intended to be. It felt like a failure.

On the Junior team, he was the starting center, also called the 2-meter man, and their first tournament was in the Can Am Mex in Vancouver, Canada in March. The Juniors beat the Mexican national team by 1, the Canadian national team by 2, and only lost to the USA National 'B' team by 2. The tournament also included a game against the powerful Hungarian National team, featuring a player then considered to be the best in the world – Tamás Faragó. At 6 foot 4 inches and 230 pounds, Faragó was intimidating to say the least. He had formidable legs and a powerful eggbeater kick that allowed him to move in the water like a fish on steroids.

Tamás Faragó

During the match with Hungary, Terry was 'tooled' by Faragó on more than one occasion. By the end of the match he was impressed by the famous Faragó. Although he had been beaten, in the back of his mind, he made it a goal to earn the title of world's best for himself one day, and he understood fully that the only way to do that would be to help Team USA become one of the world's top teams. Although this was a respectable beginning, Terry was left wanting more.

The night after the final game, Terry was packing for a morning flight home when he received a call from Barbara Kalbus, the USA Team Manager. She informed him that plans had changed and he was told to get ready to fly to Rio de Janeiro the next day to join the USA 'A' team for a series of games against Brazil. Terry knew full well that those games were essentially the qualifiers for the 1980 Olympic Games.

This moment was everything he'd dreamed of for the past 10 years and yet – that quirky little shadow called doubt - reared its debilitating head: was he ready for this next phase? The long, lonely flight to Rio was a restless, sleepless journey - accentuated by the solitude. While the rest of the team had flown together and were already there, Terry was the latecomer and he knew that the second he landed, he'd have to perform by drawing from the reservoir of hard work. Imperative, too, was the need to inject his play with the kind of flair that would win the coaches' attention - and more importantly – win the respect of his new teammates. His dad's and Coach Irwin's words resonated deeply as he focused on excelling.

Arriving in Rio the next evening, Terry's first priority was to overcome the jet lag and sense of disorientation. The new world of USA 'A' team water polo began with an interesting early morning view: after a night of tossing and turning in the same room as his assigned teammate, Terry awoke to find a beautiful, naked Brazilian woman getting dressed and eventually leaving the room. Apparently she'd been his roommate's guest during the night. As he left the room 30 minutes later, he smiled wryly and muttered to himself, "this might be a pretty good gig".

He joined the team at breakfast and the welcome he received was an essential force – one that helped to assure him of his readiness. The team appeared to be really happy about his arrival and within the first practice session, Terry felt the ease of belonging. He calculated in his mind that he was the missing piece of the team puzzle. Disappointingly, the day before the team's first qualifier, they were informed that the games in Brazil would no longer serve as official Olympic qualifying games. Instead, the Pan Am Games in 1979 would serve that purpose. Undeterred, the team took the task seriously and treated the competition as part of the season's exhibition schedule.

So began Terry's long relationship with Coach Monte Nitzkowski who immediately put his new player in the starting line-up for the first exhibition game against Brazil. Just one week previously, Terry had been on the Junior National Team and now, he was a starter on the National Team. It was a hugely irrevocable moment of reckoning.

Ken Lindgren and Monte Nitzkowski

Play ensued and on the first possession, Terry tactfully turned his defender and had him sent to the penalty box with an exclusion. That set the stage for the first 6 on 5 (men) of the game where Team USA scored. This was a crucial confidence maker for Terry, who then knew that his teammates trusted him, and as the game progressed, he imbibed all the signs they gave him - signs that conveyed to him their trust and respect. Instead of trying to grab the spotlight, Terry was exceptional at controlling the offense and drawing exclusions – thereby affording his team multiple scoring chances. He also excelled at making assists so that any one of the team's talented shooters had more scoring opportunities.

The consistency of his performance at these exhibitions earned Terry a permanent spot as a starter on the National Team. Though elated at the news, he experienced that confusing mixture of emotions when one is at the cusp of success: it's a combination of fear and passion, which when managed and balanced, becomes the perfect ignition fuel. There was a healthy fear in his new level of success but Terry debated in his head whether it was real or if it would last. This was accentuated by the feelings of heart-pumping excitement - fed by a passionate drive that emanates from knowing that this is what one loves doing.

Even though Monte respected Terry and tempered the number of times he'd rebuke him, his style of coaching was fear-based – even if he didn't intend it to be that. One of his ideals was Bobby Knight – University of Indiana Basketball Coach who was famous for his temper tantrums, yelling and throwing bench chairs out onto the basketball court when he disagreed with a call.

Monte excelled in long-winded sermons. A 5-minute piece of information would at times take him 30 painful minutes to deliver and he didn't seem to notice when his team was looking at the trees with glazed eyes. A typical national team weekend workout schedule – before full time training – was 2 hours on a Friday night followed by a 30-45-minute meeting. Saturdays were long, physically demanding days: 5 hours in total were spent in the pool followed by a Monte dissertation. Sunday was a similarly rigorous schedule. Then there were the mid-week workouts - 2 nights per week. It was a grueling schedule that had to be balanced with the players' universities' academic demands.

One of the team members who consistently received the brunt of Monte's wrath was John Siman. John was a full-time member of the 2nd unit or "nut squad". After playing a game in Budapest, Hungary, Terry and the rest of the team sat in stunned silence as Monte ripped into Greg Boyer for his terrible play. The team knew that they had all played poorly but Monte was singling out Greg - perplexingly. Finally, John Siman said matter of factually: "Monte, I don't think that Greg played that poorly". After what seemed like a minute, a stunned Monte began his pre-explosion ritual by turning red, and then he fired his rockets at John for about 10 minutes before ripping into each one of the team members. Terry remembers leaving the pool deck feeling disconsolate and dejected -although there was a sense that he needed to stay closer to his teammates.

Later in the trip after a game in Belgrade, Yugoslavia, the team witnessed probably the worst personal bashing they'd ever watched a teammate receive. Monte was furious with John Siman, who had not played well, but Monte never forgot anything and he was still steaming that John had challenged him in Hungary. He told John with flaming adjectives just how badly he'd played. As if that weren't enough, he decided to press his point home even further by saying, "John, when they circumcised you, the doctors threw away the wrong piece."

After that humiliating tirade, the team felt an empathetic twinge of pain for John, and they united around him defensively. In their opinion, Monte had crossed a line. Perhaps that was Monte's tactic: to hammer the men so hard that it would make them rely on each other more and become a closer team.

He didn't pick the best moments, though. Once, during a severe thunder storm, Monte jostled for dramatic effect with the weather; just as the rain came pelting down, he'd raise his voice even more vociferously and yell while spit burst forth from his mouth. Barely a word was audible in the thunderous noise, and another one of Monte's speeches became lost in space. The more Monte thundered on, the more the team united and turned to humor to alleviate what could have been a simmering pot about to explode.

Monte was a gifted coach – no question. He was exceptional when it came to game management and strategy. He put together incredible scouting reports on all the teams the USA played, and he consistently challenged his players with game situation drills in practice. He was also responsible for developing a style of play that was unique to USA water polo: a fast-paced counter attacking game with mobile centers - a game that suited Terry well.

Making it onto the National Team meant that Terry would have to make peace with Los Angeles traffic and its parking-lot freeways. Training took place in either Long Beach – which was preferable from Malibu – or Newport Beach – 4 times a week. Traveling to Newport Beach could be a cruel 3-hour drive in congested traffic and on one or two rare occasions, while he was gnashing his teeth with impatience while stuck in traffic, Terry almost succumbed to the temptation of turning back to Malibu – thereby missing training.

Those were the critical testing times when he had to decide how badly he wanted his Olympic dream. Monte was sometimes not easy on Terry; even after he plowed his way through the worst of Los Angeles traffic to get to practice, Monte would summarily punish Terry for being late – something that he found disheartening given the effort he had made to be there. This made Terry all the more grateful when Dave Myers and Doug Demirelli were able to commute with him from Pepperdine. Ride sharing relieved some of the pressure and helped everyone to focus on the goal. Also, this allowed the players to study or prepare for tests the next day in class. It was a delicate balancing act.

Dave Myers proved to be an incalculably valuable friend to Terry through those years. The Myers family invited Terry to their home frequently and treated him as one of their own sons. Mrs. Myers' meals had a particular gourmet appeal to a ravenously hungry pair of water polo players who needed quality food and quantity – to drive their turbo submarine engines.

Unfortunately, Dave never made the 1980 Olympic team even though he was talented as a great outside shooter. A situation on the team concerning Dave was Terry's first experience at witnessing something he knew was wrong, but he felt uncomfortable about speaking up because he wanted to fit in and not confront anyone. Basically, he never really stood up for his friend, a decision that to this day, he regrets.

Dave's nickname on the team was 'Gomer' after the famous television character, Gomer Pyle. The name was not intended to be a compliment and usually the team used this nickname behind his back. It was flat-out bullying. Dave received the barbs from all sides; unlike Terry, he was not a member of the first unit – the starters – who were Monte's favorite players. Dave was in the 2nd unit – the so-called 'nut squad'.

Terry would be enjoying another one of Mrs. Myers' delicious dinners while Dave's father was at the hospital, watching his son being stitched up, patched up or being cauterized after another bloody nose from one of the many blows he received in practice that day. Sometimes those blows weren't accidental and Terry felt a deep sense of unease about it. Despite the absence of Dave at the dinner table, and the obvious worry Mrs. Myers was experiencing, she still gave Terry a 'goodie' bag full of cookies to take back to his Pepperdine dorm.

In the summer of 1978, Terry was chosen as one of the top 11 players who would travel to the World Championship in Rome and represent Team USA. This was his first really major tournament with Team USA and so it was an immensely important baptism. It was also his first encounter with the unfortunate politics that has been endemic in the sport for decades.

USA was knocked out of the medal round of a game that appeared to be 'fixed' in order to keep them out of medal contention. 'Fixing' is done by manipulating the system. In this instance, a deal appeared to have been struck between the Romanians and the Soviets – in order to cut out the USA. Quite simply, the Romanians and the USSR played to a prearranged tie – costing USA the bid into the final 4.

Team USA chose to turn the frustration of the politics into an important catalyst. Instead of being demoralized, it served to improve their game more as they were determined to prove that they were a force with which to be reckoned in the world of water polo – in the same echelon as the best teams. Monte would often tell the team that in order to compete with the best teams in the world, Team USA had to be 3 goals better than them in the water. This was to make up for the officials' seeming prejudice against them.

Proving their worth came at the right time: in 1979 Team USA placed 2nd in the World FINA Cup and won the Pan American Games to secure their bid to the Olympic Games in Moscow. Terry and his teammates were elated – especially the older players on the team who experienced the disappointment of not qualifying in the 1976 Montreal Olympics. This was the dream...the moment that they had all sacrificed so much for...and it was imminent. The Pan American Games was the first "gold medal" that the USA team had won in international competition in years. This called for a significant celebration afterwards - Terry's first immersion into the team's penchant for playing hard and celebrating hard.

In keeping with celebratory tradition, some respectable Puerto Rican rum from the Pan Am's host city flowed, and most of the team members began to lose control of their quick reflexes - fairly rapidly. Terry found himself in the company of one of the girls from Team USA's synchronized swimming team and he woke up next to her on the hotel lawn the next morning, unsure of why they were there while watching rats the size of rabbits scurry around just a few feet away. It was a new era and definitely a new chapter in the Schroeder water polo annals, and one that needed to stay in San Juan, Puerto Rico.

With a rigorous training schedule ahead of them, 1979 was the all-important preparation year for the 1980 Moscow Olympics. Every vital component that made this team powerful and formidable was augmented by hundreds of hours of intense practices. They were cohesively committed to going to Moscow – to earn a gold medal. The odds were extremely good: they had beaten the favorite team, Russia, 3 times in the lead-up to the Olympics.

U.S. President Jimmy Carter brought the sledgehammer down on that dream in March of 1980 – when he decided that the USA would boycott the games. The reason behind it – the standoff between the USA and the USSR over the issue of the Afghanistan invasion – persisted while Carter and his USSR counterpart, Brezhnev, showed the world just how intransigent and unrelenting they could be. It was an inconceivably painful experience – the first major piece of adversity Terry had to face.

The acceptance portion took a long time as Terry cried himself to sleep for months after the shock. It would take several months to work through the agonizing disappointment and the sense of injustice. Determined to eventually see the light at the end of the dark tunnel, Terry began to emerge from the chrysalis by the end of 1980. It was a new day and bitterness, he realized, was debilitating.

It was time to shake off the victim chains and empower himself by having a plan and being committed to what could be – at the 1984 Los Angeles Olympics. He resolved to look up and forward. Incredibly, 9 of the 11 players from Team USA would put their lives on hold and commit to train – in pursuit of a gold medal in 1984.

Terry Schroeder playing Water Polo for Pepperdine University

CHAPTER 4

The Pepperdine Pool

There is a destiny that makes us brothers; none goes his way alone, all
that we send into the lives of others comes back into our own
- Edwin Markham

September 1, 1978: In-between the exceptionally rigorous training that goes into Olympic preparation, it's easy to imagine that it was all sweat and no laughter. That couldn't have been further from reality. One of Terry's relaxation outlets was fishing. The entire Schroeder family, Bob, Pat, Terry, Lance and Tammy, headed out on mini fishing trips to Lake Cachuma - about 45 minutes from Santa Barbara - whenever they could steal away from the rigors of life.

In August each year, they did their National Geographic excursion to the mouth of the Klamath River near the Californian Oregonian border where they fished for salmon. There's a real art to salmon fishing that elicited Terry's and Lance's competitiveness and their collaboration. They would work together to find the hottest fishing spots in the middle of the shoulder-to-shoulder fishing (combat fishing); this happened when the salmon were running. Sometimes, either Terry or Lance would sacrifice himself by casting his line over the neighbor's lines in the water - creating a tangle that opened up a place on the shore for the other brother. It was a great form of teamwork that almost always worked. Occasionally, the boys would get yelled at but the scolding was definitely worth it when they headed back to the campsite with a limit of king salmon in tow.

Back at Pepperdine, Terry was learning to embrace a more balanced and less rigid life. He and his water polo friends on the swimming team became specialists in having artful fun (apologies to the real artists). They formed the unofficial 'Cousteau Society' – named after the legendary aquatic adventurer, Jacques Cousteau. So determined were they to become fully-committed Cousteaunians that they visited the official 'Cousteau Society' in Los

Angeles and equipped themselves with all the stickers and memorabilia that they could find. Their stash of Cousteau-engraved insignia made their allegiance to the great explorer all the more official as they returned back to the Pepperdine campus.

Once back in their habitat – the pool – their goal became to explore under water while the rest of the swimming team was training hard core. While the serious swimmers were sprinting over them in their assigned lanes, the underwater explorers - members of the esteemed Cousteau Society - blew bubbles and drew dolphins and sharks at the bottom of the pool - using colored chalk.

When they'd done advancing Jacques Cousteau's underwater cause with their self-amusement antics, the art of enjoying a Jacuzzi became a particular specialty for the boys. During their 06h00 morning workouts, they'd swim to the shallow end of the pool, discreetly hop out and crawl on their bellies to the Jacuzzi. They luxuriated in the frothy warm bubbles until Coach Rowland discovered what they were doing and yelled at them to get back in the water. There were no floodlights at the pool deck at that time so in the semi darkness of early winter mornings with just enough fog on the water to disguise their whereabouts – nature provided the perfect foil. Out of the 25 swimmers at the deep end, 2 - 3 could easily escape – undetected – leaving the serious 22 to swim back to the deep end. If the set was 10 x 200 meters, the really crafty escapees could skip the first 3 - 4 before Coach Rowland discovered their hijinks.

1980 PEPPERDINE WATER POLO (Left to Right) Top Row—Assistant Coach Keith Cruickshank, Erik Luchs, Lance Schroeder, Pat Padilla, Kevin Outcalt, Dave Chase; Middle Row—Bob Evejene, Bill Shandor, Ken Lamkin, Rob Moore, Rick Rowland, Pat Meany; Front Row—Assistant Coach Tim Elson, Kerry Kemp, Scott Hellwig, Captain Terry Schroeder, Jon Sterkel, Brian O'Connor, Head Coach Rick Rowland.

1980 Pepperdine Water Polo team

On other occasions Terry and other members of the Cousteau Society, who were becoming as skilled as Harry Houdini in disappearing, would sneak onto the pool deck - hide under the cover of the water polo goal backing, which used to be a solid blue. That provided a perfect vanishing location for 15 - 20 minutes. On one occasion, Coach Rowland stood right there and shouted, "Where did Schroeder go?" while Terry was within three feet of his shoes. The Cousteau Society didn't let up and simply shook their heads innocently while giving Coach Rowland a bewildered look. It took a lot of control for one of them not to give away his presence with an unsuppressed laugh.

The typically mild-mannered, slow-to-anger Terry made his own personal history one night at Pepperdine. After an evening out, he returned to the Upsilon dormitory, looking forward to a good night's sleep before practice the next day. His room had a spectacular ocean view and the only downside to its positioning was a pay phone booth directly outside the room (and the light post). Whenever the phone rang, one of the men in the suite would have the good manners to answer it. But on this particular night, nobody woke up to answer the late night caller. Mildly irritated, Terry clambered out of bed and put an end to the ringing by greeting the caller who wished to speak to Julie. Since there were no girls in the men's dorms, and Julie was definitely not present, Terry hoped that the caller had listened to his explanation and that would be the end of that. It was not to be. Five minutes later the same person called back. Terry emerged from bed a second time. Despite being told again that this was a Pepperdine University's men's dormitory with no women present, the caller rang back a third time, this time after a ten-minute interval, just enough for Terry to be on the cusp of sleep. Two more futile attempts at sleep were interrupted by Julie's persistent pursuer, and this time, Terry lost his cool-headedness.

Unaware of his own strength, he picked up the phone receiver and yanked it with unremitting force. The entire pay phone – which was fairly large – came crashing off the wall and fell on Terry's right leg before hitting the floor with hundreds of dimes everywhere. It was like a Las Vegas jackpot bonanza except that blood was rapidly oozing out of the deep leg wound, and Terry had no chance of being inconspicuous at this moment. Determined to minimize the drama, he tied a towel tightly around his leg and went back to a disturbed sleep, hoping that his leg would miraculously heal itself through the remainder of the night. As it turned out, the wound was deep and the 12 stitches that were inserted cost Terry some valuable water time.

But the mainstay hijinks in the summers usually involved the Cirque du

Soleil evenings off Pepperdine pool's high diving board. During these high-flying evenings, the water polo team vied with each other for the most spectacular aerobatics – moves that might even have impressed Greg Louganis for their sheer, brazen chutzpa. The high-flying belly floppers then night-capped the evening with a midnight Jacuzzi under the glistening stars. It were as if the men owned the pool – or for that matter – the campus.

Terry Schroeder playing Water Polo for Pepperdine University

One mischievous evening, Terry and his water polo teammates made a deal with the baseball team to have a massive food fight in the cafeteria. Corn-cobs, apples and hamburger patties went flying through the air. The incident had Terry called into Dr. Howard White's office – the President of Pepperdine. The visitation turned out to be dinner at Brock House, which was the President's official residence, and Dr. White's staff prepared the largest steak Terry had ever seen. The conversation moved in rhetorical circles as Dr. White tried to have Terry explain the logical reason behind the food fight. There was none and Terry felt like a fool as he devoured the massive, juicy steak like it was his last supper.

But the importance of that dinner was not lost on Terry. Dr. White took an acute interest in Terry's wellbeing and he had a particular interest in Pepperdine's athletes – proof of which was that he watched virtually every game across the sports spectrum. As Terry climbed the food chain of USA water polo, Dr. White supported him wholeheartedly and always had an open door policy. But what particularly impressed Terry about Dr. White was the quality of his leadership. Unlike some of the egotistical people he had watched, Dr. White set a new, higher standard in leadership: he was humble and he had a genuine servant heart.

Throughout his time at Pepperdine, Terry found Dr. White to be an essential role model – someone he admired and respected enormously. While Dr. White didn't always have the answers, he was humble enough and curious enough to spend time with people from whom he could learn and grow. He always asked, "What can I do for you?" It was Dr. White who was responsible for the Olympic Water Polo games being held at Pepperdine for the 1984 Los Angeles Olympics, and his leadership and commitment saw it through to resounding success. On numerous occasions, he hosted the USA team and the entire Schroeder

family at his residence. Terry looked up to this kind, generous man who cared about everyone - and viewed him as a second father. It was fitting and special, therefore, that when Terry married his wife Lori a few years later, he asked Dr. White to conduct the service in the Pepperdine University Chapel.

One of Terry's special friends at Pepperdine was John Wasko, the team's characterful goalie. A rule unto himself, John developed a passion for airplanes. While Terry, Lance, and their respective roommates Jon Sterkel and Pat Padilla all knew the careers they were going to pursue, John had, up until then, been largely directionless.

Terry and Pepperdine University's Dr. White

Terry, Jon, Lance and Pat spent many happy afternoons with John on the Pepperdine grounds, flying little gas-powered control line planes (controlled with a handle attached to the wing of the plane with strings). Becoming increasingly more proficient at controlling the action in the air through deft ground navigation, the airplanes could be flown upside down while doing flips and other tricks. There were some spectacular crashes which usually required starting over with a new plane.

Flying airplanes afforded the 5 friends a uniquely special bonding time; they even snuck into the gym on some nights and played out kamikaze scenarios in which the planes would end up stuck in the volleyball net like a bug in a spider's web. The sight of that tickled their funny bones so much that they collapsed on the gym floor laughing – the kind that worked their core stomach muscles to the point where they hurt the following day.

One of the most admirable qualities about John Wasko was that he had to make up for his size in the water polo team by working that much harder. He was feisty, committed and the team looked up to him.

Once Pepperdine installed floodlights into the pool area, it was John's decision to switch the lights off at night so that the team could practice shooting in the dark. He figured that not being able to see was the best way to shoot and defend with a sixth sense - in the same way that a blind person's hearing can compensate for the visual loss. The problem, though, was that the guys were shooting the balls at 50 – 55 MPH. Lance Schroeder had a deadly left-handed shot and on one occasion, he broke another goalie's arm with one hit. John's face endured more punishment than it should ever have received, and when hit, he would make a bellowing sound like a seal. The problem was that the Malibu neighbors heard the bellows and assumed that there must be a seal in the Pepperdine pool because they had definitely heard the animal's cries of distress. Animal Welfare calls were made, and none of the neighbors realized that it was simply poor John in pain. That silly occurrence provided important levity that saw the team through some tough times.

Once John knew that his goal was to become a Navy pilot, he buckled down to serious studying in order to attain the grades he needed. He and Terry were in sync when it came to their unremitting determination to achieve their goals. John achieved his dream and after college, he flew helicopters for the U.S. Navy. Terry was elated for his friend.

A few years later, while Terry was in his last year at chiropractic school, John's father called him to share with him the devastating news that his passionate, engaging friend was flying his helicopter over the ocean during a training exercise when it crashed. John and his crew had drowned. The wound of loss was exacerbated knowing that the very element that John felt so comfortable in – water – was the element that took his life. Swimmers don't fear water and so it's almost incomprehensible for them to imagine losing their lives in something they instinctively know how to navigate. Years later when Terry became a coach, in John's honor, he initiated the John Wasko Water Polo Invitational at Pepperdine University. The tournament was held every year for 20 years in John's memory as a reminder to all of how he overcame adversity and powered through situations which were never easy – in order to succeed.

Terry Schroeder representing Pepperdine University Water Polo

Bill Dryer, Terry Schroeder and Lance Schroeder graduating from Palmer Chiropractic

Lori Bell's graduation from Palmer Chiropractic

CHAPTER 5

The Confluence of Olympic and School Waters

A soulmate is the one person whose love is powerful
enough to motivate you to meet your soul, to do the emotional
work of self-discovery, of awakening
- Kenny Loggins

August 1981: Lori Ann Bell began her graduate studies at Palmer West
School of Chiropractic in 1981, the same year that Terry embarked on the
same study path at the same school in Northern California. Originally, Terry's
plan had been to attend Palmer School of Chiropractic in Davenport, Iowa, but
providence provided an infinitely better plan when Palmer opened its doors in
Northern California, and Terry was rescued from a lifestyle in Iowa that was
about as foreign to him as a polar bear living in the Sahara Desert.

Beyond just the massive adaptation to weather and habitat, water polo was
almost non-existent in Iowa and the geography of his positioning would have
cost Terry his Olympic dream. Saved from the icy temperatures of the Iowa
winters, he arrived at Palmer West invigorated and charged for a loaded schedule that would prove to be punishing at times. Between training for the 1984 Los
Angeles Olympics and keeping up with his heavy graduate school responsibilities, organization and a photographic memory were key survival strengths.

Providence also provided another key survival strength in the form of Lori
Ann Bell, the tall, blonde aerobics instructor with the body of a goddess and
plentiful brains to garner her a place in chiropractic school. God was exceptionally generous in His gifting. At that stage Terry wasn't aware of how much his
cup was going to runneth over, but the shrewd Schroeder eyesight did take a
mentally-accurate note of Lori's considerable physical assets. Since the Olympics were unwaveringly Terry's top priority, and each of them was dating someone else at the time, the love sparks remained in hibernation amid the obstacles.

Terry had just returned from visiting his girlfriend's family in Hawai'i. Her
mom wanted to make a special dinner for them so she made a beautiful London

Broil. Terry was agog with anticipation: at last a protein-packed, sizeable meal to feed his 12 - 15,000-calorie-a-day appetite! When the plate was passed to him first, he scooped the entire splendid chunk of meat onto his plate – and only 30 seconds later did he notice that everyone was staring at him. After his girlfriend's mom gasped, Terry realized that he had to do a surreptitious return of the prodigious protein to the serving tray so that others could eat. Although it was funny at the time, it was probably the beginning of the end of that relationship.

Always the game tactician, Terry began to configure a pursuit plan for Lori once Lance joined him at chiropractic school. Employing Lance's bold, outgoing nature, he instructed his brother to attract Lori's attention in class by throwing raisins at her from his lunch box. Lance even broadened the scope of his flying objects to paper airplanes or anything that was light and harmless. His target accuracy was perfect and Ms. Bell became aware that her attention was being sought. But putting two physically-attractive specimens together can result in a rapidly imploding scenario because of too much electricity racing ahead of the important stuff – the characteristics and features that are ultimately so much more meaningful in a relationship. Terry and Lori avoided becoming remnants of a firecracker burnout; instead they became friends and maintained that innocent interaction for a considerable time.

As they built up a deep and rich friendship, Terry recognized how much he admired Lori: she had a sweet innocence about her and everything she said and did was authentic. A young woman with the purest of intentions, her smile was infectious and she laughed easily and joyfully. Above all, her beauty lay in her kindness. The undeniable physical chemistry they felt for each other was kept in

Lori Bell

the freezer courtesy of Baskin-Robbins ice cream. Originally Lori was a quarter term ahead of Terry at Palmer but she sustained a serious injury to her knee while teaching aerobics, and the ensuing surgery caused her to drop back by one quarter.

This was perfect positioning. She was now in Terry's microbiology, biochemistry and chest x-ray interpretation classes. There was a considerable amount of chest interpretation that they both would have liked to explore out of class - but the timing wasn't right. Instead they took frequent study dates at Baskin-Robbins where temperatures were sensibly controlled below zero. This was necessary on two cold fronts: aside from cooling the always-present basic instincts between them, the chiropractic course load and tests were rigorous – sometimes 3 in one day and so they visited their favorite stalactite cave two blocks from campus to study and compare notes while enjoying some scoops of their favorite ice cream. Their friendship grew as they studied together and learned more about each other. Those Baskin-Robbins days were invaluable pressure dispersers in an academically rigorous environment and they also provided a foundation for a lasting relationship.

It was Terry's dry sense of humor that endeared him to Lori. He sat behind her in class and pretended to be the perfect student. That guise was soon expelled when Terry started to imitate the professors. He'd lean forward and mimic them in Lori's ears. Her reaction was just perfect. The painting was taking shape. During a microbiology class, Terry excelled in the comedian department: he took a micropipette of Dr. Phil Banda's homemade wine and embarked on his experiment. When he'd finished, Dr. Banda noticed that there was hardly any wine left in his student's Pyrex beaker. Terry kept his taciturn expression intact and appeared just as bewildered as Dr. Banda at this evaporation scene.

Above all, Terry's shyness had a heart-warming effect on Lori. She knew that despite his Olympic stature, there was nothing vain or conceited about him. During an anatomy class, the professor chose Terry to take off his shirt. As he did so, the entire class began calling out "woo-hoo" chants and Terry's face went crimson. As the chants continued, the crimson hue deepened. This was not a man comfortable being on show in such an objective way. Lori chalked it up as another important attribute.

As the 1984 Olympics approached, Terry had to attend more training camps and his traveling commitments doubled. The pressure to be ready for that pinnacle moment meant that he had to spend large amounts of time away from school. Lori and Lance did everything in their power to cover for him by taking notes and keeping his homework up-to-date. They assiduously became Terry's A Team – the essential force without which he could never have coped. Upon his return from traveling they'd coach him through the information he had missed in class. His photographic memory kicked in when he needed it the most, and Lori and Lance were his proverbial backbone.

In the meantime, having ended one relationship, Lori had started to date Les – also known as Superman because – yes – he resembled Superman. Both Lori and Superman were not only studying at Palmer but they were in the fitness industry so they attended certification seminars and classes together. Months later, Terry broke up with his girlfriend, and Les was then that crazy obstacle to his desires. He had to figure out a way to re-direct Les' energies elsewhere. The opportunity arose during a friendly intramural flag football game.

Chiropractic school organized these intramural sports so that students could interact with fellow students who weren't in their classes. Terry appreciated them for many reasons: it was a welcome release from the pressure of international water polo, and it was a congenial environment in which to make new friends and socialize with a wide array of interesting people. It was also an opportunity to play with Lance; their sibling competitiveness had never waned.

But for many, the games constituted the sum total of extra mural activities on campus so the students often took them seriously and passions became intense.

There were two main teams in intramurals: the 'Never Sweats' - made up of many really good college athletes and the 'Never Say Never Bulldozers'. Lance and Terry were responsible for naming the Bulldozers team; it was intended to stoke up their adversaries and create more fire in the competitions. No matter which sport it was - basketball, softball, ultimate frisbee, soccer or flag football - the Never Sweats usually won.

In 1983, the Never Sweats – all pimped out in uniforms - and the Never Say Never Bulldozers – wearing plain yellow t-shirts - faced off in the Palmer intramural flag football championships. There was more at stake than just a football championship. Unlucky for Les, the campus had rallied around Terry because he was the only student on campus preparing for the 1984 Olympics and they were proud of that representation from their school. In their eyes, Terry was 'the man'.

Les was the captain of the Never Sweats but the second piece of misfortune for him was that nearly everyone on campus knew that Terry was in love with Lori. The well groomed, dark skinned, handsome Les was up against many obstacles including chants for victory that ran in Terry's and Lance's Bulldozers' favor against Les' Never Sweats team.

The game was physically intense and like most intra-murals sports, the athletes played both sides - offense and defense. Terry was playing defensive line and tight end. He caught a couple of touchdown passes and the game was rivetingly close with both teams possessing the lead for chunks of time. In the final quarter with the Bulldozers leading the game by 6, Terry found himself blocking Les as he rushed the Bulldozers quarterback. This was the official clash of the Titans and the crowd earnestly awaited the victor.

Terry laid into Les without constraint and just as his forearm touched the upper part of his face – albeit it partially accidentally - Les fell to the ground bleeding from the nose while holding his face in obvious pain. The game ended shortly after with the Bulldozers securing the championship. The crowd erupted with supportive fervor and Terry felt somewhere deep inside his soul that perhaps the victory would score some points with Lori. While Les went off to the plastic surgeon to fix his nose, Terry contemplated how he was finally going to take his relationship with Lori to the next level. Unbeknownst to most, Terry had every right to pursue Lori because Les wasn't in a position to be pursuing a relationship with her.

Before Terry and Lori finally had their official first date as a couple, they had solidified a substantially strong friendship – one that would help to tide them through many of life's future challenges. Terry truly believes that this foundation was critical to their long-term success as a couple. Mere physicality is fleeting and porous but it's the soul connection – wrought from years of solid friendship - that is inestimably valuable.

Shortly after the big intramural football victory, Terry and Lori began their official relationship. Even while dating, they poured sensible ice on any impetuous impulses by continuing to build a relationship built on much more than physical love. That patient bedrock of a solidly intact friendship developed markedly.

As Palmer finished another quarter, and finals ended, Terry and Lori took a big step: they booked into Napa Valley for the weekend. The much-anticipated getaway took place auspiciously at Dr. Wilkinson's Resort and Spa in Calistoga, Napa Valley. Finally they were able to take the lid off their suppressed desires and feelings; fireworks erupted, the birds sang, the earth fell off its axis briefly, and the rainbows emblazoned a few hallelujahs across the Northern Californian sky. Terry and Lori were officially in love.

The Never Say Never Bulldozers

Former Yugoslavia

CHAPTER 6

Navigating the Heavy Surf of Eastern Europe

It makes one better to have had hardships and to have overcome hardships and not to blame anybody else for your mistakes
– Maureen Forrester

15 June 1981: Eastern Europe is - unquestionably - the home of the strongest and most powerful water polo teams in the world. When the Soviet Union's Lenin, Stalin and a cadre of their ideological apostles inculcated communism throughout Eastern Europe in the 1900s, conventional religion was swept away and in its place, the Eastern Europeans turned to their own religion – water polo.

Two of the water polo powerhouses that have dominated the world are Hungary and Yugoslavia. The latter broke up in the early 1990s after the collapse of communism, and a bitterly fought civil war. No longer known as Yugoslavia, the area is now Croatia, Slovenia, Serbia and Montenegrin. Now that they constitute not one – but 3 powerful water polo countries, they may one day win all 3 medals in the Olympic Games. They were close to doing that at the 2012 London Olympics when Croatia won the gold, Serbia the bronze and Montenegro was 4th place. The only medal missing was the silver.

Their own rivalry is unparalleled: when these countries from former Yugoslavia meet in the pool there is national pride at stake and the fans show up in droves. In the most recent 2016 European Championship held in a transformed basketball arena in Belgrade, the opening match between Croatia and Serbia drew over 11,000 water polo crazy fans. The stadium had to be opened up for the finals which featured Serbia and Montenegro. The near record crowd of over 16,000 fans proved how important the sport is in Eastern Europe.

A brief summary of Yugoslavia's history gives some insight into the traumatic past few decades: After communist Russia's victory at the end of World War II (1944 – 1945), Yugoslavia was set up as part of the communist master plan with a set of republics: Slovenia, Croatia, Bosnia and Herzegovina, Serbia, Montenegro and Macedonia – all underneath it. Each of the republics had its own branch of the League of Communists of Yugoslavia party and a ruling elite.

There was a period of relative stability in Yugoslavia with a fair amount of economic growth in the 1960s and 1970s, but that all came crashing down upon their leader, Tito's death, in 1980. A strict autocrat, Tito was essentially the founder of the second Yugoslavia, which was a socialist federation that lasted from 1943 to 1991. However, he defied the Soviet hegemony and he began his own socialist program. He suppressed his people and crushed any nationalist sentiment. After his death, tensions between the Yugoslavian republics flared up. By 1991 the country had disintegrated into a series of inter-ethnic wars that lasted the rest of the decade.

After two Olympic finals in 1984 and 1988 featuring the USA and Yugoslavia, the two favorite teams heading into the 1992 Barcelona Games were these same two teams. The 1991 World FINA Cup proved to be the final time that Yugoslavia and the USA would meet in international competition. These two teams would battle in the semi-final of the tournament and once again the game would end in a tie and go to overtime. This time the USA would win and then go on to defeat Spain in the final to win the World FINA Cup and become the favorite team going into the 1992 Olympic Games.

Apart from having to sit out the 1992 Olympics because of their civil war, the former Yugoslavia has always held a proud water polo tradition. Croatia (part of the former Yugoslavia) took the silver medal in 1996 and the gold medal at the 2012 London Olympics. Serbia won the bronze medal in 2008 and the bronze in 2012.

But when it comes to the results, particularly at the Olympics, Hungary is the most powerful and most successful water polo country in the world. They have won a record 9 Olympic gold medals including 3 in a row in 2000, 2004 and 2008. Additionally, they have won 2 silver medals and 2 bronze medals. The stats speak for themselves.

If one were to draw a comparison between Hungary and Yugoslavia, Hungary has had a less tragic, less violent history since World War II. In fact, from the 1960s to the late 1980s, Hungary was often referred to as the 'happiest barrack' within the communist Eastern bloc. During the latter part of the Cold War, Hungary's GDP per capita was 4th only to East Germany, Czechoslovakia and the Soviet Union itself. The Hungarians enjoyed a more liberalized economy, a less censored press and less restrictive travel rights. However, in the 1980s, their living standards dropped dramatically due to the worldwide recession and communism's failure. By 1989, the Soviet Union was in steep decline and a younger generation of reformists saw liberalization as the solution to economic and social issues.

Having had a less anarchistic period than Yugoslavia between 1950 and 1991 does not mean that the Hungarians have not suffered. They have – very much so. Nobody in Eastern Europe has had an easy life. From an American's perspective, it's hard to fathom what their strongest water polo rivals have endured and experienced: large scale death in wars; families split up with re-drawn-up borders and ethnic divides; repressive regimes; military invasions and countless social ills that emanate from heartless governance. Only the tough have survived the turmoil in Eastern Europe and they have a kind of elevated fortitude that makes them almost invincible.

One edifying day, Terry sat down with Yugoslavian water polo player, Ratko Rudić, whom he played against between 1978 and 1980. Ratko would go on to a very famous coaching career - coaching Yugoslavia in the Los Angeles 1984 Olympics and the Seoul 1988 Olympics wherein they took home both gold medals. This was followed by another gold medal with Italy in the 1992 Barcelona Olympics and finally a gold medal with Croatia in the London 2012 Olympics. He holds a spectacular record of achievements. He also coached Team USA from 2002 – 2006 before moving back to Croatia.

Yugoslavia's Ratko Rudić in the 1980s Olympics

Ratko and Terry were discussing various countries' merits and in a moment of absolute clarity, Ratko looked at Terry intensely and said, "The problem with the USA athletes is that they do not know how to suffer." One of the world's greatest tennis players, Martina Navratilova, echoed that sentiment when she said, "Eastern Europeans have suffered and they are tough. They are not spoiled like Americans and they are prepared to go through greater hardship to achieve their goals."

The most famous water polo match in history is the 'Blood in the Water' semi-final match between Hungary and the Soviet Union at the 1956 Melbourne Olympics. Tensions had been running high between the Hungarian and Soviet water polo teams before the games because the Soviets had taken advantage of their political control of Hungary to study and copy the training methods and tactics of the Olympic champions.

At the time, the Hungarian water polo team was in a mountain training camp above Budapest. The Hungarian Uprising against the Soviets had just broken out and the team was able to hear the gunfire and see smoke rising from their beloved city below – all while they were preparing to defend their Olympic championship title. Eight weeks before the start of the Olympics, they were secretly moved to Czechoslovakia to avoid being caught in the crossfires of the violent revolution. The players only learned of the true extent of the uprising and the subsequent Soviet crackdown after arriving in Melbourne, Australia. Naturally, they were all anxious for news about the safety of their family and friends.

The Soviet army went in to crush the Revolution in Budapest, Hungary, and they didn't do it lightly: they used air strikes, artillery bombardments and tank-infantry actions. It was a thorough crushing. What followed during this "Blood in the Water" match at the Melbourne Olympics was the spilling over of a real-time war.

In this semi-final match, The Hungarians led the Soviets by a score of 4–0 with a little over a minute to play. The game had been a physical battle with blood being shed from players on both sides. Legend has it that the color of the pool was a light shade of pink due to the blood loss from the players. Officials called off the game before the end when a Soviet player, Valentin Prokopov, punched Hungarian player, Ervin Zádor, in the face above the water.

Given the animosity between the Soviets and Hungarians, the water polo officials were concerned that the Hungarians in the crowd were going to react violently to Valentin's actions against one of their own.

Ervin Zádor injured in the "Blood in the Water Match"

When Ervin emerged from the pool with blood pouring down his face, pandemonium ensued between the players and the crowd. It was like a volcanic eruption and the spewing lava was the simmering anger and animosity that had been brewing for years between the two countries. The game was emblematic of years of volatility in Eastern Europe and nobody involved in aquatic sports will ever forget it.

After the match, Ervin explained how important the game was in terms of salvaging pride for his beleaguered country, Hungary: "We felt we were playing not just for ourselves but for our whole country", he said.

Ervin went on to seek political refugee status and he defected to the USA immediately after the Olympics. It was an agonizingly difficult choice because he knew that by leaving Hungary, he was closing the door on his Olympic career. Hungary took the gold medal at that Olympics, and had Ervin stayed on with them after 1956, he most assuredly would have earned even greater Olympic prominence since he was only 21 years old – nowhere near his prime. After moving to California, Ervin went on to coach USA's Mark Spitz in swimming. He died in 2012 at the age of 77 having lived the majority of his life in California.

Apart from it being a metaphor for the times, The "Blood in the Water" story at the 1956 Melbourne Olympics also illustrates how physically violent water polo can be. Surviving the abuse meted out – both under and over the water – has made it one of the toughest sports in the world. In the last few decades, it's become more physically challenging and more aggressively played. Terry laments the route the game has taken: "Water polo should be about skills, technique, and strength but instead it's become increasingly about holding, grabbing and neutralizing the skilled players. It has become a wrestling match in the water that affects the flow of the game. It is not the same game it once was."

Terry's personal history with Hungary and Yugoslavia is substantial. In order to be the best, one has to play against the best, and so the USA team endeavored to play the two powerhouses whenever they could. Besides these teams training and playing against one another, individual players from Team USA have played and trained professionally in Europe whenever possible. The Eastern Europeans take water polo far more seriously than the U.S.; they pay their players professional salaries so that they can devote themselves to the sport full time. It's a luxury that the Americans wish they enjoyed, although, today, many on the USA national team have spent time playing professionally in the high level leagues overseas in order to improve their own game.

During Terry's 15 or more trips to Hungary with the USA team, he studied his opponents assiduously for tactical moves, positioning and overall game strategy. The water polo culture there is like no other and every visit is an opportunity to immerse oneself in the greatest water polo thinking tank in the world. There is an important tournament each year in Budapest called the Tungsram Cup and it normally has included the top 6 teams in the world. When Terry took over the captaincy of USA Water Polo in the 1980s, he made sure that his team made that top 6 list consistently.

One of the best-known Hungarian water polo players is Tamás Faragó. Interestingly, many of the top Hungarian players in the 1980s were announced as doctors during competitions in Hungary – and given the way they played, they certainly may have had doctorates in water polo. Tamás Faragó was actually an attorney; there was Dr. Csapo, with "surgical hands" on 2-meter defense, and Dr. Szivos, a 6 foot 10 inch giant who may have had a PhD in 2-meter defense.

But Tamás Faragó was a character of exceptional note: he looked like a gypsy and he wore his hair down to the middle of his back. He was an impressively solid 6 foot 5 inches and about 245 pounds. His powerful legs made him an exceptionally dangerous player, and Terry unequivocally rates him as the best player he's ever played against for several reasons: he could do so many dynamic and original maneuvers with the ball; he moved laterally like nobody else, and he was an all-round masterful tactician at the game.

When Terry played Faragó the first time in a tournament, two things had a mesmerizing effect on him: Faragó had the ball on the perimeter and was preparing to shoot. As Terry moved towards him in a shot-blocking position, Faragó moved laterally about 2 meters before Terry even had time to react. From the instant space that his deft 2-meter lateral move produced, he made a beautiful, perfect shot and goal. Terry stared at his opponent in utter awe.

In the same game, Terry went to set a pick on Faragó - to try to free up another player – but Faragó wrapped his one hand around Terry's neck, then looked at him with laser-beam focus and said in broken English "no pick". Terry knew instinctively that those words came loaded with a ferocious warning. Intimidated at first, Terry looked to find a solution without being choked out. But then he decided to earn Faragó's respect by fighting it out. By the end of the game, Faragó gave him the subtle signals that indicated to Terry that he had won his respect. In water polo parlance this is a critical psychological victory. It was somewhat of a relief for Terry, though, that Tamás

Faragó wasn't a center guard so he didn't have to match up with him too often in future games. For a man his size, his skills were unbelievable.

Dr. Csapo, Hungary's 2-meter guard in the 1980s, was 6 foot 6 inches tall and 250 pounds of brick-hard muscle. Appearance-wise he looked more like a middle linebacker than a water polo player. He had a unique and punishing way of guarding center. He would put one hand up - to show the official that he was not fouling Terry - and the other hand would go between Terry's legs where he would grab onto his manhood. Terry's pain threshold indicated that Csapo was serious, and his minute of agony elicited two thoughts from him: either he was going to die in the pool right then (worst case scenario) or he would never be able to father children (less severe scenario).

Terry's battles in the pool with Csapo became an all-out war of survival. Even though aggression is alien to Terry's nature, he had no choice but to enter into a no holds barred physically aggressive relationship with Csapo to stay alive. He would poke Csapo in the eye – or try to grab his thumb and break it, or punch him in the throat. On one occasion after the ball had turned over, Csapo had significantly hurt Terry and he knew that if he didn't respond with an equal wake-up call, he would forever be Csapo's slave. But the plan was to do it with equanimity because if Csapo witnessed Terry flinching from pain or livid, he'd notch it up to a mental victory over him.

After the ball turned over, Terry torpedoed down the pool with volition and speed. Slightly in front of Csapo, he shrewdly looked to see if the referee's attention was elsewhere; in mid stroke, he elbowed Csapo above the bridge of the nose with such force that he thought he may have broken his own elbow. Certain that he had delivered the blow that would immobilize Csapo, Terry looked back to find the bloodied face of Csapo smiling at him – as if nothing had happened. At that moment he was convinced that he was up against the James Bond villain, Jaws. In *The Spy Who Loved Me* movie and *Moonraker*, Jaws is the massive, brutish assassin who dispatches people with smiling metal teeth and never feels any pain when someone strikes him back forcefully.

As far as Terry remembers, Csapo never showed any of his opponents that he was intimidated or affected by them. He was one of the few players whom Terry knew he'd always have to battle but thankfully, at some point Csapo mellowed out – possibly because he had come to respect Terry through the years of physically battling each other in the water. Perhaps that mutual respect or fear allowed both players to focus on playing the game and helping their respective team to victory.

There were other Hungarian players who provided Terry with plenty of movie-worthy encounters. Dr. Szivos – the 6-foot-10-inch center defender - was not only vertically huge, and an older veteran, but he had a wingspan of over 7 feet. He was the only international player that Terry felt he could not successfully turn because he could not get outside his wingspan. The amphibious Szivos was completely different when he was on land: he wore thick coke bottle glasses to compensate for his exceptionally poor eyesight, and he walked around awkwardly. But once he jumped into water he transformed into Superman. It didn't take Terry long to recognize that Szivos had a ritual: each time Terry played against him, Szivos's tradition for the first face-to-face encounter with his American opponent (which occurred after Terry had swum down to center with him at defender) was to say in minimal, sternly-mouthed, heavily-accented English, "Hello Terry". Then it was game time and there would be no more pleasantries.

One of the reasons Hungary is credited with being the strongest water polo country in the world is that it has plenty of thermal water which – certainly before the days of heated pools - made it possible to play the game in winter.

Eger - a town in Hungary where there is a famous pool with a rock bottom - is one of those thermal spring waters, but the problem is that it is often difficult to see the bottom or for that matter 2-3 feet down. To players who have a healthy respect for the creatures that frequent large pools of water, this can be slightly intimidating not knowing what is lurking below. In 2005, the Hungarians built a new pool in Eger that resembles a church with a steeple – a fitting symbol to the religion of water polo there. When filled to capacity, the stands at the new pool in Eger easily hold 5,000 faithful fans.

Yugoslavian player Ratko Rudić was someone that Terry would come to know pretty well in the ensuing decades ahead. His relationship with him started as a player in 1978.

In his playing days, Ratko was an attacker and a formidably strong player. He knew and read the game exceptionally well and he was crafty and smart. Once, when the USA team was training in Belgrade, Terry incurred a severe rib subluxation that left him in severe pain and barely able to breathe for 3 days. He knew that he needed an adjustment and so he kept requesting for a chiropractor. Finally, the manager from the Yugoslavian team triumphantly announced that they had found a chiropractor and that the team captain, Ratko, was going to drive Terry to the hospital to meet the chiropractor.

Ratko loaded Terry into his funny little European vehicle and proceeded to demonstrate that his talents in water polo didn't extend to his driving abilities. The picture of these two huge water polo players fitting into the tiny little automobile was a visual illustration of how to drive in the fetal position. Their spines curled over, the two men careened down the streets of a crowded Belgrade with Ratko's hand permanently on the horn as he shooed cars off the road and honked at pedestrians to leap out of the way. If the traffic came to a standstill, the impatient Ratko would simply steer his vehicle onto the sidewalk and drive on it.

With Terry's rib subluxation and the severe pain he had been in for the past 3 days - he was relieved when Ratko finally pulled up at the hospital - to find that it actually felt slightly better. Now that the two men had become more intimately acquainted through the car ride, Terry felt he could ask Ratko a personal question. He looked at the many scars on Ratko's face and inquired, "water polo?" Ratko shook his head back and forth and said, "no – many car accidents!" This response did not bode well for the return journey.

The experience in the hospital was not in the realm of comforting. As Terry was taken down a corridor, he saw people lying on gurneys looking like they were dying. He was taken into a room with a doctor who, in fragmented English, explained that he had visited California and had met a chiropractor once. Not willing to risk permanent damage, Terry decided to take matters into control by talking the nice Yugoslavian doctor through an adjustment he was happy to learn. The cordial collaboration worked. After the hazardous journey with Ratko back to the hotel, Terry found himself able to train and play the next day.

After that cozy getting-to-know-you hospital ride, Ratko's and Terry's friendship was sealed for decades to come. When Terry took over coaching Team USA in 2007, he gave a lot of deserved credit to Ratko for what he had achieved coaching the American team from 2000 – 2006.

The Hotel Metropol in down-town Belgrade was a very convenient hotel for training because it was a short walk to the main pool in Belgrade. This was normally where Team USA trained while in Yugoslavia. The problem was that it sat on a busy street corner that was invaded by heavy truck traffic going right by Team USA's window all night long. After suffering through countless sleepless nights from the cacophony of engines roaring, horns blowing, brakes screeching and sirens blasting, the American men became convinced that the Yugoslavians had tactically and deliberately put them in this hotel so that they'd arrive at scrimmages the next day exhausted and sleep deprived.

Resigned to not being able to sleep, the team would stay up most of the night at the Metropol playing board games like Risk, dealing cards or sitting and telling stories. The team could always count on Joe Vargas to have a tale to tell and many of these sleepless nights turned into hours of laughter. Fatigue would eventually catch up to them all and sometime in the early morning hours they would pass out for a maximum of 3 to 4 hours of sleep. That was no way to take on the skilled and feisty Yugoslavian team, and they knew it. After a time the Hotel Metropol took on the reputation as the 'No Sleep Inn'.

In contrast to this, Yugoslavia had its extraordinarily beautiful moments. Team USA took a boat trip along the Yugoslavian coast and they stopped at each port city where they played games. It all seemed a picture of perfection except for this potentially perilous problem: the boat was wooden and interim team manager, Chuck Metz, suffered from narcolepsy – which is a chronic brain disorder in which the person cannot control his sleep-wake cycles. Unfortunately, to complicate this situation, Chuck was a heavy smoker; a smoker with narcolepsy in a wooden boat - that's a potentially fatal combination. He fell asleep many times while smoking, necessitating members of the team to be on vigilant watch for lit cigarettes that suddenly rolled onto the deck. A quick stomping remedied the imminent drama.

There were other dramatic incidences associated with this famous boat ride along the scenic Yugoslavian coast. Tim Shaw, who was a member of

Boat rides along the Yugoslavian coast

the 1984 Olympic team, was also an Olympic swimmer. His credentials made him spectacularly popular with swooning women who commandeered his attention. On one particular night, he basked in the female attention a little too long – missing the boat the next day because of his romantic expedition. As the boat motored out of the harbor, a frantic Tim Shaw came running onto the shore – waving his arms pathetically and shouting for any of the players to help convince Coach Monte – to take mercy on him and come back! Fortunately for Tim, the boat came back and picked him up, but the punishment was severe: Monte sliced into him and as the words flew they were coated in extra spitballs – a sure sign that Monte was particularly upset.

The Yugoslavian adventures were numerous. On one of the boat stops, the team played on an island in a pool that had exotic stringers with lights over the water. The lights were intended to make the field of play more brilliant. But nature has a willful way of interfering with man's plans; at the height of the game, a severe electrical storm struck with such ferocity that the lightning knocked out all the lights on the entire island. In order to prevent a few water polo players from being skewered by lightning, the officials called the game off and ordered the players out of the water. After drying off their toned bodies, they coordinated a tactic to make it back to the boat on an island that had become pitch black.

When lightning lit up the sky, they would sprint towards the boat, and when it was dark, they would freeze like statues. This red light/green light adventure made the journey back to the boat feel like one of those silly games you play as children except this wasn't a game – and every time the sky crashed with another volt – the men felt nature's power imprinting itself decisively. Once everyone was back on the boat, they laughed off their high-riding emotions.

On November 9, 1989, thousands of jubilant Germans brought down the most visible symbol of division at the heart of Europe – the Berlin Wall. For two generations, the Wall was the physical representation of the Iron Curtain, and East German border guards had standing shoot-to-kill orders against anybody who tried to escape to the west. But just as the Wall had come to represent the division of Europe, its fall came to represent the end of the Cold War. Communism was a tried and tested failure and there was no choice but to concede the defeat of a fallen ideology.

U.S. President Ronald Reagan developed a uniquely special relationship with the Soviet Union's leader, Mikhail Gorbachev, and in his famously impassioned speech at the Brandenburg Gate near the Berlin Wall on June 12, 1987, Reagan challenged Gorbachev with the words, "tear down this wall." He implored Gorbachev to do it as an emblem to increase freedom in the Eastern bloc through 'glasnost' (transparency) and 'perestroika' (restructuring). During this period of welcomed détente between the USSR and USA, Mikhail Gorbachev would visit Ronald Reagan in California in the most unassuming way. He'd arrive by helicopter on billionaire David H. Murdock's Ventura Farms in Thousand Oaks, and stay in a quaint yellow hidden-away cottage on the property. Maybe that in of itself spoke volumes about Gorbachev's character and unpretentious nature.

The jubilation felt around the world on November 9, 1989, as the Berlin Wall came crashing down was inestimable. Back at the White House in Washington D.C., President George H.W. Bush and his National Security Advisor, Brent Scowcroft, watched the unfolding of events animatedly - both of them acutely aware of the historical significance of that moment.

For the water polo world, this day had massive consequences – good and bad – depending on how you gauged it. The numerous ethnic groups that comprised Yugoslavia held historical animosities towards each other stretching back hundreds of years. While these animosities were put aside after World War II, they were not, however, forgotten and when nationalist politicians needed to create a power base, they merely had to promote nationalist symbols and myths, and encourage the discussion and exaggeration of past atrocities. This created a deadly snowball effect that proved unstoppable.

The decline of communist ideology in the rest of Europe led to the severe weakening of Yugoslavia's crucial unifying factors. The country was also reeling from the severe 1980's global recession which found them carrying a foreign debt of $US 20 billion.

Slovenia and other relatively economically prosperous regions started to push for economic and political change and they mobilized forces for change. Long significant to the Serb nation, Kosovo became the catalyst for the revival of Serbian nationalism. Led by the Serbian Academy for Sciences and Arts, from 1986 onwards, many prominent Serbs claimed they had been the victims of consistent discrimination in Yugoslavia.

The bitterly-fought 1990's civil war in the region produced untold hardships for its people as Yugoslavia split up into Croatia, Slovenia, Serbia and Montenegro. Oftentimes, while Team USA played against their Eastern European rivals, they'd witness the players burdened with worry before or after a game – wondering if their loved ones had perished back home in the war.

It was difficult to watch as former teammates from Yugoslavia seemed to now have a real dislike for each other that translated into some very hard fought physical battles in the pool. In the 2007 World Championship in Melbourne, Australia when Serbia played Croatia in the semi-finals, the crowd was crazed. It was as if every Croatian and Serbian immigrant who now lived anywhere in Australia - had traveled to this game with one thought - to settle the score and prove who was better. The battle in the pool was one of the toughest games that Terry ever witnessed and to top it off, there were fights in the crowd that rolled into the nearby streets after the games. Mounted police and riot squads were called in to control and calm the situation. Croatia beat the Serbs and eventually ended up on top of the podium as the World Champions – much to the Serbians' disgust.

On one particular trip to Serbia and Montenegro, those countries split when Team USA was in Belgrade. The USA Embassy in Belgrade was attacked and the USA team members were ordered on lockdown in their hotels rooms for 24 hours. The following day, the teams were scheduled to train in Montenegro. Overnight, the Serbian and Montenegrin teams had been split into two. When Team USA trained, they faced a new Montenegrin team with many new faces. The amazing part of this situation was that the team did not miss a beat. They were as strong as ever in the water - a testament to how much water polo talent exists in this region of the world.

This time of civil war and turmoil seemed to have wrought a heightened level of resilience in the already hardened, stoical Eastern European players. Perhaps Ratko Rudić had hit the nail on the head when he said, "American athletes don't know how to suffer." He knew in too raw detail how much his people had suffered through these years – and maybe the suffering has augmented the gene pool and the national pride in water polo – to make the accomplished Eastern Europeans the toughest, most resilient water polo players the world will ever see.

USA Water Polo 1982 at University of California Los Angeles (UCLA) pool

CHAPTER 7

Preparing for the Los Angeles 1984 Olympics

Swimming with the Pod

Discipline is the bridge between goals and accomplishments
– Jim Rohn

July 28, 1984: After the arcane disappointment of the 1980 boycott, most of Team USA's water polo players emerged pulverized - recoiling into their private coral caves to replenish their energy resources and ameliorate the massive quotients of time spent away from their families and work commitments. This cave period was a crucial time of reckoning where each player had to gauge his own desire and stamina for another Olympics. For two years each of them grappled with committing to that all-in zone – a zone that unremittingly demanded 100% of themselves.

Part-time practices took place in Long Beach, Southern California, and at Stanford University in Northern California with the team split up depending on the vicinity of their abodes. The only time they merged together was on the weekends when either the Northern Californian players would fly down to Southern California or vice versa. The incessant airport transfers each weekend took their toll - depleting the energy reserves of men who juggled full-time studies or job commitments during the week. Meanwhile, many of the European teams enjoyed the enviable luxury of being immersed in full-time, professional water polo. It was a sore comparison and Team USA was painfully aware of their comparative shortcomings in the rigorous preparation.

In 1982, the huge wake-up splash pelted them. The lack of full–time preparation became ruefully apparent at the 1982 World Championships in Ecuador. Team USA placed 6th behind the Soviet Union (gold), Hungary (silver), West Germany (bronze), Netherlands (4th) and Cuba (5th). The officiating also appeared to be hostilely pegged against the USA.

Although somewhat dispirited and dejected, the team returned to California with the notion that they were not that far off from their target. For a team that had only trained part-time they had finished this tournament one goal away from the medal round. Returning home, they all held onto a belief that with a full commitment they could win a gold medal in the 1984 Olympic Games in Los Angeles. Sometimes losing teaches great lessons and the overwhelming sentiment on the team after the World Championships was a strong belief that they had the potential to beat anyone.

Eight of the thirteen 1984 Olympic team members came over from the 1980 squad and were highly experienced at what it took to be in the best shape of their lives. Olympic D. day was July 28, 1984 and not a day could be wasted. The team motto became, "Within every struggle in life there is opportunity". Imperviously united, they were intent on proving to the world that they could rise to the top. They knew the rapacious sacrifice it would entail and the training consumed them. With every victory against a European opponent, their emerging strength solidified the podium possibility. It was never going to be easy but struggles made them better people – like a catalyst effecting superlative performance.

Each of the members of the Olympic team was a superstar at his respective university. One of the keys to winning a gold medal would be to mold these superstars into a team where each player had to play a specific role. Perhaps this role would be very different from the role they played on their college team. This sacrifice of playing a different role or a smaller role would either make or break the team. Ultimately, it would be up to the coaches to blend these superstars into a cohesive team. There was no doubt that these players made up the core of perhaps the best water polo era that USA ever enjoyed between 1980 and 1992.

In the team there was Kevin Robertson, the fast, quick lefty whose attacking skills and super quick release made him a very valuable playmaker and goal scorer. Out of the University of California at Berkeley (CAL) he was also a great passer and set-up man on the 6 on 5. Having a left-hander at the 6 spot is critical for 6 on 5 success and Kevin was as good as anyone in the world at this spot. He read the defense well and either took the proper shot or made the proper pass. Kevin also provided speed on a team where the counter attack was a significant weapon. As a left-hander, he also had to defend one of the opposing team's best attackers, and Kevin was able to do this admirably even though he was usually one of the smaller players in the pool. Terry particularly enjoyed playing with Kevin. Having joined the national team together in 1978 as the two youngsters, they shared a special bond and both of them would go on to be excellent team-mates through the 1988 Olympic Games.

Gary Figueroa was a naturally gifted great scorer on the team out of the University of California at Irvine (UCI). He had an uncanny ability to see the play before it happened. No coach can teach that. A man of sol-idly decent principles, Fig loved to have fun; how-ever, come game time, he was all business. Even before he received a pass he would carefully watch the goalkeeper and be able to "read" the situ-ation as to whether or not to shoot, and where to shoot. Of course, Fig was an offensive-minded scorer and he would usu-ally shoot if there were even the slightest of

Kevin Robertson and Terry Schroeder

openings to the cage. Sometimes this earned him the wrath of the coaches. He did score a high percentage of his shots and played a crucial role at the 1 spot on the 6 on 5 – making him critical to the team's success. Figgy was certainly one of Terry's favorite targets to look to pass to when the team needed a goal.

If ever there was a player who was unquestionably loyal and 100% com-mitted to the team's success, it was certainly Joe Vargas. A standout at Uni-versity of California Los Angeles (UCLA), he had a surplus amount of energy and moved incessantly. He was not one of the team's high scorers but he kept the opposing team's defense on edge all the time with his unpredictable, constant movement. This often displaced the defender as they chased after Joe – thereby opening up a teammate who could then score. This was what being on a successful team was all about. Joe might not receive credit for the goal but he made things happen around him because he created chaos for the defense. From a teammate's perspective, Joe was a good friend and a respected, tough player.

John Siman, Gary Figueroa, Joe Vargas and Jon Svendsen

Chris Dorst was also one of the best goalies in the USA. Unfortunately for him, his role became that of a backup to Craig Wilson, which gave him limited time in the water, but he took on the role without ever complaining, and became one of the team's best cheerleaders. He was always positive and always available to help a teammate. His comedic timing was also perfect: when the team was depressed after a tough game or training, Chris provided a reason to smile. Super easy with whom to get along, he hailed from the water polo bedrock of Stanford University and married a Stanford swimmer, Maybeth Linzmeir. They went on to produce three daughters who all became strong water polo players.

Chris Dorst and Terry Schroeder

John Siman was a veteran out of Long Beach State University. He was a defender and captain of the "nut squad". The nut squad was made up of the game time non-starters on the team. Their role was to push the first group every day in practice and they did. They often took the heat from Monte which made their role that much more difficult. This group may not have received much credit along the way, however each of these non-starters was essential to the team's ultimate success. Terry and John clashed in practice every day; they made each other better by going as hard as they could against one another. Some days John would get the best of Terry and other days, Terry would get the best of John. They became good friends in the process. The sacrifices that the men have to make when committed to the Olympics played out in John's personal life. His first wife left him while he was on a European training trip – probably because she was not able to handle the immense toll that the Olympics takes on relationships. John went on to marry Natalie, a beautiful, friendly and outgoing lady – and one of the team wives who really opened her arms to Lori. After the success of the 1984 games, John did a snickers bar commercial.

Doug Burke – known as 'Dougie' - was Terry's roommate along with Jon Svendsen during their 3-month full-time training prior to the games in 1984. He was an adept attacker, shooter, and 6 on 5 specialist. He had a quick release shot that was deadly to opposing goalies. He tended to be a cerebral thinker and was quiet. Like a few others, he battled with Coach Monte in the sense that he disagreed with the way Monte handled certain situations. Terry regarded Doug as a great roommate whose cooking and baking skills were much appreciated. Another Stanford graduate, Terry and Doug have maintained a special friendship to this day.

Jon Svendsen – "Sven" – was the team's 1980 captain, and no doubt Terry and Jon's friendship was tested after Terry took over the captaincy in 1981. A strong defender with a powerful outside shot, he put the team's needs first and wanted the gold medal as badly as anyone did. He was willing to sacrifice the captainship if the team and coaches felt it would afford them all a better chance

Terry Schroeder and Doug Burke

Craig Wilson and John Siman - 1984 Olympics

of attaining that goal. In and out of the water, Jon was one of the toughest players on the team. He was certainly someone that you wanted to be on your team, rather than having to play against. Although, his role may have changed slightly between 1980 and 1984, he was one of the veteran leaders on the team and he was willing to play the role that the coaches asked him to play and con-tribute to the team's success in every way he could. During his college days, Jon played for the University of California at Berkeley.

Craig Wilson - 'Willy' – was arguably the best goalkeeper in the world at the time, and one of the best athletes on the team. He was one of the fastest swimmers, had the strongest legs, and could throw the ball as hard as anyone on the team. He is also credited as being one of the pioneer players in the USA who began to go over to Europe in order to play water polo professionally. He played in Italy for many years and enjoyed a successful professional career. Craig came from the University of California Santa Barbara (UCSB) where he helped Santa Barbara win an NCAA title in 1981. Incredibly, Willy did not begin his water polo career until he was at UCSB. This is a testament to how gifted he was as a natural athlete. Craig was the leader of the team on defense.

Peter Campbell was a bit of a loner who oftentimes came into practice on his bike and barefoot. He was a water polo junkie and came from the University of California Irvine (UC Irvine) along with Gary Figueroa. The team reckoned he slept with a water polo ball every night. They nicknamed him 'Chewbacca' – after the Star Wars character who was big, hairy and laid back. His primary position was that of defender; however, he really was an all-around utility player. A good outside shooter, Peter barely ever showed any emotion and for that matter rarely spoke. Although not as socially electric as others on the team, he still played an important role in the team's chemistry and success.

Drew McDonald was one of the team's most serious players. A great defender, nobody in the team wanted to incur Drew's wrath. He was intense and meant business. His expectations of himself were high: every practice was a make it or break it situation for Drew. He wanted to be the best and he wanted the best for the team. If someone scored on him, he would often erupt with self-inflicted frustration during practice. He was a cerebral player who really studied the game and made calculated plays. Committed and serious about his role in the team, Drew was ultra-reliable.

Since he was one of the prime defenders, he and Terry would battle every day in practice. However, on the road against anyone else in the world, he was fiercely protective of Terry, and this was proved particularly in an incident when a Dutch player punched Terry in the mouth during a match and fractured a couple of his teeth. Drew promptly responded and unequivocally terminated the Dutchman's game.

In another incident, while playing against fellow teammate James Bergeson during a practice session, Drew dispatched James with two separate blows: the first blow sent James off to the emergency room to be stitched up; the second blow (a few days later) hit James in the exact same spot where he'd previously been stitched up - opening up the wound again. Tempers flared at this second blow situation – leaving James seething with Drew. Some heated words were exchanged but eventually sensibility reigned when both players realized that challenging one another was part of their task. Sometimes, it would cost them some blood! A Stanford graduate, Drew went on to carve out a very successful financial services career. Terry has remained close to Drew through the years and oftentimes calls him for advice, wisdom and inspiration.

Jody Campbell was a lovable joker, prankster and party man who played with the heart of a lion. His attitude was that he would do whatever it took to win, and since water polo wasn't like tennis with courteous manners, he played toughly every game. He was also a center on this talented team and gave the USA squad a tough-to-defend 1-2 punch at the center spot along with Terry. The two centers had very different styles and complemented each other very well. Terry would beat an opponent with strength and technique while Jody would grab, hold and finesse his way to a goal or an earned exclusion. Another Stanford man, Jody always kept every team member on his toes.

He loved to ask a teammate or even a teammate's wife to smell something. His "hey does this smell funny?" line became routine and then when they would smell it, he would promptly shove it up their noses. This was how he welcomed Lori onto the team. Above all the play, when it came to serious game time, Jody was someone that you wanted on your team. He would do anything for his teammates and he had a massive heart that found a way to win.

Tim Shaw was an Olympic swimmer who won a silver medal in the 1976 Olympics in the 400-meter freestyle. At one time he held three world records in swimming and in 1975, he won the Sullivan Award for the best all-around amateur athlete in the USA. A great water polo player out of Long Beach State University, his place in the team was not without its controversy. Both his parents worked for USA Water Polo and that brought on the inevitable bias theories. Tim provided speed to the team in an era where the counter attack was one of Team USA's biggest weapons.

Terry's election as team captain for the 1984 Olympic team happened organically without question. There wasn't a specific vote: it was a simple assumption that the best man for the job would naturally take on the role. According to Doug Burke, Terry became the unquestionable leader of the team because of the way he carried himself. Doug describes him like this: "The great thing about Terry is that he never demanded to be the leader. Actions always spoke much louder than words with Terry. What he did – in a metaphorical sense - was tell everyone that he was going to climb up the hill, and if any of us wanted to join him, we could. People are much more likely to follow a natural leader when they do the work themselves and set the pace while giving others the choice to join in. How could you not follow him? Here was this completely dedicated man who conducted himself with dignity – who never yelled or lost his composure. Terry had so many admirable traits that all of us in the '84 team respected. He was an intelligent, cerebral player who was ferociously loyal to the team's best interests."

Terry had been Captain of the Pepperdine University Water Polo team for 3 years. Inspired and influenced by the Pepperdine President, Dr. Howard White, he exercised humility and never resorted to vocal outbursts. His teammates respected him for his honesty, his 'lead by example' style of captaincy, but most of all for his integrity and disinterest in attention seeking. The fact that he was also one of the best players in the world was the icing on the perspective.

Terry knew only too well that most of his teammates came with excellent leadership credentials from their respective colleges – and so the team dynamic was one where many of the players rose to the occasion when multiple layers of leadership were necessary.

But it was Terry's emotional and physical strength that particularly impressed his teammates. It didn't matter how badly he was hurt in the water, he never showed it, and he never lost his cool. Jody Campbell remembers only one time when Terry ever showed that he was angry in the pool. While the two of them were playing against each other in a Stanford University versus Pepperdine game, Jody kept goading Terry by shoving him in the chest. Finally Terry had had enough so he unleashed his best right hook onto Jody. The blow stunned Jody physically and emotionally, and while he sought to regain his composure, Terry simply turned around and languidly swam off into the horizon. Even then he refused to show any emotion. He was the team's level-handed rudder who led with formidable physical and mental strength. Jody still takes pride in the fact that he was one of only two people in the world who ever upset Terry enough to actually get punched! He wore the punch as a trophy.

Head Coach Monte Nitzkowski knew the game. He was also an excellent swimmer and represented Team USA in the 200-meter butterfly in Helsinki, Finland at the 1956 Olympic Games. He was Team USA Olympic Water Polo coach in 1972, 1980, and 1984. His team won the bronze medal in 1972 and was about to add another podium medal to his résumé. Monte is credited with being the godfather of USA water polo. He impacted the game in his host country monumentally by bringing new tactics to the game which were incorporated into the rule book. Since Eastern Europe dominated water polo and its tactics, Monte gave a much-needed voice to the USA – and penetrated the eastern bloc echelons who ruled the game with an iron fist. Monte was one of the first to really develop the counter attack offense which became one of the USA's biggest weapons. He also should be credited with bringing more movement and flow into the game which was healthy for water polo. He led the team during the golden years of USA Water Polo and should be given a great deal of credit for doing so.

Jody Campbell describes Monte's complexity like this: in 1980 and 1984, he hated having Monte as a coach because his objective was to break everyone down mentally – so that if they cracked – Monte would know that they were not tough enough to be an Olympian and they would be off the team. Monte firmly believed that winning at the Olympics was about mental toughness and grit. He didn't want to discover in a gold medal final that one of his players was about to implode with an emotional breakdown. He wanted those who might crumble out of the team equation before the Olympic Games – and he tested the men's resilience by inflicting them with intense physical training and mental humiliation.

In 1980 he told Jody, "You don't deserve to receive an Olympic ring – but when you get it – I want to take out the stone and shove it up your ass!" All these years later, Jody holds no resentment towards Monte for those abrasive words. He believes that the modus operandi made him mentally stronger all round – but at the same time – he also remembers seeing great and gifted athletes quit because they couldn't handle Monte's coaching style.

Ken Lindgren was the Assistant Coach - also known as 'The Preacher'. Everyone loved Ken and he proved to be a perfect balance to Monte. Soft spoken and easy to approach, he was always reasonable. He knew that Monte was loquacious but he never went against him. He always had Monte's back and never overstepped his boundaries – something Terry respected and admired. Monte and Ken would later put on a highly successful camp in Long Beach, California called the 'Camp of Champions'. They remained close friends, enjoying lunch once a week until Ken passed away in 2013. Monte spoke at his funeral and even played a song on his Ukulele in honor of Ken. It is not easy being an assistant coach whose role it is to back the head coach at all costs. The assistant may not always agree with the tactics or the strategy outlined by the head coach, but he needs to support the coach in front of the players at all times. It takes a special person and Ken was incredibly loyal to Monte for his entire tenure.

Rich Corso was the goalkeeper's coach or rather the "goalie babysitter", as Terry put it. Rich came into the program looking to help wherever possible. The team's two goalies, Craig Wilson and Chris Dorst, were driven and did not really need a coach although they probably liked having someone looking after them specifically. Truth be told, he did a great job of keeping the goalies focused and getting them in the best possible physical shape. Rich went on to enjoy a successful coaching career winning multiple high school championships at Harvard-Westlake. He finally landed at University of California

Berkeley (CAL) where he coaches the women's team.

Manager Terry Sayring – known as "Sunshine" – was the ideal manager. He was loyal to Monte, Ken and the players. He would do anything including give money out of his own pocket to help the players be successful. Often was the time where he'd buy the team ice cream or a beer after tournaments or training. He always maintained a good finger on the pulse of the players – and sometimes knew more than Monte or Ken because he hung out with them and was more "in the trenches" with the players. Terry was a high-level college referee who officiated competently and fairly. He loved the sport and did everything he could to make it better. Even today he is still involved as a referee evaluator at the NCAA level (National Collegiate Athletic Association). Terry is one of the kindest and most generous people ever involved with USA water polo.

The 1984 team was made up of many singularly colorful characters that have immortalized their legacies with their never-to-be forgotten antics. Joe Vargas made his mark and marked his territory internationally. Out of the water, he maintained his preference for hot, humid environments with his cross-continental conquests of women. So successful was he in the art of seduction that he far out-eclipsed all the other players – and that's not necessarily an enviable legacy. Upon Joe's departure from some countries, some of the women who fell for his charms may well have wanted to punch him in the guavas or inflict some other critical bodily injury.

Women of all nationalities were – in the initial stages of meeting Joe - utterly smitten by the beguiling tanned knight whose particular penchant was chambermaids. Whoever cleaned Joe's hotel room – be it in Belgrade, Madrid, Rio or Naples - usually succumbed to Joe's wanton charms. Young señoritas giggled and blushed in their little dresses with white French lace aprons - while caving in at their knees. Women in the eastern bloc countries declared their volcanic love for Joe within hours after their first nostrovia toast. Language was never a barrier. The effect he had on the fairer sex defied scientific logic – but it was real – and it was always dramatic, emotional and worthy of its own reality show. Mostly always living on the edge, Joe was an exciting, enticing, adrenaline-charging party animal whose instincts propelled him. His actions in the pool echoed his land behavior. He brought energy to every game and was exciting to watch - no matter what had happened the night before. Fathers of every nation soon learned to lock up their daughters – away from Joe.

During one of the team's many trips to Hungary, one story about Joe remains immortalized: with strange bacteria abounding in the Eastern European countries, the men often succumbed to stomach infections and that's where one of the team's most famous doctors, Dr. 'Feelgood' came into the picture. His timing, though, was not his strong suit. Once, during an ultra serious team meeting between the players and Coach Monte, Dr. Feelgood barged into the meeting and blurted out to Joe Vargas, "do you want orals or suppositories?" This was code for Joe obviously needing a form of medication to settle his stomach but Dr. Feelgood's social skills must have been snuffed out under the weight of his academic skills. His "do you want it in the mouth or butt" question produced peals of ribald laughter and for the first time in his history, Joe blushed and was truly humbled. As serious as the meeting had been, even the coaching staff had a good laugh.

Oftentimes, Joe Vargas' partner-in-hijinks was Jody Campbell. The reason was obvious: Jody had that rare ability to metamorphose the molecules in a room when he moved in with his gargantuan, irresistible personality. When Joe felt like it, he enlisted Jody in some of his spontaneous romantic exploits.

One evening in Puerto Rico, after the two men had finished playing with the team, they navigated themselves towards a bar non-accidentally. As luck would have it, the lady serving drinks at the bar was decidedly attractive, so Joe unabashedly inquired what time she was due to finish work. Loyal to his friend, Jody, he asked the lady if she had a friend who could make this a happy foursome soirée. The two men were so committed to the evening's promises that they waited a full five hours for the shift to end! Finally, success was in sight. The water polo bodyguards accompanied the two ladies on an illustriously memorable night – leaving behind their DNA as a farewell to the town and the fleeting meeting with Puerto Rico's feminine side.

Jody Campbell's ability to galvanize everybody into his larger-than-life presence has never waned through the years. Just as he injected much-needed levity into the 1984 team when they most needed it, he continued to rouse their spirits at his animated annual New Year's Eve parties for all his water polo teammates and their spouses. Nobody ever wanted to miss Jody's parties. Even on the most glum nights, Jody was sure to help others see the brighter side: the lighter side of life. Where there was darkness, Jody always sowed humor and fun – and his teammates rallied around his positivity magnetically – as if it were a survival instinct. Jody was a bit of an adrenaline junkie. He liked to experience life at full throttle - and a few times he crashed and burned - injuring himself pretty badly. There is no doubt that his personality gave him that sixth sense ability to rise to the occasion when the stakes were highest. Jody shone at critical moments in the game.

In a similar but distinct channel, Craig Wilson deserves huge recognition. If ever there was a personality whose glass half full optimism was infectiously effective – it was most definitely Craig's. A character that genuinely loved life, Craig was always that joyful, positively motivated teammate who made the most of every circumstance. It was impossible not to enjoy life in Craig's company; he'd find a reason to celebrate even in an alleyway.

In all the years that Craig has played water polo, coached it, and continued to maintain his contacts with the legions of people he's met through the aquatic world, you will never hear a bad word said about him. He looks for the good in people; he strives to focus on the diamond in the rough. He was the team's goodwill ambassador around the world. No matter how hard fought a game might have been, Craig was usually out making friends with his opponents that night after the game. Where others rued their lot in life: the result of the water polo game; the unfairness of a call; the end of his water polo career, Craig has always sought the constructive channel – the one that allows him to swim away with gratitude and epically satisfying memories. There are few people who possess that uncanny ability – or maybe Craig has thoughtfully worked at it – because he knows that regrets and anguish are debilitating, useless burdens in life's journey.

The team's goodwill ambassador cracked the ice with the Russians long before the fall of the iron curtain. Tensions usually always ran high in and out of the water between the American and Russian players but it was Craig who ventured into Checkpoint Charlie territory – and helped to put an end to the distrust and enmity between the two countries.

While the USA team was playing at the Tungsram Cup in Budapest, Hungary in 1984, a banquet was held for the players at the end of the tournament. The Russian table was sequestered at one end of the room while the Americans sat at the polar opposite. Without any hesitation, Craig made his way across the border and greeted the Russian players with cheerful alacrity. At first he encountered a stunned version of KGB silence – but when he immediately brought up a topic of mutual interest – vodka – the rock-hard ice started to crack. Within seconds, one of the Russian players responded in English, "Room 523".

Excited at this new prospect, Craig enlisted the companionship of Joe Vargas, and the two men made their way furtively to the fountain of plentiful vodka. The Russians welcomed in their political foes without any qualms and Craig was about to begin a fantastical journey of discovery.

One of the Russians, Erikin Shagayev, who had visited the U.S. in 1982 for the FINA World Cup, had met a friendly, vivacious girl at the Pepperdine University track in Malibu, California. It was there that she had offered to show the Russian team around the Southern Californian landscape. The Russian gentleman now wished to express his gratitude to the girl in Malibu by asking Craig to deliver a gift to her when he returned home. He said he would do it with absolute pleasure. A few weeks later Craig met the hospitable girl named Maria, gave her Erikin's gift, which was a ring, and fell instantly in love with her. Craig and Maria married two years later in 1986.

Two weeks after their wedding, Craig and the team flew to Moscow for the Goodwill Games. Quite spontaneously and serendipitously, Erikin Shagayev happened to be in the stands where Craig was sitting, and the two friends ran into each other. Of course Erikin inquired about Maria, and Craig responded gleefully, "She's now my wife!" After Erikin extended his congratulations, a Sports Illustrated writer, who was sitting behind them, couldn't resist eavesdropping in on the conversation. He went on to write a Sports Illustrated article in which he said: "Soviets Take the Gold; Wilson Gets his Girl".

As far as water polo went, when Craig was in the goal, the team knew that they had a chance to win. No matter how poorly the offense was playing, the team knew that the opposing team would struggle to score many goals and therefore USA always had an advantage. Craig would often say, "the ball looked like a beach ball". Obviously when a water polo ball looks like a beach ball, it is going to be much easier to block.

The stories surrounding the team's worldwide journeys with teammate Kevin Robertson are also awash with memory-firing imagination. A polite description of Kevin would be to say that he was an ultra-discerning eater. Put more bluntly, he was picky to the point of making eating in foreign countries almost impossible. So afraid was he of foreign delicacies that he insisted on traveling with an extra suitcase of food on every trip around the globe. The staple features in that case were American peanut butter and Tang orange drink. It goes without saying that Kevin was not going to take any chances on food that he was unsure about (which was about every meal outside of the USA), so he enlisted his trusty jar of peanut butter to provide him with much-needed calories, and sometimes he would find fresh bread to accompany the only food he trusted. Every once in a while, a jar of jam or jelly made the trip to round out the delicious and very safe peanut butter and jelly sandwich. Of course, this was to be washed down with a large glass of Tang.

Putting water with his Tang also provided Kevin with much anxiety while traveling. In countries that have suspiciously poor filtration systems for their water, Kevin always avoided drinking what he assumed was contaminated water, and once he witnessed teammates becoming ill by simply brushing their teeth with water out of the faucet, he was convinced that all foreign water was dangerous. This necessitated him bringing bottles of U.S. water in his suitcase, and when the team all saw workers at the hotel in which they were staying – filling bottles of water with hoses in the back alley – they too asked Kevin if they could drink his imported stash.

During this period of time, Mexico certainly fell into the 'don't trust the water' category. During the team's trips to Mexico City, one particular incident had them lining up for Kevin's water stash. They were at the Can Am Mex Tournament (Canada, America and Mexico) when John Siman became so sick with Montezuma's revenge that he ended up in a Mexican hospital – dangerously ill, severely dehydrated and precariously hanging on to what little interiors he had left. When he finally emerged from his ordeal, he told stories of having a shot of antibiotics with a needle designed to be used on horses. The next trip, Kevin brought a second suitcase of water. John Siman vowed he would never again return to Mexico City.

Eating in places like Belgrade, Yugoslavia, Budapest, Hungary, Sophia and Bulgaria in the 1980s brought on its own set of ratatouille nightmares. Financially challenged, the team had to eat whatever was dished out to them, and as they perused the lumps of red meat sitting in sludgy gravy for all three meals of the day, they were genuinely concerned about the constitution of the red meat. The "mystery meat" was enough to scare everyone on some occasions. Kevin, of course, could barely look at some of the meals without feeling ill. As his teammates gulped down their mysterious, sinewy stew, he watched them – his face contorted in disgust - as he sat down to another meal of peanut butter and Tang.

It was only Germany that produced a marginal change in Kevin's suspicions about the safety of food and water. When the team was on a training trip there, they visited a local beer garden where the owner triumphantly announced: "Beer is food!" Delighted with this newly discovered German knowledge, many of the men in the team drank more beer than usual on the trip for their hydration and nutrients. Even Kevin drank a few more beers than usual on this trip - happy for the very first time to supplement his Tang.

Craig Wilson was the diametric opposite of Kevin in the food stakes. Eager to savor the delicacies of all the host countries, Mr. Ambassador dove into everything that was offered on his plate – ignoring all the erudite cautionary tales offered him by Kevin. Once in Japan, he ate more than one entire sea slug and followed that with a true delicacy: "baby sparrows". What revolted Kevin even more was the manner in which Craig devoured the sparrow. Holding it feet first, he began with the bird's head - and the feet went into his mouth last. It was snake-like: repulsive in every way. Craig was never shy about food consumption. Raw food, dirty-looking morsels - all made their way into his mouth. Contrary to all predictions, Craig rarely became ill and was one of the healthiest members of the team.

Once back in home territory – California – Kevin made up for his lack of food consumption and often invited his teammates to enjoy prodigious quantities of food at his home. Terry often stayed with the Robertson family in Orange County, California during the weekend trainings, and he never left hungry. On many occasions the men would frequent one of Kevin's favorite food emporiums close to his home - a Mexican restaurant – Mi Casa - that served mass helpings for a reasonable price. Their supersized burrito would leave each man in a veritable food coma for the rest of the evening – making it a definite after-practice treat. It was like a food orgy that hung over into the next day's practice.

Doug Burke and Terry entered into their own private food challenge at a time when they were training six hours a day and going six days per week. During these days of full-time training, the team members were basically training, eating and sleeping. A normal day consisted of a light breakfast, then one and a half hours of weights, followed by two and a half hours in the water. This was followed by lunch, a nap, and then preparation for the evening practice. Another two and a half hours in the water was followed by a huge dinner, and then some time to talk and prepare for bed and another day of training. This required tremendous focus and discipline.

Food and sleep were critical components to the lives of water polo machines. One day, Terry and Doug decided to count the calories that they were consuming. Their record was over 15,000 calories in one day. Of course, dessert consisted of an entire tray of homemade peach cobbler and a half gallon bucket of vanilla ice cream shared between the two of them.

Terry and Doug shared a room for the final 3 months of full-time training prior to the 1984 Games. They entered into many deep conversations about water polo, life, girlfriends, and of course, Coach Monte. The two learned to lean on each other for support and comfort. They became close friends with a huge amount of respect and love for one another. Doug was justifiably terrified that he might be investing in all of this training – only to be cut by Monte at the end. He was tortured by this thought and it cost him many hours of restful sleep. Doug was a perennial "nut squad" player who struggled at times with confidence because he was often broken down mentally by Monte.

During one stretch, Doug suffered a broken bone in his hand, and attempted to come back from the injury too soon in order to get back in the water – to try to prove to Monte that he was tough and deserved to be on the team. He felt pressured to do this and as a result, ended up re break-ing his hand and having to take another four weeks off of training. It was a self-defeating situation exacerbated by his fear of Monte. Terry enjoyed Doug's company and did everything he could to encourage him and help him make the team. Doug loved to bake and cook. After the Olympic Games he would open up his own bread-making company and grow it into a super successful business before selling it off and retiring in Oregon.

As the Games neared closer, Monte seemed to be feeling more pressure to be successful. This meant that he turned up the heat on the team mem-bers. Some were close to quitting and this is ultimately what Monte wanted - to weed out the weak. However, through his rants and at times rages, the team learned to rely inescapably on each other. Many were convinced that this was Monte's master plan all along – to inculcate so much fear into the men that they turned to each other in unity.

It was a precarious gamble that Monte played and one that could have backfired on him at any moment. Only a month before the Olympic Games in Los Angeles, the 1984 team was close to mutiny. Players were asking for Monte's head and many were at the point of not wanting to play for him at all. As captain, Terry felt the enormous pressure to keep the team together and as they talked it through, they decided to ride it out together. Having been through so much by this time - the pact was to lean on each other and win or lose – to unite. That cohesiveness was a matter of survival - and as a team – they proved to Monte that they were strong enough to endure his tsunami lashings. They had won their battle with Monte: they were determined to fight with everything they had – perhaps shock the world – and win that coveted gold medal. It was a painful but triumphant realization.

Each player on the 1984 team was a colorful character – worthy of his own entire book. The 13 that made the final cut were the right 13. In the pro-cess of training and traveling together they became a deeply-bonded family. Now they had to prove themselves in the water - at Pepperdine.

1984 Olympic Men's Water Polo Team

1984 Olympic Men's Water Polo Team

Terry Schroeder at The White House with President Ronald Reagan and
Nancy Reagan after the 1984 Los Angeles Olympics

CHAPTER 8

The Arrival of the Los Angeles 1984 Olympics

The Most Memorable Waters

Individual commitment to a group effort – that is what makes a team
work, a company work, a society work, a civilization work
– Vince Lombardi

In 1982, while Terry was at Chiropractic school, he received an unexpected
call from a woman who identified herself as Robert Graham's secretary.
Since Terry's focuses in life were a chlorinated 50-meter pool and studying
courses like neuroanatomy and organic chemistry, the name 'Robert Graham'
failed to ignite any significant awe-coated recognition. He was unaware that
the famous sculptor was the genius behind the Duke Ellington Memorial, in
Central Park, New York, and F.D.R. (President Franklin Delaware Roosevelt),
by the Cherry Tree, in Washington D.C. Just those statues alone are known
for their monumentality.

But Terry was about to learn of Robert Graham's particular partiality for
nude sculptures. Married to famous actress and director, Anjelica Huston,
their Venice Beach, California home was filled with nude statues and in a
Vanity Fair interview, Anjelica went on to relate the story of when Maria
Shriver, California's First Lady at the time (husband Arnold Schwarzeneg-
ger was Governor of California), visited Robert's and Anjelica's Venice home
with her "very Catholic" mother, Eunice. Eunice was the sister of President
John F. Kennedy and Senators Robert F. Kennedy and Ted Kennedy. She's also
the legendary pioneer of the Special Olympics.

As Eunice walked around the home - she surveyed nude women splayed
everywhere and remained proprietorially tight lipped. According to Maria,
when Eunice left, she said a quiet prayer for the artist and "his poor wife!"
Upon Robert's death in 2008, Maria delivered the eulogy at his Catholic

Requiem Mass and added a touch of warm humor relating Eunice's story.

Back to 1982 and the matter at hand, Robert Graham had been commissioned to design and sculpt an "Olympic Gateway" to the 1984 games at the Los Angeles Coliseum. The gateway was to consist of a 9-foot-tall headless female and male torso – true to life and entirely naked. The delicate question was posed to Terry: "Are you interested in being the nude male torso?" Convinced that this was the typical kind of prank call that his teammates had probably set up, Terry exercised cautionary restraint and requested that the 'joke' caller send through more information. In the meantime, in case it wasn't a joke, he turned to Lori and his parents for their opinion. Lori's opinion carried a lot of sway: she felt it was an honor and something he could show his grandchildren one day but keeping true to hers and Terry's lack of affectations she asked jokingly: "who's going to clean the pigeon poop off the statue every day?"

With trepidation, Terry steered his trusty Mustang with the red seats down to Robert Graham's home and studio in Venice Beach. While there he was asked to strip so that Robert could take a slew of pictures of his assets at every angle. Unaccustomed to strutting au natural in front of a stranger, Terry's awkward bell rang loudly. Robert then informed him that he was still interviewing other prospects and would let him know the eventual decision.

A few weeks later, Terry received the green light call: he was the uncontested male model choice. The objective of the statue was to create a human body that represented an Olympic ideal. The 'no head' part was done deliberately because the ideal was the focal point – not the person. Anxious to get to work immediately, Robert requested that Terry travel to Venice Beach a few times a week for a few months. The logistical juggling this entailed was complex: With school in Northern California, Terry compromised with one extra-long afternoon session per week before attending Southern California practices. After practice, he'd fly back to school for classes the next day.

Modeling for Robert Graham entailed an evolution of various stages of discomfort to comfort. The initial stages seemed pointless as Terry stood there – stark naked - while Robert played with his clay. No one came into the room at first, but before long, Robert's secretaries began to feel the spirit of the artistic integrity of the project, and so they walked in freely – pottering around nonchalantly while Terry stood in his birthday suit.

Unaccustomed to the artistic eccentricities of someone as gifted as Robert Graham, Terry encountered an unexpected surprise one day. With more than 20 hours logged modeling for the gateway and just as he thought the statue was taking shape and looking awesome, Robert went into a raging artistic spiral, threw the clay to the floor and said, "I have to start over again".

Desperate to recalibrate the lost time, Terry began to bring his study notes to the modeling sessions. As Robert started all over again and molded his masterpiece, Terry erected a lectern far away – because Robert didn't want any object to be in any close proximity to his crown jewels. So, with his biochemistry notes propped 3 feet away and off to one side, Terry had his first taste of long-sighted studying. 60 hours later, the task was completed and the water polo model had managed to incorporate some academic enlightenment into the process.

The Statue of Terry Schroeder

The back story was that Terry took out a loan and paid Robert a sizable chunk of cash to enhance the size of certain parts. Actually he didn't: he'd never sink to that level although it was a thought! The eventual 9-foot statue was converted into bronze and it stands in perpetuity outside the Los Angeles Coliseum.

But before the statue's official unveiling, the thrilling MI6 mystery to the story was especially riveting in light of the fact that Terry had managed to keep his big secret under wraps all those months he was driving to Venice Beach to pose before water polo practice. Not once did he let up to his teammates where he'd been – proving that he had great potential for the U.S. Secret Service.

The secret was eventually exposed by Robert Graham's friend, Robert Helmick, who worked with USA water polo and the United States Olympic Committee. Once the secret was out, it spread like wildfire, and Terry had no chance with his teammates, who had been waiting for a moment like this all their lives.

In early 1984, the male and female bronze statues were unveiled at the Gateway to the Coliseum. When Terry and Lori arrived at the ceremony, accompanied by hundreds of dignitaries, the statues were covered with drapes. Terry breathed a sigh of relief. Shortly thereafter, the statues of Jennifer Guyana and Terry were dramatically exposed, and Terry turned crimson as the cameras clicked away at his unphotoshopable reaction. The full reality of what he had done hit home: He was naked in front of the world! There was no hiding on that one. But that turned out to be the exceptionally mild portion of what was to come.

Terry's statue was manna from heaven to a mischievous group of team-mates who thrived on golden opportunities. The thesaurus had to amend their definition of 'ribbing' after the 1984 team had finished milking the young Schro's new reality. According to Jody Campbell, the scenario was that much more tantalizing because of all people who could possibly be on display – with no clothes on – Terry was fruitfully perfect! His conservatism and his shyness played right into their hands. "Had it been Joe Vargas", said Jody, "there would have been no reaction. In fact, Joe would have paid somebody to put himself on display in the buff. Not Terry. He was the last person in the team who was into any form of showmanship and we just loved it."

The team stayed in the University of Southern California (USC) dormitories – the Olympic village - and trained in the Coliseum pool every day. During the 2-week Games, they walked past the statue daily, and they wasted no time in pulling pretty women over to stare at it while gesticulating wildly at Terry. In fact, they ceased calling him by his real name. Instead, they referred to their captain as simply "the statue". To this day, the 1984 team reunions are inflected with hilarious jokes about the famous bronze statue by that guy named Robert Graham. It would be remiss of them not to keep reminding Terry of the shades of red he turned then, and still turns.

The 1983 tide washed in before anybody had time to think. Right off the diving block, there were two proving-ground tournaments: The FINA World Cup – which was held at Pepperdine University, Malibu that year – and the Pan American Games in Caracas, Venezuela.

The FINA World Cup was a test event for the Games and the host country took on that responsibility. The top 8 teams in the world played in a round robin type tournament. Another breaker wave struck Team USA as they came in 4th. Once again, the Soviet Union won the gold, which stung since the USA had only lost to them 7-6 in a game that could have gone either way. They tied 6-6 with Italy, who won the bronze, but a very bad loss to West Germany (7-3) cost them any chance at a medal. The West German machine was well oiled by their star lefty - Frank Otto. The indomitable Frank was a goal-scoring titan, as was the West German center, Hagan Stamm, who played with spectacular prowess.

Hagan would later become the Head Coach for the German team in the Beijing 2008 Olympics. Team USA usually matched up well with the West Germans; however, on this particular day in Malibu, the Germans had domi-

Pan American Games 1983 in Caracas with Drew McDonald,
Joe Vargas and Craig Wilson

nated the contest. Offensively and defensively, the USA's game was still not firing on all cylinders. They could put together a couple of great quarters a game but were not consistent for the entire game. Although frustrated with their finish, Team USA knew that they were close to being right in the mix with the top teams. Much hard work lay ahead.

The 1983 Pan American Games in Caracas, Venezuela were the Olympic qualifiers, but the USA was already over that hurdle since they were the host country for 1984 – an automatic qualifier. The conditions in Caracas were reminiscent of a 5th world country. The athletes spent a week coughing up gray dust that they inhaled from the unfinished cement floors. Most of the toilets were out of order, and there was no air-conditioning in a hot, stiflingly humid climate. Only the Pan American countries took part in the competition so the USA rolled through the

Germany's Frank Otto

tournament without any problems, beating Puerto Rico, Venezuela, Mexico, Colombia, Brazil, Canada and finally Cuba in the gold medal final.

Once they'd won the tournament, the team decided to celebrate – even if it was a small achievement with the Pan American teams. Some might say that they swam away from discipline and better judgment. Their excuse was that since the town was a mess, they might as well join the mess and throw all caution to the wind. On their last night in Caracas, they decided to paint the town red, so they weighed down a couple of taxis and bounced their way down the street to the not quite throbbing metropolis of downtown Caracas.

Within hours they paid the price: Joe Vargas – for the first time since his 18th birthday - was in no fit state to play his usual Don Juan role with the Venezuelan ladies; instead he threw up all over everyone in the taxi – including the poor driver. The rest of the men endured their own self-induced form of suffering the next day.

As the year marched on and ended, the pressure-cooker situation was approaching boiling point. In May 1984, the USA team began full-time training - just three months away from the Olympics. They all moved to Orange County, California and trained 6 hours per day 6 days a week. They had 12 weeks in which to produce a massive miracle. As captain, Terry did his best to steer them to what was about to become the USA's first return to the Olympic podium after an absence of 12 years.

The prerequisite of taking the game to levels of absolute excellence requires each team member's ability and willingness to sacrifice a part of himself and work with others in order to become the best possible team. Selfishness is the death knell of any high level team. Magnificent play is produced when each team member surrenders himself and gives everything to being the best possible teammate. This alone brings about a seismic shift in the group's performance. The same principle applies to corporations and communities as well. Selfishness is always self-defeating. Selflessness is the key. There is no room for egos or individuals. Water polo is a sport that requires all the pieces to be working synergistically for any degree of success. Each player must know his role and do his job.

In order to arrive at that impermeably solid, united front, the first thing that the1984 team had to accomplish was learning to trust one another. After that, the building blocks of respect could take shape. When it comes to Olympic level performance, practically every player in the top 8 countries has oceans of ability. That's already a given. But that defining mental edge comes from a team that works together as trustworthily and fluidly as a team of heart surgeons who are battling to save a human life. It's also about recognizing and celebrating team members' differences and working with each other's strengths. Blaming others, negativity, showmanship and vanity have costly consequences.

While having each other's back, it's essential during pressurized situations to develop that split-second clarity of thought that is in the team's absolute best interests. A crucial example of that is in the 6 on 5 situation. In a limited time frame, the offensive team with six men has the opportunity to score because the defensive team is one man down with only 5. The 6 on 5 situations are a true measure of how well the team is working together.

A risky or ill-advised shot by a player attempting to pad his personal stats can kill the team. In order for the 6 on 5 to be successful, team members must be looking to set one another up with 2-3 consecutive passes that stretch the defense and make them move out of position. When the 6 on 5 is working correctly, the team with the advantage might score 70-75% of the time. On the other hand, when it is not working well, the team with the advantage might score only 25-35% of the time. As a general rule, the bigger the tournament is – the more important the 6 on 5 becomes. Success on the 6 on 5 usually determines whether a team wins or loses the game.

The other critical factor is a team's belief in itself and its goals. That collective, positive attitude sets the stage for success. Conversely, doubt and a lack of confidence all have a crippling effect on the team's performance.

This team had an edge in all of this. The 1980 boycott had been extremely painful but it had brought the team closer together. They had been through a huge loss together (8 of the 13 players) but they had survived the experience and grown through it. It was a competitive edge that even they did not fully understand at the time.

In that critical 3-month period before the Olympics, the rewards of full-time training began to pay massive dividends. The team was playing exponentially more strongly by the week. By this time, General Secretary Chemenko announced that the Soviet Union was going to lead an Eastern Bloc boycott of the Los Angeles Olympics in retaliation for the USA boycott of their 1980 Olympics. Yugoslavia emerged as one of the gold medalist favorites along with West Germany, Italy, Spain and the Netherlands. The competition – despite the Soviet exclusion - was still going to be tough.

In June 1984, the USA hosted Yugoslavia in a series of exhibition games and beat them 3 out of 5 games, tied one and lost one. It was a promising curtain raiser for what was to come. They also traveled to Europe and placed 2nd at the Tungsram Cup in Budapest, Hungary – the biggest and most competitive tournament in the world where the top 6 teams are invited. The team was beginning to believe in itself and there was a surging feeling that they could actually go all the way.

Because Budapest in the 1980s lacked the social amenities that it boasts today, Team USA – whose attention span out of the water in 1984 was like a group of 4-year-olds in a playpen – became easily bored. Boredom usually leads to pranks – and this was no exception. With nothing to do in the evenings, the team hung out of their 8th floor windows and dropped coins on the sidewalk. When people rushed to go and claim the coins, the men waited with their trashcans filled with water, and then poured out – from the 8th floor - prodigious quantities of moisture onto their unsuspecting targets.

However, it was Terry who often took mischief to another level. The public image everyone had of him being a super controlled, perfect cherub - was his alter ego. Once away from the public's eye, Terry led the mischievous charge. Instead of just throwing water down from the 8th floor, he added American ketchup to the mixture – and the red deluge that cascaded down on the unsuspecting coin grabbers below - was cinematically dramatic.

When they weren't doing that in Budapest, they would get a light bulb filled with some type of liquor. The Tungsram company – who were sponsors

Members of the 1984 USA team taking a break from grueling practices

of the tournament - was an electrical company, and so the smart 100-watt veterans in the team figured that a light bulb - filled with liquor – would become an apt participation prize for being in the tournament. Every year, they ceremoniously handed out the liquor-filled light bulbs to each team member. However, in 1984, they ratcheted it up a notch by deciding to make the bulbs into Molotov cocktails. Fortunately for them, they never blew up anything or set anything on fire. Since then and out of necessity, Budapest has installed lots of night-time activities for visitors. Wisely, they also no longer give the competitors the liquor-filled light bulbs.

The party tricks were often deliberately insti-gated relief from a tough day's training or play. One night, after a demanding

Members of the 1984 Olympic Men's Water Polo team enjoy a reprieve from the Olympics

tournament in Frankfurt, Germany, Terry and his teammates were invited to a magnificent medieval castle in the beautiful German countryside. This wasn't just a casual invitation. It was a prestigious invite issued by the local Mayor and other dignitaries were to be present.

Always known for their exceptional discipline, the German Water Polo team accompanied the USA guests to the medieval castle. During that era in the sport, Germany's Frank Otto often remarked, "In the 1980s when there were no inter-net, mobile phones, and we were often very far away from home, it was easier to stay much more focused on the team and the game." But that single-minded, serious determination seemed to only apply to the Germans on this particular night. Hoping that this country foray would be a historically significant occasion for their American friends – they were not expecting what transpired.

As the USA men arrived at the castle, it was as if they rocketed back to their childhood time capsules. Entranced by the castle's imaginative pros-pects they enthused as they noticed the super cool moats and drawbridges in the middle of this black forest – everything that little boys dream about. The creative potential of the environment was too marvelous to ignore.

Terry claimed that John Siman was the instigator of this particular inci-dent: he ended up holding Rich Corso – their goalie coach - upside down - off the castle wall with the moat below. Distressed while being held, Rich flailed dramatically, which made matters worse.

A week later when they returned to California, Rich insisted that his NCAA (National Collegiate Athletic Association) championship ring from the Univer-sity of California Los Angeles (UCLA) fell off and dropped into the moat while John and the other culprits were holding him upside down. Afterwards, when the men went through their pictures at home they came across a dramatic picture of Rich being held off the moat – flailing - with the ring on. Then they looked at pictures taken a day later, and Rich's ring was still on his finger. It appeared that he wanted to make the team feel badly about losing his championship ring.

Despite training and playing hard - there were often nights when team members tossed and turned about on their beds restlessly. Jet lag was often a sleep inhibitor or just being in an unfamiliar, foreign bed created sleepless nights. Even the beds' lengths caused discomfort for the players who were too tall for the average length of the beds.

When sleep eluded them, instead of tossing and turning, the men stayed up laughing and telling stories - listening to and watching some of the veterans. As time went on, Terry's natural course was to gravitate after hours to the men who did not 'party' so hard. Kevin Robertson, Gary Figueroa and Doug Burke were not big drinkers; like Terry they recognized they needed more sleep and rest to function well the next day. This is not to say that this group was made up of perfect little angels. Quite the contrary, all of the team members were fond of having a good time; some, however, had more endurance when it came to partying, and Terry was not one of them.

On occasion, a few of the men would stay out till the early hours of the night having a bit too much fun. The next morning as they guarded each other in drill sessions, they reeked of alcohol. However, as the Olympics approached, much less of that was going on. Wholly dedicated, many of the team members had chosen not to drink at all during the final 6 months of Olympic preparation. They were determined not to blow this chance – having already experienced the fragility of the 1980 Olympics.

Riding the crest of a solid wave of positives including results and team camaraderie, the united, impenetrable team had morphed into a tightly-knit family, and they couldn't wait for the start of the Olympics. They knew, without any doubt, that they had an excellent chance of winning the gold medal. Every day in training, they amped up the intensity and challenged each other to try harder: to stretch themselves way beyond any boundaries and discover vast quantities of untapped potential. Hungry and focused, they were like race horses bursting to get out of the gates. The day finally arrived!

The Opening Ceremony of the 1984 Los Angeles Olympics proved to be a significant highlight in the entire team's life. Terry recounted the day in his journal so that he would never forget the skin-chilling details:

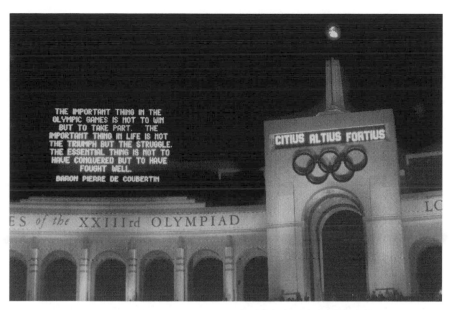

Olympic motto- Los Angeles Coliseum 1984

1984 Los Angeles Olympics
Opening Ceremony

Olympic Flag at the 1984
Los Angeles Olympics

John Siman, Joe Vargas and
Craig Wilson

Terry at the 1984 Los Angeles
Olympics Opening Ceremony

July 28, 1984

Earlier today we all loaded onto busses at the village that would take us to the Coliseum for the Opening Ceremonies. As I looked around, I felt in my heart the connection I had with each of the coaches and my water polo teammates who were on the bus. After all, many of us had worked together preparing for the 1980 Olympics and experienced together the subsequent devastating letdown of the boycott and of having to stay home. As our bus arrived at the unloading and organizing point for the Opening Ceremonies, I could sense a growing anticipation and excitement from all the athletes. There was a sense that this was going to be something special. We waited with nervous energy for our turn to enter the stadium. As the host country we would be the last to enter. I could feel my heart pounding as we were finally called and began our march towards the Los Angeles Coliseum.

We reached the tunnel that would lead us on to the field and all of us were inexplicably happy. But the rush of emotions that were about to hit us would magnify our feelings a hundredfold. There were 521 people in the US delegation alone. Our team was about three quarters of the way back from the front lines of team USA. We knew when the US flag bearer entered onto the field because the crowd erupted and, as far back in the tunnel as we were, we could make out the chant of 100,000 people shouting, "U S A, U S A, U S A." The noise from the fans hit us like a wind rushing through the tunnel and as we approached the opening of the tunnel, the chanting was so motivating it was hard not to push past those in front of us and run. As we emerged from the tunnel I was so full of emotion – it was an explosion of senses and to this day I can remember looking around and seeing happy tears streaming down the faces of so many of my teammates. I don't remember the details of walking around on the field, filing around the track (it really felt more like I was floating around the track) – some of it is a blur, but I'll never forget the enthusiasm of the crowd.

On the field, we looked around at the other athletes; I could sense that all were carrying in their hearts the same pride, the same joy, each hoping for the gold, all hoping to make their country proud. One thing every Olympic athlete shares is the knowledge of what was sacrificed to get to the Games. If you were standing on that field, you had probably put your life on hold; perhaps struggled in relationships, missed family gatherings and pushed yourself mentally, physically and emotionally to the limit. There was a strong sense of team as we stood together with Team USA. All of us had waited for this opportunity and for the moment to finally be here – and to have a chance to do it at home - was amazing.

As the torch entered the field, I was overcome with everything it stood for. Athletes around the globe refine their bodies and excel at their sport in an effort to compete while also promoting peace and supporting global community. As I watched the torch enter the stadium and begin the final hand offs between athletes as it was carried around the track, it saddened me for a moment that the Olympic ideal was so tarnished by politics. This time Russia and the other Eastern Bloc countries were not represented. But there the rest of the world's top athletes stood, each representing their country's athletic cream of the crop, watching the torch, watching that symbol that represents the true spirit of the Olympics. The torch was handed off 3 times inside the stadium before it was finally given to Rafer Johnson, who then ran up the final set of very steep steps. As the flames engulfed each ring, I knew my teammates were feeling the same thing I was: "This is real. We're really here. This is our chance to win the gold and make our dreams come true." The Olympic flame was lit and I could feel the fire burn inside my heart. At that moment, I realized that my dream had come true; I was an Olympian who, over the next two weeks, was going to have a chance to compete for the gold medal. We hugged each other and waited 5 days and nights before our first game.

While the Opening Ceremony was emotionally impactful – USA's 1984 Water Polo team had to inject some lighter moments in the otherwise grand occasion. Since Jody Campbell could always be trusted to provide those moments of levity, he unintentionally found himself caught up in this cameo scene: As he was entering the stadium with the crowd shouting "USA, USA", he decided to take a detour into the bathroom while the rest of the American athletes had already gone under the tunnel. While there, he met Carl Lewis, the 9-time American gold medalist in Track and Field. The two men soon realized that they'd have to run to catch up with their American teammates. Carl Lewis had no problem accomplishing the 100-yard dash in a few seconds. Jody, it turns out, wasn't made for land speed, so he flat-footed his way trailing behind his new mate, Carl. By the time he caught up to the group, he was in a significantly compromised breathing state while Carl looked as fresh as a stallion.

Photo Courtesy Los Angeles Times

1984 Olympics: Craig Wilson (goalie) and Jody Campbell.

USA water polo received unprecedented media exposure at the 1984 Olympic Games and in the months that followed. The sport of water polo had - at last – been introduced to millions of people and it won the hearts of many Americans. Thanks to Dr. Howard White's hard work, all the water polo games were held at Terry's alma mater, Pepperdine University. It seemed that everything was destined in the right direction: with an ultra-familiar pool in the mix, Terry felt comfortable about all the variables lining up perfectly.

Craig Wilson had his own strategy for attracting media attention for water polo. He quickly figured that if he hung closely to some of the superstars of the Olympic Games during the ceremonies, he was sure to be spotted on television close to Carl Lewis, Mary Lou Retton, Edwin Moses and Rowdy Gaines.

If there's one thing Los Angelinos definitely excel at – it's the ability to put on an Oscar-worthy performance. The Opening Ceremonies in 1984 didn't disappoint – no matter the athlete's nationality. That sentiment was emotionally articulated by star German water polo player, Frank Otto. He recently said unequivocally: "Many people say that the best moment in life is attending the birth of your children. I witnessed my kids coming to earth, so I can say: big nonsense! The greatest moment in my life was marching into the Coliseum of Los Angeles and the stadium was packed. Everything I had dreamed about as a young athlete lived up to my expectations in that moment."

The Olympic water polo competition consisted of 12 teams – 3 brackets of 4 teams each. In the bracket with the USA was Greece, Brazil and Spain. Team USA had fared well against these teams but they were concerned about the Spanish team who had a young and upcoming superstar named Manuel Estiarte.

The star Spanish player was making huge waves in the water polo world while being the top goal scorer in many international tournaments.

The team had 5 days off in the village prior to their first day of competition. These were difficult days of waiting for their moment especially after the emotionally charged opening ceremonies that had the adrenaline pumping through their veins.

Opening day is always a nerve-wracking time as each athlete wonders if he or she is ready. As Terry sat in the green room with teammate Drew McDonald, they had a conversation about that. Drew

Spain's Manuel Estiarte

asked Terry if he was ready and his reply couldn't have been more affirmative. Terry knew – without the interference of any doubt - that he was physically and mentally prepared and that he had done everything humanly possible to prepare for that moment. Team USA beat Greece on the opening day 12-5, a promising icebreaker.

After another fairly easy game against Brazil, it was time for a true test against the up-and-coming Spanish team. The game was tight and Manuel did everything he could do to help Spain. In the end, Team USA had used 4 different defenders to try to stop Estiarte. Three of them had fouled out with 3 exclusions and Spain earned a total of fourteen 6 on 5 opportunities. Some giant saves by Craig Wilson and some great 5-man defense helped the US team survive and win the game 10-8. With the win the U.S. team advanced to the medal round.

Drew McDonald and Chris Dorst
at the 1984 Olympics

First up in the medal round was the Netherlands. This team was loaded with three great left-handers. Historically, Willy (Craig Wilson) struggled with the outside shooting of the left-handed players and Team USA barely held onto an 8 –7 victory. This was another test of the heart and soul of the team – and they passed.

Two days later, Team USA would face off with Australia in the 08h00 game. This is always a tough time to play. Team USA utilized their home court advantage and spent the previous night at Pepperdine University in the graduate apartments. A quiet environment led to an early bedtime and a 04h30 wake-up call. The first thing the team did was head down to the pool

Terry Schroeder preparing and playing at The Olympics

for a 20-minute wake-up swim. After that they went back to the apartments on campus and had a home-cooked meal before their pre-game meeting. By game time, the team was pumped up and ready to face off with Australia. Team USA destroyed the sleepy Aussies 12–7.

Next up was the West German team that had crushed the Americans at the FINA cup in the Pepperdine pool just months before. The USA players knew that they had their hands full with the likes of Frank Otto and Hagen Stamm but Terry felt confident that the team was ready and his conversations with his teammates were more positive than ever. There was no doubt in his mind that the team could beat the Germans – having watched them play in a few games leading up to this match. He had studied their defenders astutely and felt like he had their numbers. Jody and Terry spent some time before the game discussing how to beat their defenders. The two USA centers both had great games - drawing 9 exclusions between the two of them. Terry had two goals and Jody added one. Drew McDonald had a huge play during a 5-man defense situation that saved the game near the end. He had shoved the German post player below the water with perfect timing. As the off-balance German player shot the ball, it flew over the cage. USA won the game with another 8–7 victory.

Having defeated all their opponents, they had finally made their way to their dream game: the gold medal final against Yugoslavia.

Statistics showed that Team USA was scoring close to 80% of their 6 on 5 opportunities and limiting opponents to just over 25% of their man-up situations. The statistics bode well for the championship final and proved that the team was working brilliantly together.

Terry's captaincy strength was leading by example in the pool. Consistent, rock solid and always emotionally intact, he calmed players who became flustered or angry with referees or players. He knew that it was vital to let go of any negativity – or it would impede and interfere with the level of play in the next crucial minute. But Terry's leadership encapsulated much more that: he made the team great by showing love, respect and trust at every training session and in every game. When the pressure mounted as the gold medal game approached, the team looked to him to be that calm force in the storm. The stakes were inordinately high and Terry's emotions were inordinately controlled. Any emotional dislocation at this point would be disastrous for the team.

When it came to irritations building up in the pool because of a bad pass or some other miscue, Terry halted the insidious blame game by taking quick responsibility for the breakdown in play. That helped defuse situations and even if it were not his fault, it would help to keep his teammates in the moment. Coach Monte was excellent in his role as a knowledgeable game expert and passionate tactician. However, when it came to Monte's emotions going awry, Terry consistently softened that effect and brought down the team's blood pressure with his extra calm demeanor. Right to the end, his responsibility was to keep his team sensibly focused on the scoreboard – not the fairness or unfairness of an official's call or a bad play.

Never before had Terry been tested in a leadership role like he was in the gold medal final game against Yugoslavia. August 10, 1984 will go down as the one of the most brutal days of his water polo life. The night game at Pepperdine University started out perfectly. The home crowd was particularly energizing, the stands were full and people lined up on the streets – supporting from behind the fence. The Americans were comfortably up 5–2 against Yugoslavia after a full three quarters had been played.

Going into the gold medal game against Yugoslavia - 1984 Olympic final

In the 4th quarter, things went rapidly awry and Yugoslavia scored 3 goals in succession. At 5–5, Terry knew that if they didn't reply with another goal, Yugoslavia would win the Olympics based on goal differential. In other words, in a tie, the team with the best goal differential would be declared the winner. This was definitely a flawed system – as the critical difference in goal differential between USA and Yugoslavia came down to their respective games against Spain.

Team USA had beaten Spain 10–8 while Spain was still very much in medal contention. Yugoslavia had beaten Spain 14–8 after Spain had been eliminated from any medal contention. Therefore, Spain had no motivation to play hard against them. In fact, the Spanish players had all gone out to "party" the night before they played Yugoslavia. Unfortunately, these were the rules that faced the team in 1984. Today it's quite different: In all the major tournaments, teams now play with either a penalty shoot-out or overtime after a tie.

With about one minute to go near the end of the game, the ball was passed to Terry at the center position and he was fouled hard. The Yugoslavian defender who had fouled Terry - thought that he was being excluded - and on tape, he is actually seen swimming to the penalty box. Terry then passed the ball out and received it right back - and shot the ball into the goal

Terry Schroeder - 1984 post gold medal game against Yugoslavia

for what he thought would be the game-winning goal. The crowd erupted with fervor. However, just then, Terry noticed the referee blowing his whistle assertively while calling off the goal. Instead, the referee had called an offensive foul on one of the American players on the perimeter. The game ended 5-5 and Yugoslavia won the gold medal based on goal differential.

Terry and the team were inconsolably devastated and their free-flowing tears were evidence of that. The USA took the silver medal. An extra dose of coarse salt was rubbed in the wound when they heard from a USA administrator that the Spanish referee spewed forth these words after the game: "Screw the Americans" as he walked off the deck. Since so many calls by referees during the game can be determined as 'subjective', the sting of what might have transpired in that gold medal final, had they had a more impartial referee, became a searing, open sore, and the scar of that comment will reside with Terry and everybody in the team for the rest of their lives. The men struggled to smile for the cameras with their silver medal loss.

While Terry and the team recognized the relevance of having taken USA Water Polo back to the podium for the first time in twelve years – they so desperately played their hearts out for that gold – and it seemed to have been achieved in that final minute. Therein lies the excruciatingly difficult adjustment. These are not men who settle. Their natures will always be - to set rigorously high standards for themselves - and Yugoslavia winning the gold on goal differential was not a decisive win. The abolition of that rule after this incident in the 1988 Olympics was proof that even the Olympic committee saw the flaws in a goal differential scenario.

Apart from the 'what could have been' heartbreak, the positive, incalculably valuable story that came out of the 1984 Olympics was the quality of the team's relationships with each other. They didn't just become a cohesive team who trusted and respected each other. They became a close family who genuinely loved each other as brothers.

Doug Burke describes the golden chemistry of the group like this: "We were all very different characters but we never let character differences or flaws get in the way. We concentrated on respecting each other's skills as water polo players. We complemented each other in the water and the team's overarching goal was always in the best interests of the group. We'd played together for a long time and we grew into a mature family who didn't let petty differences interfere with the bigger picture. I know that I played for the team because I enjoyed it so much. Our interaction was the most fun imaginable and I am exceptionally grateful for the experience. It was a unique and special time and we trusted each other to have our backs." Under the nurturance of Terry, those deep bonds that formed back then are as strong today – over 30 years later.

Doug Burke's personal appraisal of Terry's leadership is encapsulated in these words: "Terry was a mature, cerebral player who dug as deeply as any other player I know. He was completely dedicated to the team's success and showed us, by example, how to stay focused on our objective. He helped unite us in strength and purpose – and was an integral part of what made our team close. "

Immediately after the Olympic Games, the USA Men's Water Polo team were invited on a 5-city tour across the country, and everywhere they landed, they were treated like gold medalists. The tour began in Los Angeles at a breakfast with President Ronald Reagan and First Lady Nancy Reagan.

Terry Schroeder (back row right) at The White House with President Ronald Reagan and Nancy Reagan

President Ronald Reagan congratulating the athletes

President Ronald Reagan congratulating the athletes after their 1984 podium victories

Pat and Bob Schroeder join the street celebration after the 1984 Olympics

Terry Schroeder speaking at the celebrations at the White House
and Washington D.C. at the post 1984 celebrations

Spending personal one-on-one time with such a charismatic President was a thrilling experience for the men and their ebullience is reflected in the pictures taken. From Los Angeles they traveled to Washington D.C., New York City, Florida and finally, Dallas, Texas. Feeling like celebrities in chartered jets was a whole new dimension for the men in golden armor, and they reveled in this new-found luxury – knowing that it would be short-lived.

The Washington D.C. visit was a particular milestone in Terry's life. He was chosen to represent the entire USA Olympic Team and speak at a celebration outside of the Capitol Building. About 10,000 people attended and they all shouted the familiar "USA" cheers. Terry lights up as he speaks of that experience: "I was a bit nervous but that was soon replaced with extraordinary pride – because I realized that Americans were proud of us and it felt so good to be a part of that. While we were in New York City, we were in a ticker tape parade. I still recall fondly that feeling of being smothered with ticker tape as we cruised down Broadway in a classic convertible." The parade in New York was the largest that had been held since Neil Armstrong came back from his moon walk – in 1969.

A few weeks later, the team was invited to partake in numerous commercials - one of which was a milk commercial. However, they weren't warned about the number of hours they'd have to hang around and wait on set – for 30 seconds of fame. As their attention spans began to wane, things were bound to become interesting as the hours wiled away.

When they noticed an enticing Jacuzzi nearby, their amphibious instincts led them to the tub where they sat around waiting for a few more hours. However, somebody on set stupidly offered them beer as part of the hospitality package. All went well in the 1st hour. By the 5th hour, their coordination skills were deteriorating and taking any form of direction from the producers - became challenging.

On the second day of shooting, Craig Wilson was picked to be the person who drank all the milk in the locker room after their game. The problem was that while doing 54 takes, he had to drink all 54 glasses of milk – and this is when he discovered his unfortunate lactose intolerance. While no one was looking, he excused himself from the studio after each take and threw up the milk in the dumpsters outside. As the day progressed, Terry, who had the easier part of staring gleefully at Craig while sipping his milk, kept wiping the frothy milk residue from his moustache while Craig did the diametric opposite of what the commercial touted: it espoused that water polo took so much out of their bodies that milk was a necessary nutrient replacement to the exertion. Sadly for Craig, he almost needed a stomach pump by the end of the day. The last few seconds of the commercial shows Tim Shaw hitting Craig on the head – all part of their typical locker room antics. The commercial can still be viewed on youtube.com under 'milk water polo commercial'.

While Terry made solo appearances on ESPN with *Roy Firestone, America's Funniest Jokes*, and *Family Feud*, on another occasion, the team was invited to appear on a television series named *Glitter*. Once again they waited around for hours before being called to action. In the meantime, they invaded the catering truck and demolished every morsel of food available. The show's catering crew had never seen such vast quantities of food vanish. Clearly the advertising agency hadn't warned them about the daily calorie intake of each athlete.

But the most controversial invitation was Playgirl's one. Having seen a poster of the men and the shape they were in, the publishers at Playgirl were eager to have the entire team as their upcoming centerfold. For Joe Vargas, this was the ultimate dream come true – finally being able to show off all his assets to all the women in the world. For Jody Campbell, who was single, it was an opportunity that couldn't be missed, but for most of the team, it was crossing a line, and something they were not comfortable doing. Despite Joe's and Jody's remonstrations to the contrary, the majority team vote won, and Playgirl lost.

In all the glory of the Olympic Games, an amazing phenomenon happens. Terry explains it as a centrifugal force that pulls one in. "That force makes you yearn for more - especially after finishing so close to your goal of a gold medal. This team was left wanting." Terry felt the emptiness and the only thing that could possibly fill that void would be a gold medal in 1988.

Lori and Terry

CHAPTER 9

Love in the Water

The best thing to hold onto in life is each other
– Audrey Hepburn

March 21, 1987: The formalization of Terry's and Lori's love story – which began with a weekend getaway to Napa Valley, Northern California in 1983 as an escape from the pressures of graduate school – was about to unfold. Being almost inseparable since 1983 confirmed for Terry that Lori was the woman with whom he wanted to spend the rest of his life. That did not mean that the seas weren't rough along the way. Their relationship was tested massively with Terry being away for long chunks of time with his Olympic commitments. Young love typically requires constant assurances through frequent, clear communication – but Terry's long absences before texting and cell phone days made regular communication virtually impossible. The adaptable Lori learned that the only way their love could survive these long absences was through absolute trust. She also understood from the inception how important Terry's water polo career was to him – and the last thing she would ever do is deny him that velocity of fulfillment.

Terry respected Lori's selfless attitude monumentally. She put his needs first and never complained about his Olympic preoccupation. Their love was distinctly separate from Terry's passion for water polo and Lori never viewed it as competition. She focused her energies on appreciating the qualities in Terry that made her fall in love with him: it wasn't just the bronzed muscleman that won her love but the thoughtful, kind, gentle person who left beautiful little notes on her car windshield when she least expected it; or the loving notes he'd pop into her books at college – notes that encouraged her and made her feel cherished. They were always heartfelt - inflected with words that made Lori realize that this was a substantial man with a deeply beautiful soul.

Terry knew what he needed, and Lori was his perfect match in every respect. However, his unflinching conviction in their future went through the washer many times as his Olympic desires consumed him. In those midnight hours when his brain raced, Terry wondered how he could give Lori what she needed when his goals demanded so much of him mentally and physically. The Olympics were an unrelenting force - ubiquitously greedy in its demands and requiring a razor sharp one-dimensional focus for much of the time. In those dark midnight hours, vexing thoughts about how he could make Lori happy while training for his opportunity to win the gold – weighed on Terry heavily.

In those moments of fear and doubt, Terry eased out of this abyss knowing in his heart and in his mind that no other woman had ever understood him with the degree of accuracy that Lori had. Beyond that intricate level of understanding, she was able to physically and emotionally give her man what he needed: love, support and committed partnership in reaching their goals. She made him laugh with her irresistible sense of humor that usually incorporated imaginative fun. For all the masculinity that Terry was, Lori was his supreme feminine counterpart. Gentle, loving, nurturing and kind, she was also tall, athletically fit and physically strong. Their similar physicality was a perfect complement to their emotional connectedness. Terry also felt that Lori had "great healing hands" to take care of him when he was broken, and to hold him and heal him in many other ways.

During one of the most pressurized phases of his life where he juggled intense water polo training across the world while keeping up with his studies at chiropractic graduate school, Lori was consistently Terry's peaceful, quiet sanctuary – the safe haven to which he could retreat and let down his substantial guard. In her hands he rested in the intangible assurance of her unconditional love – something she gave magnanimously and generously. Never before had he felt so at peace with anyone. Lori loved him body and soul and she would always have his back. He knew that with unflinching certainty.

As they were both finishing up chiropractic school, Terry felt that the time was right to plan their future together and make an official commitment. But he struggled to find the perfect time that would make it special for Lori. He wanted simplicity without any pressures from outside influences. Basically, he wanted Lori to only have to answer to an audience of one. Because Terry was not the best communicator, he assumed that Lori knew that he felt that she was the right one. In reality, Lori was extremely stressed because she was oblivious to his intentions. As they grew together, these occasional misunderstandings were actually a valuable tool in deepening their relationship.

Bill Bell, Lori's father, loved his daughter deeply, and was fiercely protective of all his children. Even though Lori's nickname was "Tuffy", he knew that she had a very sensitive and vulnerable heart. He wanted more than anything to figure out what Terry's intentions were for his daughter now that they had graduated. At Lori's graduation party, the crescendo of expectations reached fever pitch. Even Lori had her moments of doubt.

Terry had been traveling and in-between, both of them were hyper vigilant about their school grades. The pressure of these commitments often denied them time for those necessary conversations about the future – their dreams and their hopes.

Meantime, what Lori didn't know was that Terry had already bought a ring and had every intention of proposing to her – but he didn't feel that her graduation party was the right moment. When the proposal did not happen at the graduation party, Lori thought that maybe it was not going to be.

The organic Schro wanted the moment to be spontaneous, intimate and unrehearsed. He didn't want an audience cheering him on; instead, he wanted a peaceful moment with his soon-to-be wife. Essentially, he wanted to surprise Lori when his heart told him that the moment was right.

The proposal was simple and unostentatious – a reflection of Terry exactly. There was no sweeping his love off to an exotic location for "reality TV". That wasn't his style, besides which, it was a relief not to be boarding airplanes again.

Terry planned his simple, happy-to-be-back-home-in-California engagement proposal that ended up paying dividends in its reception. Diligently waking up extra early that morning, he orchestrated the following romantic hour with Schroeder zeal.

It started with some deft tiptoeing into the kitchen to begin his culinary masterpiece: a fluffy, light and delectable spinach omelet with organic vegetables from their garden – Lori's favorite. The special breakfast was perfected with a slice of banana cinnamon French toast – and - Terry squeezing the ripest and juiciest of oranges to accompany the celebratory champagne. He bolstered his confidence by deducing that his lady couldn't possibly say no to the big question with a breakfast of such appetizing appeal. He had crafted some seriously romantic score points here.

But he needed to top it, so he bought the most beautiful long-stemmed rose and laid it across the tray that was already adorned with the light, fluffy spinach omelet. The pièce de résistance – the diamond ring – lay cradled around the rose stem for easy visibility.....or so he thought.

Terry entered the bedroom about to ask the biggest question of his life. Lori woke up with her usual radiant smile, grateful to be receiving breakfast in bed. Terry asked her – beside the bed – to marry him and spend the rest of her life by his side. Though fairly sure she would say "yes", it was Lori's heartfelt response that particularly touched him. Her beauty was enhanced as she responded with joyful tears cascading down her cute cheeks like a perfect little waterfall.

As Lori dove into the delicious spinach omelet awaiting her, Terry held his breath, waiting for her reaction to the diamond ring on the rose stem, but Lori never saw it. While she absorbed the best morning of her life, she didn't see the ring! Eventually, after it twinkled at her 50 times, she noticed it, and Terry muttered in his inimitably dry way, "finally!" Always quick with her comebacks, Lori answered, "Yes......finally". It was a happy declaration of touché all round.

Lori's other feelings – the ones that Terry particularly relished - soon asserted themselves; this time it wasn't the lion after the lioness; the lioness was definitely after her lion. An intensely passionate dawn – one that was vastly more powerful than any violin serenade on the Champs-Élysées - sealed the newly-engaged couple's first day together. A few hours later, Terry re-heated Lori's breakfast and demolished it with her. Mission accomplished!

When two almost perfect physical specimens come together, it's easy to focus on the obvious – the more shallow aspect of a relationship – but that would be doing Terry and Lori an enormous disservice. There was so much more to their relationship than the just the physical aspect.

The deep bond that existed between Terry and Lori then – and to this day – is cemented by a powerful soul connection that is wrought from their capacity to open their hearts completely to each other. It's a plain in which they are completely vulnerable, but that mutual generosity in being so open and honest with each other reaps massive rewards – rewards that are spiritually and emotionally fulfilling. Without that deep love and trust, Terry's and Lori's bond could never have survived the worldly pressures that have been a part of their lives for over 30 years. On the day that Terry and Lori made the decision to spend the rest of their lives together, the physicality was the least most important attribute they had going into the union. Inestimably more valuable was an immeasurably deep abiding love and friendship – one that would fill their hearts and sustain them.

An early exercise in managing the world occurred during the early days of Terry's and Lori's engagement. Terry had a friend who had volunteered to drive him down to many of his water polo practices in Orange County, California. Since the 1984 and 1988 Olympics necessitated spending many hours on the road traveling to and from workouts, Terry reasoned that being able to rest while on the road made good sense. As the weeks progressed, Terry and Lori navigated their first prickly experience. It turned out that Terry's driver had ideas beyond his mandate: he was a bit jealous of Terry's relationship with his fiancé. Lori immediately sensed that there was an undermining current, but it only became blatantly evident when the driver made a determined point of informing her that it was he who picked out her engagement ring – not Terry.

She communicated this information to Terry, and he set the record straight, assuring her that this was not the case. The experience amplified the need for both of them to be aware of people who transgressed boundaries and behaved inappropriately. This was one of their first lessons in learning to protect their circle of love. The goal was always about protecting the sanctity of their relationship and warding off influences that were unhealthy and potentially destructive.

A few months after their engagement announcement, Pepperdine University's President, Dr. Howard White, called Terry and asked him if he would be interested in coaching the Pepperdine University Water Polo team. Since Terry and Lori were committed to building their lives together, every decision that either of them made was done collaboratively and with each other present. Neither of them at that stage had any fixed plans as to where they were going to practice chiropractic. Terry was still playing on the USA national team – but he was definitely interested in coaching. After discussing their future, Lori and Terry decided that this would be a fulfilling step forward; coaching was on his radar and the invitation had simply come earlier than he had anticipated. Since Terry had enormous respect for Dr. White and trusted his judgment, he accepted the offer – thinking that he could coach for a few years while building up a chiropractic practice in the Thousand Oaks area next to Malibu, California.

It was while Terry and Lori were visiting back at Pepperdine that they arrived at the definitive choice of the Pepperdine Chapel for their wedding day. Terry had a deeply soft spot for the school and Lori understood in her caring, sensitive way how much exchanging their vows there would mean to him. She also loved the chapel. It represented – geographically – the mid center between their two families: Lori's family was in Pasadena, California, and Terry's was in Santa Barbara, California. It seemed like the natural meeting point where they would join the two families together. The more Lori came to know the depth and goodness in Dr. White, the more she too grew to love him for his strength and integrity. Terry and Lori asked Dr. White if he would marry them at Pepperdine, and he said he'd be honored to do so. They were both thrilled. This was going to be a particularly special wedding.

The March 21st, 1987 wedding date was imminent. Terry's bachelor party – which took place a week in advance for sensibility's sake - did not evolve gently into the good night. In retrospect, it should have been held a month in advance considering the injuries and aftermath. None of the side effects was the result of alcohol or wild partying. Instead, it was Lance's wrestling. Ever the competitive brothers from childhood, and because Lance had some wrestling experience from his high schools days, he commandeered his big brother to a full-scale wrestling match that etched into the night for more hours than was healthy.

As the after party progressed, it was the brothers' unabated determination that produced a fairly beaten up and sore groom and best man. But Terry's souvenir of the occasion was – unfortunately – a lot more visible than Lance's: a huge rug-burn was the central feature on his face – not the ideal scenario 6 days away from the most photographed day of his life. A week later, with the rug-burn still beaming, Lori's family, who were experts in the beauty business, did some technical magic in the make-up department. It elevated the definition of the efficacy of make-up concealers.

The most significant day of their lives arrived with special touches and humor-filled moments that were pricelessly memorable. Besides his best man Lance, Terry's groom's men were teammates from USA Water Polo. It made natural sense to include the aquatic brothers with whom he had shared so much in the past few years, and trimming the size of the wedding party down to 9 was a tough decision. Once again, young love and a lack of communication caused a misunderstanding that thankfully was amended: Terry's sister Tammy, whom he initially thought would not appreciate the experience of being a bridesmaid, was immediately brought into the wedding party when Terry's assumption was proven wrong. Lori had thought all along that Tammy should have been in the wedding party from the beginning, and this was another learning curve for a young couple figuring out how to communicate effectively.

The wedding morning began ominously as the heavens opened and the rain poured down relentlessly. While Southern California rarely has rain, apparently that day was the exception and it looked like the moisture wasn't going to recede. In some ways it seemed fitting that there should be so much water around for a water polo-dominated union – but no bride wants to be drenched just before she walks down an aisle. Besides all that, water is a logistical hassle when maneuvering long dresses and lace trains out of cars.

But a few hours before the wedding ceremony, nature cooperated magnificently. The sun broke out and it turned out to be one of the most majestic days ever in Malibu. A beautiful rainbow painted the blue sky and the setting couldn't have been more impeccably staged.

In the morning, the ever-active athlete in Terry had him shooting some basketball hoops with his close friend, Ken Bastian. They shared a meaningful heart-to-heart talk about the significance of the day. It was typical of the kind of substantive conversation that Terry always enjoyed with Ken – a man whose integrity he held in the highest regard. Ken's words resonated deeply with his friend as he said, "Block out all the distractions of the day. The surrounding stuff isn't important; what's important is that you focus in on Lori. Look into her eyes and when you speak your vows, make them all that matters. That's what this day is about - yours and Lori's heartfelt words to each other. Let each word sink into your soul and help you focus on her and why you love her. Remember those words and that moment - especially when things get tough one day". Ken's

influence in Terry's life was huge. He was that supremely wise rudder person who helped Terry to become a better man each day of their friendship.

Bill Bell opened his beauty salon generously to his daughter and the entire bridal party so that they could look and feel their best. Tammy had other plans and perhaps as a small protest for initially being left out, she decided to color her hair purple for the wedding. It probably wasn't the color that Bill Bell would have picked out for her but she actually did look pretty good.

Lori shimmied into her voluminous Lady Di wedding gown – a high fashion

Ken Bastian, Lori and Terry
on Wedding Day

statement in the 1980s. She loved it except for the limitations it imposed when she had to hustle to the bathroom after her limousine driver lost his way to Pepperdine University and arrived 20 minutes late for the wedding. It turned out that the real limousine driver called in sick on the wedding day so an under-qualified replacement in a red sweater took the helm and somehow managed to get lost on his way to one of the most prominent locations in

Malibu. Getting lost was incomprehensible given Pepperdine's tall palm trees that are beacon land-calls to anybody who is unsure of what chapels with stain-glass windows look like. Hopefully the stand-in driver found his calling elsewhere after the wedding and doesn't work for Uber today.

Lance, Terry, Bob and Ian Schroeder

Surrounded by the people who meant so much to them both, Terry and Lori couldn't wait to exchange their vows. As Bill escorted his daughter down the aisle, Lori let her tears of supreme happiness flow freely. Never before had she felt so at peace about a major decision. She knew with the greatest sense of clarity that this was her life partner and the man she loved completely unconditionally.

Terry's face instantaneously lit up as he saw his bride approach. Clichés genuinely put aside, Lori was the stunning princess he knew he was marrying, and no other woman came close to her. This was the partner with whom he wanted to share his life and it was the best decision he ever made. As Lori said her vows to Terry, God gave her the strength to give her tears a two-minute break. She relaxed into what needed to be done and her words of commitment were voiced without any distractions.

The ceremony was deeply moving and it ran almost without a hitch until one of the bridesmaids, who turned out to be pregnant, fainted and fell to the floor. She

recovered quickly and her embarrassment was the principal injury.

The wedding reception afterwards produced an exuberant
party that ran into the early hours
of the morning. In Terry's toast
to Lori he said, "My dream is to
make you happy; to complement
you and to complete you. I am so
proud of you and I want to wake
up in 50 years' time to your beautiful smile next to me." Their first
dance was to Chicago's 'You're the
Inspiration' followed by Kenny
Loggins' 'Forever'.

Considering the array of
highly energized, characterful
people at the wedding, the evening antics produced a few scenarios that could have made the

Lori and Terry at their March 1987
Pepperdine Chapel Wedding

press headlines. One of the soon-to-be 1988 Olympians, James Bergeson
(and a recent alternate on the 1984 Olympic team) became so buoyed up
with the fun of the occasion that he forgot that he was at Terry's and Lori's
wedding. He did, however, remember that it was his birthday, and so he
began to bask in the belief that this was his birthday party. He thanked everyone around him for attending his birthday celebration and swept Lori's sister,

Lori and Terry – Wedding March 1987

Lori and Terry's first wedding dance

Robin, onto the dance floor, where he promptly lost the fight with gravity and they ended up splayed on the floor. It was a horizontal rendition of the dance they were supposed to be doing vertically. But that was just the start of the expeditious reception revelry. A few hours later, Lori's dad, Bill, had to pull good-time James out of a Los Angeles police car. As James began to sober up with his new reality, the details of how he came to be in a police car became a better-to-forget-about secret.

The wedding reception that never ended - March 1987

When Terry and Lori finally made it to their room to spend their wedding night, the jokes were still on them. One or several of Terry's teammates had managed to gain access to the wedding boudoir where they booby-trapped it by short sheeting the bed. Luckily for the pranksters, it happened to a bride and groom who appreciated extensive humor. While Terry and Lori laughed at the bed-altered circumstances, they rectified it in record time so that they could progress to the important business of consummating their marriage. Terry recounted that moment with delight: "Even in that wedding night moment, my teammates were right there with us!" Again, Terry appreciated Lori's unfailingly good nature in seeing the amusing aspect of what might have irritated another bride. He married a trooper who knew how to ride with the waves.

The honeymoon that followed was in the A+ realm. Terry and Lori arrived in Fiji to be transported onto Turtle Island – the same island where the movie 'Blue Lagoon' had been filmed. But film footage and pictures did not do it justice. Being there was the only way to truly appreciate the island's mesmerizing natural beauty with its turquoise warm water and soft white sand. Even the sea breeze was the perfect temperature. There were 6 beautifully-appointed huts around the island – all open air with a welcoming island breeze blowing through.

Terry's and Lori's hut offered them expansive privacy – so much so that they were able to wear their birthday suits for much of the day. Had they known about the seclusion, they would have brought very little luggage. The newly-weds fished, went horseback riding and snorkeled naked in the most beautiful environment while their bodies experienced sunburn in parts where the sun usually does not shine.

The island was owned by an American but was run by local Fijian people. All the honeymooners and couples on the island came together for just one meal per day in the evening. Meeting them was invigorating and it was great to share the day's experiences with new acquaintances. On one occasion, they all decided to go clamming in the Fijian mud and a huge mudslinging war broke out. Terry had the distinct advantage of still being in Olympic shape and with a pretty formidable arm intact, he dominated

Idyllic honeymoon on Turtle Island, Fiji, 1987

the messy fight and was able to protect Lori. Later on, Terry found out that one of the people he had blasted with mud after the fight broke out - was the Mayor of Pasadena. Oops...so much for a career in politics.

But it was the emotional relevance of the honeymoon that was especially poignant to Terry and Lori. While sharing with each other their dreams for the future, they spent hours each day in bed clinging onto each other – so grateful that they had found this profound love that meant so much to each of them. They couldn't get enough of each other emotionally. Each moment of each day was filled with a sense of absolute completion and a magnitude of contentment that nobody could have described to them. They felt it in their cores. Having been separated for so many long periods due to international water polo, they drank in every moment; appreciated the luxury and significance of finally being together intensively. They were two souls uniting in the most meaningful sense. Their union made each of them individually better people and it was inconceivable for either of them to imagine a life without each other.

There were so many brilliant moments that Turtle Island captured. The simplicity with its close-to-nature harmony fitted the newly-weds perfectly. They didn't need fancy restaurants or superficial accouterments. In the early mornings – they'd wade out into the ocean and feed the fish that surrounded them. They were able to fully disconnect from the world and its pressures as they focused on each other.

Later on, they were dropped off on a beautiful, deserted private beach in the morning. They spent the day bathing in the sun on the soft sand, talking about their dreams and snorkeling in the beautiful ocean. At a pre-arranged time, a little skiff arrived to bring them lunch: lobster washed down with champagne. It was hard to top that combination of love, scenery, sun and a perfect lunch menu. As soon as they had quenched their appetites, they returned to snorkeling and playing in the water like happy dolphins – only to proceed to the next most natural of callings – some warm, afternoon lovemaking.

Terry wanted to live on the island with Lori forever. He'd always wanted a simple, natural life, and this honeymoon amplified the things that were so important to his wellbeing. Being surrounded by the warm blue ocean that sparkled in the sun brought an immense sense of peace to Terry. Water always had and always would be a huge part of his life; it was a medium that resonated with him completely. He was with the beautiful woman that he loved more than words could adequately describe, and Turtle Island was pure and absolute bliss.

The newly-wed Schroeders did interact with other people occasionally; this time Terry elected to enjoy playing some basketball with the natives islanders while Lori watched and laughed. They in turn became so enamored with their new American friend that they insisted that he and his bride experience KAVA - a root that assuredly would make Terry and Lori feel terrific. Not wanting to seem ungrateful at the offer, they obliged by trying a little of the root but drew a firm boundary after they witnessed the island owner – who was always chewing on something similar – looking stoned most of the time. That was not what Terry and Lori wanted or needed. Instead, they relished every fully conscious moment – moments that gave them a greater sense of wellbeing than they had ever felt. They had each other and that was all that they needed.

When their week on Turtle Island ended, Terry and Lori headed to Nadi - the main island of Fiji where they stayed for a few more days. It was an anticlimax after the perfection of Turtle Island – marked by an infestation of mosquitos that relentlessly attacked Lori in their parasitical quest for human blood. After Lori got eaten alive, Terry decided it was time to return to Los Angeles a day earlier than scheduled - but not without stopping on their way to the airport for a traditional Indian meal which turned out to be so blisteringly spicy that they spent the whole flight home breathing fire and mopping their top brows from sweat.

But as much as life seemed blissful then, Terry and Lori innately knew that their marriage would not always be honeymoon perfect. Although young and in love, they'd encountered enough in life to know that there would be challenges and many imperfections along the way – and they were emotionally mature enough to take on the realistic post honeymoon phase.

To this day it saddens both of them to see many of their friends opt out of their marriages when they encounter rough seas. Terry and Lori meant their vows sincerely and they were determined through their marriage to learn, grow and put aside their selfish, ultimately self-defeating whims. Lori knows that she didn't choose Terry because she needed a muscled Olympic hero. What she married was a man with the biggest heart and the kindest soul who shows her every day what deep love really is.

Turtle Island remains – to this day – a place that Terry and Lori will always cherish. For perpetuity's sake and to assist in averting possible poaching of the sea turtles on the island, they carved their names on the back of one of the sea turtles. The empathetic thought was to save his shell with the inscription – in the hopes that no poacher would want a shell with someone's drawing. They circled their initials on the shell with a heart – with the intent of their love serving as a kind of symbolic protection. Hopefully the Schroeders' turtle is still alive today – enjoying a long and safe life in the beautiful waters of Turtle Island.

Terry with President George H. Bush - 1986 Goodwill Ambassador

CHAPTER 10

1988 Seoul Olympic Games

A Familiar Current

Competing is exciting and winning is exhilarating, but the true prize will always be the self-knowledge and understanding that you have gained along the way
– Sebastian Coe, 4-time Olympic medalist

17 September 1988: Aquatic athletes share a mystical bond: their affinity to the power of nature in its purest form – water. From conception where a baby is soothed and comforted by the surrounding amniotic fluid in its mother's stomach – to adulthood – aquatic athletes need water to sustain them and they share an unspoken understanding of the bliss that they feel when they're surrounded by that all-healing medium. That first dive into its depths elicits a childlike smile and it permeates and produces an "I've come home" feeling that transcends mere scientific explanation. Gliding through water is peaceful and effortless to these amphibious people who embrace their fish-ness – knowing it's an integral part of their biped journey.

Terry has always thrived in water. He discovered its calming properties during his early swimming days in Santa Barbara. The rhythm of swimming - particularly during pressurized times when life became frenetic – has always given him a sense that his life is in order. With each stroke that enters the water, a gentle cadence of rhythm is produced that is similar to a musical beat. That soft, gurgling sound of the water's movement accompanied by the feeling of it flowing all over his body, has always led to a soothing sensation like no other. There is a quiet peace in water – far from the noise of the world. From his early days, Terry seemed to understand that even when the training in the water was brutally intense, the medium still produced a healing power. Water has always allowed him to go inwards and focus on what he wanted in his life.

Just as dolphins and seals joyfully dive, duck and play in water, so too do swimmers and water polo players. Muscularly strong – they glide easily through water with little strain on joints, muscles or tendons. The elongated and graceful muscles of these aquatic athletes propel their bodies with almost effortless speed and aerodynamics that create an enormous source of satisfaction. That smooth, frictionless ability comes from years of dedicated training, and even though doing thousands of laps is monotonous and challenging in its sheer repetition, there's not a single swimmer who is going to tell you that he or she doesn't feel the magical quality of the water. The reality, though, is that there's also a conflicting love hate relationship with extreme swimming training. It's often painful – but it's a means to an end – and water polo athletes recognize that it's the necessary platform to be able to excel in the sport they love.

The surety of the lanes' black lines underneath a swimmer feeds that disciplinary need; but most of all, it's the glorious feeling and the sounds of the little ripples and splashes that feed right into a aquatic athlete's soul. Even the stress of training is reduced by an aqualete's ability to find a quiet place even under that pressure.

Add to that an exceptionally fun game with a ball that combines soccer, basketball and hockey in water – and the enjoyment of the interaction of teammates – and you've pretty much devised a recipe of competitive perfection. Water polo players who have reached the heights of Olympic participation relish all the elements of the game. Their love for what they do more than makes up for the years of sacrifice and pain.

Picture this scene: the players pull themselves out of their beds every day, oftentimes when it's still dark outside, and even though their bodies tell them that they should sleep in a few hours, their dream tells them that this is a necessary sacrifice that has to be made. They drag themselves to the aquatic center, look at the 50-meter pool to begin swimming laps, and then approach the edge of the pool with a "here we go again" mantra running through their heads. It is in that moment of "jumping in" that a choice has been made to plunge in and train in a cold environment. Although at times there is hesitation, the athletes know that it is in the water that they will make their dream come true.

Within a few minutes, the team members are synchronized into groups as they enter into the rhythmic phase of fitness training. Their torsos strengthen with each stroke, and the familiar sounds of their environment produce an at-home feeling. But it goes beyond that: frequently during these early morning workouts, the surface of the water is shrouded by a soft coat of mysterious mist which contributes to making the place feel like a sanctuary - a quiet, hidden place where the team members' arm strokes begin to work in unison – each limb lifting and deftly immersing itself in the water. The pool becomes the men's church – a place they go to for quiet meditation and comfort; the place that elicits a necessary rhythm – one that reminds them that things are working as they should – and that life is in order – devoid of chaos. It's a very special place and its relevance is usually only fully appreciated later in life.

Team USA, destined for the Seoul 1988 Olympics, was largely made up of new players. Veterans from the 1984 Olympics included Craig Wilson, Kevin Robertson, Peter Campbell and Jody Campbell. Terry's return as captain was the much-needed rudder for a relatively new team, and he was committed to doing everything he could to create the magical feeling that existed with his teammates in 1984. By now, he was in that comfortably assured phase of having mastered the art of juggling Olympic training with chiropractic school commitments. He had set up a system that worked for him – and he was all the more confident during the 1988 Olympic preparation that he could handle the double-loaded pressure.

The new teammates, who brought with them a fresh spurt of energy and youthful vitality, were going to have to cope with a new level of pressure - relatively quickly. Even players who are gifted with uncanny abilities can fall apart if pressurized situations send their nerves into a tailspin. Experience is usually the crucial elixir for those nerve-racking moments, and it was Terry's task to shepherd the new Olympic prospects by teaching them how to stay mentally focused – no matter how difficult the circumstances or situation proved to be. At the same time, most of these players were used to playing and winning at the highest level available in the United States – the NCAA (National Collegiate Athletic Association).

James Bergeson was an alternate player from the 1984 team. Known as Bergie, he was a teammate with Jody Campbell and Alan Mouchawar at Stanford University. Both Jody and Alan consistently egged on James to do something silly and he usually caved into their dares and in doing so provided a lot of laughter for his teammates. Bergie made the history books at Terry's and Lori's wedding. A great attacker and all-around good player, Terry felt that he should have been on the 1984 team – when instead, he was an alternate. He was a utility player. Strong in the water and able to score from the drive, post up or outside, he was a weapon that Team USA needed in the pool. Bergie had been a part of the USA system for many years and he had an uncanny ability to score big goals.

Douglas Kimbell – known as Big Doug - was an impressive 6 foot 9 inches tall and a center defender. He played at Long Beach State University; a team that was in the same conference as Pepperdine – so Terry and Doug were familiar foes that became great teammates. Every day in practice, Terry and Big Doug battled it out and gave each other a significant physical contest. In less polite words, they beat the living daylights out of each other. Terry credits Doug with making him a better player and Doug credits Terry with making him a tougher defender. They both brought out the best in each other. Doug was a great outside shooter and one of the best defenders in the world between 1986 and 1992.

Edward Klass went by the name Craig. He was a utility left-hander from Stanford University and was physically formidable. Craig was primarily an offensive center at Stanford, however on the national team, he was converted to a defender. Craig had great speed and was extremely strong in the water. He could post up on offense and he gave the team depth on the 4/5 side of the pool along with Kevin Robertson. While Kevin was fast and small in stature, Craig provided size and brute strength on the left-hander's side. With his size and power, Craig could battle with the opponents' big men and hold his own. Craig went on to become a successful Physical Therapist.

Alan Mouchawar – known as Mouch – was another Stanford star. A good attacker, Mouch was light-hearted and fun to have around. Through his years on Team USA he brought humor and much laughter to the team. He was an attacker with a wicked shot. Perhaps not the biggest player in the water, he was deceptive and could match up well with any opposing player, and would usually find a way to win. Jody, Bergie and Mouch could have been the 3 Musketeers with some of their escapades. They each brought life and energy to the team and played a significant role in the team's success. Mouch was also not short on brains. He went on to become a very successful anesthesiologist. Tragically, Mouch lost his brother, Larry Mouchawar, another water polo star, to suicide in 2013.

Jeffrey Campbell was Peter's younger brother. Another defender and utility player on the team, Jeff was quiet and fairly subdued out the water, and he was another water polo junkie from UC Irvine. If Peter was the quiet one on the 1984 team, Jeff made Peter look like a big talker. Perhaps a bit stronger than Peter in the water, he was a great utility player who could play an offensive or defensive role on the team.

Greg Boyer – being the competitive person that he is – actively participated in an internal team competition to see who could bring the least amount of clothes for a 2½ week European trip. This resulted in his nickname of 'Stinky' because he won the contest by wearing the same shirt and shorts for 18 days. The amazing thing was that despite being one of the players who enjoyed having fun and coming in later at night than most, he was a dominant force in the pool. In fact, it seemed that the later he stayed out, the better he played the next day. It was always reassuring to have Stinky on your team. He was one of those players who was not fun to guard. Whether it was accidental or on purpose, Greg's opponent usually had some bruises or cuts by the end of practice or a game. He went hard every day in practice and he challenged others to be better. From the University of California Santa Barbara, Greg was a teammate of Craig Wilson's when they won the NCAA championship in 1981. Greg was a good shooter, a tough guard and someone who could scrap with anyone. The more physical the game, the more Greg enjoyed it. Occasionally, Terry was Stinky's roommate – probably in an effort to balance his partying ways. It didn't always work. He'd barrel in late after a night out, pass out within minutes and begin snoring like a freight train. One night Terry pulled him out of the room and planted him with his entire mattress in the hallway. Stinky didn't seem to mind; he slept soundly through the night and played well the next day. Greg ended up becoming a highly-respected lawyer and is now retired and travels around the world with his wife Reenie.

Christopher Duplanty was the team's backup goalkeeper out of UC Irvine. Because Craig Wilson was such a brilliant goalkeeper, Chris or "Dupe", as he was called, didn't play much, but he was that necessary backup force. This has to be one of the most difficult positions on the team (backup goalie) as all the others players see water time every game while the backup goalie usually sits on the bench and cheers for his teammates. His best work is often done in practice when his job is to shut down the starting team. Chris was a great teammate. He went on to play in two more Olympic Games after Seoul and was actually the captain of the 1996 team. He also was an assistant coach on the women's Olympic team in 2000 and worked for Peter Ueberroth for many years after he was done playing.

Michael Evans – known as "Evo" – was an attacker and utility player who was an incredible shooter - perhaps one of the best in the world. He was a threat anytime he had his hands on the ball. He had amazing vision of the cage and scored some huge goals for the team. No one would call Mike a defensive specialist; that was not why he was on the team. He was on the team to score goals. Terry also spent some trips rooming with Evo. On more than one occasion he would catch Evo snacking in the middle of the night on a can of coke and a candy bar. It was a small vice for the Mormon who was otherwise a really healthy living guy. Easy to get along with all the time, Mike was a star on the 1988 and 1992 Olympic teams. The Eastern Europeans would later use videos of Evo's shot as a teaching tool for shooting after his water polo career was over.

Bill Barnett was the team's head coach. He was as dedicated to the sport of water polo as anyone in the USA. He loved the game and had coached high school water polo for most of his life. He was a master at capturing video knowledge of the team's upcoming competitor – which he consistently brought to every tournament with a full synopsis. Perhaps one of Coach Barnett's weaknesses was his inability to communicate well with the national team players. Terry would later say that Coach Barnett was slightly intimidated by the Olympic platform in that he had coached high school athletes for his entire career, where he enjoyed immense success at Newport Harbor High School in Newport Beach, California. He won 15 high school championships at Newport Harbor – 10 with the boys and 5 with the girls. But in 1988, suddenly he was dealing with men. He was also going through some difficult family times during this Olympic stretch (he coached in 1988 and 1992). Once again, perhaps the pressures of training 6 hours a day and 6 days a week put undo strain onto his family relationships. Socially shy, Coach Barnett usually came out of his shell with a few libations. He was different from Monte in many ways, although, he would lambast some of his players at times. He worked hard to get the team prepared and he wanted to win as much as anyone. To this day, he still dedicates much of his time to the sport of water polo.

Steve Heaston – was the assistant coach from University of California Berkeley (CAL) where he led the Bears to 3 national championships and was consistently in the top 5 in the country. Steve balanced Coach Barnett out very well. He was more talkative and easy to get along with. In fact, Coach Heaston was involved with the U.S. Junior team during the time when Terry was a member of the junior team. Terry had fond memories of Steve inviting players into his room and then on more than one occasion, taking on 3 to 4 of the junior players at one time in a wrestling match. He was nicknamed "The Beast" for his size and strength. He was always pushing 300 pounds and was a formidable physical presence. He also played the game at a high level at the center position, and he explained to Terry that what made him good at center was the fact was that he was afraid to put his head under water, so when a defender would push on him, he would fight for his life to keep his head above water. Sadly, Steve passed away from a brain tumor in 1999.

Dave Almquist was a super nice guy who served for 4 years as the second assistant coach. Terry felt close to Dave as he reminded him of Coach Lindgren – with whom Terry had connected well on the 1984 Olympic Staff.

Also deserving a mention is Dennis Fosdick, who served as the team manager between 1985 and 1988. Dennis loved his beer and just about after every workout, he provided the team with a large ice chest of cold beer for his version of "carbo loading." Dennis volunteered many hours to help the team be successful.

Ironically, 1985 turned out to be one of Terry's best years, and it happened by accident. Three weeks before the prestigious Tungsram Cup tournament in Hungary, Terry had accidentally jammed his right hand little finger. After being x-rayed, he discovered that he had sustained a spiral fracture on his 5th metatarsal. This would necessitate 6 to 8 weeks of no contact on that finger. Since this was Terry's throwing and scoring hand, it was hugely problematic. Coach Barnett decided to bring him along for the Tungsram Cup to take stats and train. This meant he would sit and watch the games and between, he'd show up at the pool to swim a set that Coach Barnett had provided so as not to lose his fitness level.

Terry's frustration levels reached fever point after a couple of days of confining restriction but Craig Wilson, always the thoughtful friend, read Terry's impatience. He suggested to him that he spend some time after swimming training - shooting at goals with his left hand. At first, Terry was disillusioned and frustrated with his weak left side, but Craig kept encouraging him and even played badly in the goal (on purpose) so that Terry could build up his confidence with his developing new weapon.

Before two weeks had elapsed, Terry knew that he would have to devise something tactically so he worked on one move in particular: he would imagine turning his defender and taking a left-handed wrist shot as he moved laterally across the cage to his left. The first week of doing this produced less than adequate results, but by the next week, his percentage of shots went up and he also noticed that he was seeing the cage a little differently. Every time he picked up the ball and moved across the cage, he would pay attention to how Craig was moving and what holes were opening up in the cage. That new incalculably valuable perspective – borne out of an injury - helped Terry to improve every facet of his game. He was more dangerous in the water all round and could turn to his left or right and finish the ball with great successes on either side. Defenders were having a difficult time against him because they did not know which side to give him. Most good defenders will play on the two-meter man's strong side, thereby forcing him to go to his weaker side. But Terry no longer had a weaker side. He'd outfoxed his most formidable opponents.

Six weeks later, the team took off for Europe to train and play in two more tournaments: one in Sweden and another in Holland. The tournament in Sweden was a 6-team tournament with the USA and Russia as the top seeds. Now fully healed, Terry was tearing it up in the tournament and playing with more audacious confidence than ever before. They beat Sweden and Spain handily before facing Russia in the finals. The finals turned out to be something special: not only did Terry score 4 of the 6 victory goals against Russia's 3, but 3 of the 4 goals were with his new left-handed weapon. His opposition was appropriately confused as to how to defend him. He had a new powerful tool that confused them profoundly.

Terry won the Most Valuable Player (MVP) award at the tournament but the unexpected icing on the top was this coincidence: a USA Navy boat was harbored at the port in Holland, and the crew came to support and watch the team play against Russia. It was unusual during this Cold War period to have any USA support from the crowds while playing in Europe – so this was a special change – to have a supportive group from back home encouraging the players in European waters. After the finals, the captain from the ship presented Terry with the ship's USA flag. It meant something really special and Terry still flies that flag on most USA holidays.

Terry torpedoed forward with his newly acquired life-changing skill – which was the result of adversity. At the end of 1985, he received another significant award. For the second time since 1981, he was voted the best player in the world by Swimming World Magazine. In total, Terry would come to be voted the best water polo player in the world on two separate years.

With 5 returning players on the team there was a chemistry that already existed. The older players helped bring the new players under their wings quickly. The team's mutual respect for each other became unbreakably strong, and humor played its reliable part in the buildup to the Seoul Olympics. As people rallied to take pictures of the USA men, they encouraged the players to take off their shirts and reveal their toned, golden torsos. The common consensus was that the men would photograph better with their muscles exposed.

But Jody Campbell had other ideas for Terry: they were training in Germany in 1986 and standing outside a hufhaus when Terry and the men complied with their audience – and removed their shirts for pictures. Just then, when Terry least expected it, Jody snuck up behind him and whisked Terry's shorts down faster than he could react. In a few split seconds, Terry was standing exposed to 101 flash bulbs going off with rapidity. He retrieved his shorts quickly while Jody soaked in his moment of accomplishment.

Fortunately this was not the era of the internet or those pictures would have been posted internationally within seconds.

1986 began on a tough note. The team began training for important world championships in March. Just a few weeks into training camp, during an intense game situation drill, a teammate elbowed Terry unintentionally in the face and broke his nose. The blow stunned Terry, and although he was pretty sure that his nose was broken, he continued to practice and went home that night in a great deal of pain. There were no trainers or doctors on deck to check on his nose, so his only at-home remedy was an alcoholic painkiller to quell the shouting nerves.

Having recently graduated from chiropractic school, Terry knew a thing or two about the human body, so he decided to take matters into his own hands by resetting his nose. He grabbed it with his thumb and index finger, gave it a yank in the direction it needed to go, and hoped the yank would restore his face's symmetry. A loud pop ensued – accompanied by excruciating pain – but the new straight line in the mirror indicated that he had been successful with his first nose job!

The following day, two black eyes and a significantly swollen face greeted Terry as he stared at the damage in reflection.

Keenly aware that practice was going to be near to impossible, Terry finally let his vulnerability be known as he informed his coaches of the unfortunate mishap. The immediate response was that he avoid contact to his face, so for 4-6 weeks, he was quarantined to swimming and leg conditioning.

His first return to the game happened when the Australians came to town for training and a couple of exhibitions games in May. The doctors recommended a clear plastic face shield to protect Terry's vulnerable nose but he declined the advice – realizing that it would be viewed as a target for his opponents. It was best that the Australians not know about his injury altogether. He made it through the next 10 days of practice with the Aussies without taking any hit to the face, and from thereon, it was never a problem.

In time, the nose topic would come to hit Terry's teammate, Doug Burke, dramatically worse. He broke his nose over 10 times in practices or games and weakened the cartilage so much that even the slightest hit would re-break his nose. The trophy for the most punishment meted out to a nose definitely went to Doug.

In August of 1986, the second most important water polo tournament in the world was to take place in Madrid, Spain. The World Championships featured the 16 top teams in the world at the time. In comparison, the Olympic Games is only a 12-team tournament.

In the preliminary bracket with Team USA were defending World Champion, the Soviet Union, Brazil and Greece. Under Terry's leadership, Team USA defeated Greece, Brazil and the Soviet Union to win its pool. A semi-final match-up with Italy was an incredible game that went down to the final seconds. Team USA would lose 8-7 and have to settle for playing for the bronze against the Soviet Union. Unfortunately, the Soviets had too much firepower for the Americans, and the final score was 10-8.

Even though Team USA's 4th place finish was their best ever finish at the World Championships, they took little solace in that statistic. Their nemesis, Yugoslavia, would take the gold. Resolved to do the work needed to close that gap, the American team left Madrid hungry and wanting.

In-between the team's rigorous training and traveling schedule, they had their moments of light-hearted relief in the hundreds of hours they flew cross-continentally. On one trip to Europe, the pilot of the Lufthansa 747 in which they were flying - came up with a novel idea that he hoped would entertain the passengers on the huge jet. He spoke through the intercom and informed the people on board that the USA Men's Olympic Water Polo team would be serving them on this flight. Flight attendants Helga and Suzy were allowed to go and relax in the galley while the USA men began serving drinks in the business class section. After that they served the hot meal with perfectly articulated scripts: "Madam; would you like beef, chicken or vegetarian?" One of the women responded, "None of those. You!" The beefcake humor accelerated the passage of time, and an appreciative audience - including husbands - joined in with the spirit of the amusement.

The biggest tournament for 1987 was the Pan American Games hosted in Indianapolis, USA. The team's training was beyond anything the Navy SEALs had ever encountered because of Coach Barnett's determination to produce the most conditioned players on the planet.

1987 Pan American Games- Team USA Men's Water Polo

The swim sets they were made to do were brutal - but – at age 28, Terry's body responded magnanimously, and he was probably the fittest he had ever been. He sliced through the water with powerful speed and he felt physically invincible one month before the Pan American Games.

But fate has a nasty habit of screwing up perfection. As Terry was routinely driving home from Pepperdine University, a car behind him wasn't able to brake in time when traffic came to a halt – and it slammed into the back of Terry's Saab with such force that his car was totaled. The explosive hit was so impactful that Terry felt disoriented and a searing pain shot through his right shoulder.

The following day, an orthopedic physician friend, Dr. Mel Hayashi, did an MRI on the shoulder and it revealed a tear in the rotator cuff and in the labrum. Dr. Hayashi recommended immediate surgery to repair the injury. This would mean missing the Pan Am Games and potentially not playing again. Terry considered his options and decided to do what he knew best: help the body to heal itself with conservative chiropractic care and aggressive but non-invasive rehabilitation. Initially, he could not even turn his head while swimming, and had to wear a mask and snorkel - but his hard work ethic kicked in instinctively, and he did reliable elastic band work and physical therapy constantly to reverse the damage. He was also adjusted 3 times per week for the first month and then less frequently as the injury healed.

His good friend and teammate, Doug Burke, encouraged him every day while he was training on his own in the shallow end (the team was training hard in the deep end). It killed Terry to be isolated and not be able to train with his teammates.

The team left for Indianapolis, and rolled through the preliminary rounds with ease. With his shoulder about 60% healed, Terry was able to rest and play only a few minutes in the preliminary round games. These games were all one-sided in the USA's favor. In the final, Team USA would end up beating Cuba 6-4 in the final. James Bergeson led the team with 3 goals. Terry scored one, which at 60% octane, was presentable. Craig Wilson dominated the game in the goals - allowing Cuba just 4 goals.

With one year to go until the Olympics, the preparation rapids ahead would entail a great deal more healing and rehabilitation for the beleaguered shoulder. The trusty snap that Terry used to have on the ball just wasn't there, and he was almost afraid to throw the ball hard due to the sheer pain and the vulnerability he felt. The injury became as much mental insecurity as it was physical – and this feeling was so alien to Terry's nature that he resolved to do everything in his power to get back to full health. The year ahead would be dedicated to a full recovery.

By January 1988 after intensive physical rehabilitation, Terry finally felt his body return to full fighting form. This was an imperative feeling that would stave off falling into the chasm of doubt and fear. Taking on the world's best players necessitated 100% confidence in his physical capabilities. Trusting in his own body – knowing that he had the power to heal it naturally – was Terry's invincible weapon as he approached Seoul.

It would be impossible to top the feeling of ecstasy that Terry and his teammates experienced in the Opening Ceremonies of the Los Angeles 1984 Olympics. They were so incredibly connected to the moment and felt the fire light inside each of themselves as Rafer Johnson lit the Olympic torch. To this day, the 1984 team still talk about the sensations of that opening ceremony. It was a moment in time that will stay with them forever in the most powerfully visceral way.

Since it was unrealistic to imagine that the Seoul 1988 Olympics could equal or exceed the previous experience, Terry concentrated all his energies on the task at hand: bringing home the gold. That was the focal point for everyone on the team. But as the opening ceremonies grew closer, Terry so wanted his teammates to be inspired – the way he had been – back in 1984. He knew that if their inner flames could be lit with a similar set of emotions like his were, they'd go into the Games with more passion. Physically and mentally they were ready to perform at their best, but the opening ceremonies seems to invoke the extra special feeling that the Olympics represents.

Before the start of the opening ceremonies, the American media – in their quest to capture the immense excitement of the athletes – asked all of the USA Olympians to seek out the TV cameras. In fact, National Broadcasting Corporation (NBC) went one step further in their instructions: they asked that as the athletes entered the field, they should all look to the right and wave so that the numerous cameras could capture their facial expressions. Unfortunately, many of the USA athletes overstepped their boundaries – leaping at the opportunity to produce their own early two minutes of fame. Breaking out of their organized lines, they brazenly pushed and shoved to place themselves in the best vantage point – and the South Koreans took note and were appalled at the behavior.

USA Athletes at the Opening Ceremony of the 1988 Seoul Olympics

The truth is that nothing could possibly compare to the previous Los Angeles Olympics. Instead of the rousing roar of the crowd shouting "USA USA", the athletes entered the stadium to a shocked and upset crowd. Beyond that, things evolved badly for the Americans.

Asians who are raised traditionally have an inflexible opinion of what they deem civilized behavior. Entrenched in their ancient culture is a stern mandate that they should always conduct themselves – particularly in public – in a humble, quiet and unobtrusive way. Showing off theatrically, being loud and any form of exhibitionism are considered exceptionally rude and distasteful behavior. Instead, the Asians revere conformity and self-effacing manners that don't attract attention to the individual. Oops....the USA athletes definitely didn't read that memo.

1988 Seoul Olympic Opening Ceremony

Terry witnessed the circus unfolding. The citizens of their host city showed their disgust in their facial expressions. It was so clear that they found the American behavior an affront to the integrity of the ceremonies and disrespectful in every sense.

After some of the U.S. athletes realized that they might need to adopt a more inhibited demeanor, they poured water onto their exuberance and tried to regroup more sedately on the field. They still had one more chance at redemption while capturing the spirit and excitement of the Olympics with the upcoming lighting of the torch.

Things were starting to look more promising as a collective sense of dignity replaced the former theatrics and everyone stood in awe as the Olympic torch entered the stadium. Terry and several of his teammates with their cameras had a wonderful view of the torch – but that Zen moment was about to ricochet into another disastrous moment. Hundreds of white doves had just been released as symbols of peace and they angelically flew over to the unlit cauldron where many of them settled for a few minutes. Shortly thereafter, the final torchbearer received the torch and headed to the cauldron to light the Olympic flame. Unable to see the top of the cauldron, he lit the torch and inadvertently skewered the doves of peace that had used it as their temporary perch.

The poor birds caught fire instantly and scorched to death, many landing on the Olympic floor next to some of the athletes. Terry and his teammates were dumbfounded as they stared at the falling, blackened birds. Doug Kimbell remembers watching the toasted birds drop one by one.

White Doves are released at the Opening Ceremony of the 1988 Seoul Olympics

The lighting of the Olympic Torch at the 1988 Seoul Olympics - Some poor White Doves accidentally died in the flames

The incident brought on unimaginable horror and catapulted every child who watched – into shock. This type of thing was not supposed to happen at the Olympic Games. As a result of this unforeseen tragedy, the 1988 Games were the last time that live birds were released during opening ceremonies. Written into the new Olympic Guidelines was a strict forbiddance of the practice of releasing birds of peace – in case they got skewered again.

The fire wasn't over yet. The day after the opening ceremonies, the American media released a story about how the USA shooting team had been able to sneak in thousands of rounds of live ammunition through the airport security. Needless to say, this was extremely embarrassing to the South Koreans and it only made matters worse. The South Korean organizing committee finally decided that the Americans were the cause of too many upsets. For the next two weeks, they exhibited their deep offence at the Americans disgracing the spirit of the Games with their media hogging and antics at the airport. Their indignation was so strong that there was talk in the local papers of them wanting to kick the Americans out of the Olympics altogether – as punishment for disrespecting and dishonoring what was tantamount to a sacred ceremony. There was no doubt that there was still a copious amount of damage control necessary.

The history between Team USA and Team Yugoslavia is an epic, dramatic adventure worthy of its own book. Between 1984 and 1988, they played each other in over 25 matches. These titanic matches brought out the best in each of them: they fought to the end – making the matches virtually even every time. Team USA won 12 times, lost 11 and had 3 ties with Yugoslavia. Unfortunately, Yugoslavia had won all of the games that mattered the most, including the 1984 Olympics and the 1986 World Championships.

Going into the Seoul Olympics produced a voracious amount of excitement when the draw came out in March, 1988: USA and Yugoslavia were not only in the same pool (bracket), but they were also scheduled to play the first game of the tournament. The spectator interest was multiplied with the two best countries in the world playing right away.

That first game, like so many of the matches the USA played against Yugoslavia, came down to the nail-biting last seconds. Bergie scored a goal with 15 seconds left in the game to give USA a 7-6 victory in the opening match. This put them firmly in the driver's seat for the rest of the tournament. All they had to do thereafter was take care of business and win the games they were supposed to win. That would automatically put them in the medal round.

In the second game, USA played Spain and things went unexpectedly awry. A month prior to the Olympics, they had beaten Spain convincingly: 16-6. On that night at the Seoul Aquatic Center, Spain's Manuel Estiarte – who was deemed to be one of the best players in the world - was on fire. Everything he threw at the cage made its way into the goal, and Spain beat the U.S. 9-7 on the strength of Estiarte's 6-goal mastery.

Terry Schroeder (10) on the offensive against Spain in the 1988 Seoul Olympics

The defeat produced a considerable amount of pressure on the USA to win the rest of their matches – in order to make it to the medal round. The next few games were must wins - and the U.S. took care of China 14-7 and then Greece 18-9.

Jody Campbell sustained a concussion in the China game and could not even remember anything about the game in a post-game interview. With today's concussion protocol, he would have been out for at least a week. Determined not to miss any games despite the concussion, Jody played on – some would say - out of his mind!

The moment of reckoning came down to their final game in the pool play against Hungary. If they tied or lost, Team USA would be in 5th - 8th position, and if they won, they'd move on to the top 4 and the medal round.

This game also came down to the final seconds. Going into the final quarter,

Terry Schroeder analyzing the game situation at the 1988 Seoul Olympics

1988 Seoul Olympics - Tery Schroeder emerges after beating Hungary

the game was tied 5-5. It was a wild 4th quarter with each team scoring on practically every possession. Hungary scored to tie the match at 9 a piece with 15 seconds left on the clock. Things did not look good for the USA. They had to score or they would be out of medal contention. That was pressure in another hemisphere.

Terry swam down to the center position and with 5 seconds left on the clock, the ball was passed to him. In that critical moment, he scored with 3 seconds left – and stealthily sealed the victory. When asked after the match how that felt, he simply said, "It felt like each and every member of my team was helping me throw the ball into the net".

Next up was the USA against the Soviet Union in the semi finals. The South Korean home crowd was clearly rooting for the Soviet Union – even though the Soviets had recently shot down a Korean passenger aircraft, killing all 269 civilian passengers onboard. The Koreans' pro Soviet support seemed to indicate that they had completely forgiven them for the travesty – and yet – the Americans remained the foe. This time the USA was on fire: they dominated play throughout and at one point they were up 7–4. They ended up winning 7-6 to move into the finals against Yugoslavia who had won the rest of their games since that first game against the USA.

The Soviet Union has always proved to be a fascination to Terry. One of the reasons he wanted to go for the 1988 Olympics was that he had to prove to himself that the USA could still get to the gold medal final – even with the Soviet Union present.

They had boycotted the 1984 Olympics, and their non-participation saddened Terry. But what made the chess game even more interesting was that the Soviets had thrown their final game of bracket play – to rather play the USA first in the semi finals in order to avoid Yugoslavia. They'd deduced – erroneously – that the USA would be the easier team to beat in the semi finals. How wrong they were. Victory was all the more satisfying when the USA beat them in that crucial game – and no doubt the Soviet's condescending assumption of their opponents fueled the USA's fire.

Even Coach Barnett finally conceded that his men had played well – and gave them a thumbs-up and a smile at his post game meeting. Affirmation from him rarely happened.

The gold medal game was set - USA vs. Yugoslavia - a rematch from the dramatic 1984 Olympic final. One important thing had changed between 1984 and 1988: there would be no tie. Instead, the match would go to overtime so that a true winner could emerge.

The déjà vu game was eerie in its similarly to the 1984 Olympic final. Just as happened in that game, the USA controlled the game early. By the middle of the third quarter, they held the lead 5-2. Having learned from the pain of the past, Terry was not about to let complacency or feeling comfortable erode the team's fire. In 1984, he felt that maybe the team had focused on winning instead of protecting the lead, and so he beckoned all his teammates to keep the lead by elevating their game.

But Yugoslavia battled back and before anybody had time to study what had just happened, the

Terry Schroeder emerges from the pool at the 1988 Seoul Olympics victorious after beating the Soviet Union in the Semi Finals

USA was locked in a tie with Yugoslavia at the end of the game. Ironically and cruelly, this time, had the rules not changed, the USA would have won the gold on goal differential (as had been the case in 1984 when Yugoslavia won on goal differential).

The game went into overtime and Yugoslavia would eventually pull away and beat the USA 9-7. Aggressive on offensive, they took advantage of every opportunity. Igor Milanović was the hero for Yugoslavia, scoring a huge overtime goal and earning a key exclusion on the Americans. "We, on the other hand," said Doug Kimbell, "were so focused on not losing, that we weren't attacking as fiercely as the Yugoslavians. We were playing a solidly defensive game while they were on the attack. It didn't work out for us, even though we wanted to win as passionately as they did."

Terry Schroeder (10) faces Yugoslavia's Igor Milanović in the
1988 Seoul Olympics Gold Medal Final

That end-game loss was more painful than Terry could possibly fathom. For what seemed like 20 minutes, he hung to the edge of the pool, stunned at what had just happened. For the second time in 4 years, he and his teammates missed the gold by the smallest of margins. The dream had once again been thwarted. The silver medal meant they'd lost the big matchup and that was so excruciatingly difficult to grasp and accept. The disappointment was physically and emotionally searing – punishingly caustic in its demolition of the team's dream.

Seoul 1988 - Olympic Men's USA Water Polo Team receive their
Silver Medals after the Gold Medal Final against Yugoslavia

Years later, Terry would share an in-deep conversation with the hero of Yugoslavia's game - his long-time friend Igor Milanović who played in the gold medal final games of 1984 and 1988. Igor was quick to remind Terry that his two silver medals were not the two golds that Igor enviably had. They respected each other enough to laugh at the little dig. However, Igor did offer Terry a very valuable perspective on the 1984 and 1988 gold medal final games in which both of their two teams fought valiantly. He said that the USA unquestionably deserved to take the gold medal in the 1984 final. However, he said that when it came to the 1988 final, Yugoslavia simply wanted it more, and they fought harder in the critical end stage of overtime. In his opinion, they deserved the win that time. Since winning the gold was what Terry had sacrificed everything for, he found it difficult to conceptualize how anybody could have wanted it more than he. It was yet another painful shock with which he would eventually have to make peace.

In 2016, with the richness of hindsight available, Igor Milanović offered another perspective on Yugoslavia's strength in the 1980s: He said, "During the time, Yugoslavia enjoyed exceptional strength because there were so many highly competitive clubs in the country that were all fighting for the championship. It gave us the necessary experience to approach very difficult games internationally. The fierce competition back home, the constant hard games we played – made us a great team. That Olympic dream all started in the 1984 Los Angeles Games. I was only 18 years old when I came to this beautiful city with 10,000 people watching us play. The atmosphere in Los Angeles was incredible, and that final gold medal game against the USA brought out the best in our teams. I scored in that game, and my fire was lit from that moment on."

Igor went on to say, "As for Terry Schroeder: he was without any doubt one of the best centers in the history of water polo. I feel for his pain in those two gold medal final games. He won my team's respect both in and out of the pool. What we noticed and admired was his strength of character: in the pool he played the game intelligently and he was never a dirty player. Out of the pool, he always conducted himself like a gentleman. I will always respect Terry for being one of water polo's greatest players all round."

The opportunity for the Americans to redeem themselves from the showmanship debacle of the opening ceremonies came as the closing ceremonies approached. As Terry was walking back to the Olympic Village – after the final game – he endeavored to put everything into perspective while learning to appreciate the achievement in the silver medal. As he was doing this, he encountered several teammates and other athletes walking in the village who let him know that all the captains from the USA teams had voted for him to be the official flag bearer for the United States at the closing ceremonies. Terry was deeply touched. No water polo player before had ever been afforded this honor – and he felt privileged and exceptionally fortunate.

Given the excruciating embarrassment of the opening debacle – the American officials who didn't know Terry were wary as they visualized another catastrophe waiting to happen with a cocky water polo playboy flexing his pectoral muscles flamboyantly for the TV cameras.

The next day Terry was summoned into the offices of the United States Olympic Committee (USOC) to receive a lecture on how imperative it was to recover from the opening ceremonies misfortunate. They impressed upon Terry the crucial importance of representing his country with dignity and with deference to the host country. They obviously didn't know their man. Terry was the quintessential epitome of the attributes the Olympic Committee sought. They had nothing to worry about.

The closing ceremonies proved to be as impactful and as exhilarating as the 1984 opening ceremonies – but in a different way. Determined not to be anything but dignified and respectful, Terry carried the American flag filled with

Terry Schroeder carrying U.S. flag at the 1988 Seoul Olympic Games Closing Ceremony

pride and with a deep appreciation of the honor involved. He walked in a distinguished manner with the full deference and discipline of a Marine Corps soldier – processing everything that had happened to his team over the prior 16 days.

It turned out that he had his work cut out for him. Unlike the opening ceremonies, the closing ceremonies are usually the time when all the athletes' emotions are unleashed from the tension of the previous 16 days of competition, and the event usually turns into a massive party on the field. After walking around the arena, Terry was determined not to join the party since his strict instructions were to remain in the center of the field until the end. So committed was he to make his nation proud that – when all the other flag bearers peeled off the line to join their respective nations for the party - Terry stood statue still where he was instructed to stay – with the U.S. flag firmly in his grip.

However, teammate Jody Campbell, who was celebrating his own personal victory of being the highest goal scorer for Team USA in Seoul, had his own agenda: He wanted the flag to be with his team, so he hijacked it as Terry was being interviewed on NBC, and ran with it to the celebrating team. After standing still without his flag, Terry changed tactic: for the first time in 16 days, he allowed the emotions he had kept bottled up - to flow freely. In the chaos of the closing ceremonies - with athletes from all the various countries running around - he set his sights on Jody and his flag. When the timing was right, he tackled him hard to the ground, and recovered the flag. This time, rather than go back to the center of the field, he joined his teammates while keeping the flag glued to his inner palm. It was a celebration of all they had experienced together and Terry felt that massive stirring of emotions inside. For the remaining 45 minutes of the closing ceremonies, Terry ran around the stadium with his USA teammates chasing after him while the flag flew proudly and high.

The Seoul Closing Ceremonies, and the privilege of holding his country's flag, turned out to be a pivotal milestone in his life. In that introspective moment, Terry learned that perspective is based on expectations and experiences. He also learned from a very practical standpoint that his athletic training was geared towards water polo and not track: his legs were killing him from all the running he had done chasing Jody and carrying his country's flag!

Teammate Greg Boyer looks back at the 1988 Seoul Olympics with an immense amount of gratitude: "Those Olympic days were the best times of our lives. Thirteen of us played the sport we loved, and we traveled across the globe forming friendships that have lasted a lifetime. The team camaraderie was something very special. We were like brothers who shared so much together. We pushed each other's limits and laid everything we had out there on the line. We played against the world's best athletes and raised our game to unimaginably high levels. The Olympics gave us a mental toughness that instilled confidence in each of us. As a result we've been able to take that confidence and translate it into business and social interactions. As for Terry, well, his strength was incredible. Although we were the same weight and age, he was stronger than I and it was impossible to sink him. He was a brilliant center who, because of his athletic strength, took so much punishment from other teams, but he never lost his composure and always remained levelheaded. I shall always respect him."

The day after the 1988 Olympic Closing Ceremonies, Terry returned home to California, resolved that this would be his final Olympics. His family and friends had been steadfastly supportive of his journey, and the sacrifices that Lori had made only served to make him love her more.

Children have a refreshing way of emitting the truth with no malice intended. The neighborhood children, who had watched Terry on their television sets, rallied at his front door upon his return – asking to see his shiny new silver medal. As each child took turns to hang the medal around their necks, Terry was seeing his accomplishment through their eyes. Their faces depicted awe, admiration and ......the truth. One young boy took the medal, looked at Terry and said, "Yeah, but it's not the gold medal". Thump back to cold, hard reality. No, it wasn't. Trust a child to remind Terry of that perspective.

What Terry knew for sure after this 3rd Olympic portion of his life - is that every Olympics brings about new perspectives – important perspectives that are integral to our human growth. While his goal has never changed – to bring home that ultimate

Terry Schroeder with Jeff Campbell, Kevin Robertson and Alan Mouchawar at the Disneyland celebrations after the 1988 Seoul Olympics of victories - the gold – he has always come back richer and with a healthier, broader perspective from the experience. There is immense value in that.

Terry's thoughts and emotions in his last 1988 journal entry:

October 4, 1988

Mixed emotions… I am so proud of my team! We battled and, although we came up short, we gave it our best shot. Another silver medal – a combination of pain and joy. The pain comes from coming so close and not quite making it happen. Too many similarities to 1984: Losing the gold to Yugoslavia, same Spanish official who does not seem to like us much. A 5-2 third quarter lead -- game ending in a tie. I can honestly say that this time round, it was better that we played out the game in overtime. Even though we lost – it was better than the 1984 heartbreak of ending the game in a tie and using goal differential to determine the winner. That is no way to award a gold medal. At least this time, we had the opportunity to play it out. Yugoslavia stepped it up in the overtime and they beat us. Like in 1984, I have played the game in my head over and over again. What could I have done differently? How could I have helped us to win the gold? I know that I will eventually find peace with it but it is difficult to not think about the "what ifs", "could haves" and "should haves." Nothing will change what has happened. I have another silver medal from the Olympic Games. I need to be proud of that medal and move on. It is time for family. Lori deserves my time and energy now. We have dreams of starting a family together and it is time to focus on that. It is also time to turn my attention to my career. Our chiropractic practice needs my attention. I have worked hard for that goal too and it is time to follow in my dad's footsteps and start helping people. I look forward to seeing the daily miracles that I know will happen in my patients' lives. It feels weird to be retired. I am sure it will be a transition. I am still coaching at Pepperdine and we are about a third of the way into our season already. The lateness of these Games (September/October) has pushed into our season and it is time to focus on my coaching too. I have enjoyed being a coach and maybe I can keep doing this for a while. I am sure it will be a great way to stay connected to water polo. What will I do with all my time? My thoughts are all over the place. I need to sit down and write out a plan… Where do I go? Who do I become now? I have been an elite athlete. That has dominated my thoughts. It is time to transition into Terry Schroeder: husband and family man. Terry Schroeder D.C., Chiropractor.

When Terry was 8 years old, he had his first taste of being a competitive swimmer with his first real coach, Ian McPherson. Coach McPherson impacted Terry in so many positive ways. After 3 months, and having experienced a couple of swim meets where he faired adequately, Coach stopped him one day at practice, looked into his eyes and said, "Are you ready to reach for the stars?" Terry really didn't know what that meant, but he responded, "Sure Coach, I am ready. What do I need to do?" Together they did what it took to reach the goals that Terry laid out for himself.

Shortly after the 1988 Olympics, Terry was informed that Coach Ian McPherson had been diagnosed with multiple myeloma, a cancer with a very poor survival rate. His health deteriorated fast. Alex Asta, one of Terry's college players, called him and told him that Ian was in the hospital and deteriorating badly.

Terry immediately drove up to Santa Barbara, not knowing what to expect. As he entered the hospital room, he was shocked to see how much weight his first coach had lost. On heavy medication to curb the intense pain, he drifted in and out of consciousness. Terry sat quietly with his former coach for about an hour. Finally, he woke, sat up despite being very weak, and after a few minutes he recognized Terry and a smile lit up his face. He motioned to him to come closer and then he simply said, "Terry, are you still reaching for those stars?" Tears ran down his cheeks and all Terry could do was nod his head to say, "Yes." Coach passed away a few days later.

Schroeder Chiropractors. Terry is 3rd generation Schroeder Chiropractors

CHAPTER 11

Swimming towards Alignment

The Doctor of the Future will give no Medicine, but will interest
his or her Patients in the Care of the Human Frame, adherence to
a Proper Diet, in the Cause and Prevention of Disease
– Thomas Edison

18 October 1988: Terry and Lori graduated from Palmer Chiropractic in 1986. Terry began to practice part-time while he was coaching water polo at Pepperdine University and training for the 1988 Seoul Olympic Games. His part-time chiropractic work was with his dad and brother in Santa Barbara. Lori began to practice in Thousand Oaks, California with Dr. Bob Dishman. After closing ceremonies in Seoul, Terry joined Lori fulltime at Dr. Dishman's and it is there that they began to build their chiropractic practice and life's work together.

The professional impact that Terry's dad had made on him during his childhood was profound: The Schroeder family home was where Dr. Bob Schroeder had his office, and Terry recalls people filing in there looking broken and in pain. An incident that stands out vividly in his memory is that of a man who physically collapsed after walking in the door. Twenty minutes later, after Dr. Bob had worked on him, he was laughing and walking effortlessly. That was the scenario with most people who came to see Dr. Bob, and Terry was resolved that he too wanted to perform these physical miracles – just like his dad.

There was never any pressure on the Schroeder children to follow in dad's footsteps. However, growing up with a chiropractic lifestyle and seeing patients' lives changed in front of their eyes almost every day made choosing chiropractic as a profession an easy decision. Terry, Lance and Tammy would all follow their dad's lead. Dr. Bob would often teach his children life lessons when he spoke with them. Two of those life lessons Terry absorbed resolutely: Work hard at work that is worth doing and: bring out the best in others. There was no question that their dad's work as a chiropractor was physically demanding and hard work, but the joy of seeing positive change in people's lives everyday made it very meaningful and fulfilling.

The chiropractic lifestyle was inculcated deeply into Terry, Lance and Tammy in every respect. They knew that eating healthfully, exercising frequently and getting adjusted regularly allowed their bodies to function at their optimum level. The Schroeder family medicine cabinets were always empty because Dr. Bob and his tribe never resorted to taking pills for a quick fix. Instead, they learned to trust and believe in the body's natural ability to heal itself. Terry, Lance and Tammy were noticeably healthier than other children their age and while their classmates at school were often sick, they weren't. To this day, Terry has had a total of two shots in his life: one was an antibiotic to help resolve an infection that he brought home from Europe, and the other was for severe pain after having a minor surgery. He's never taken an aspirin, Advil, Tylenol or any other over-the-counter medication.

As Terry's teenage years progressed, Dr. Bob would adjust his son regularly. Many of those childhood adjustments stand out. On one occasion, Terry was in excruciating discomfort and felt almost disoriented after a very physical water polo tournament, so Dr. Bob adjusted his atlas – a powerful adjustment under normal circumstances. The immediate change in his body astounded Terry. His body and mind were realigned and he felt as though the power

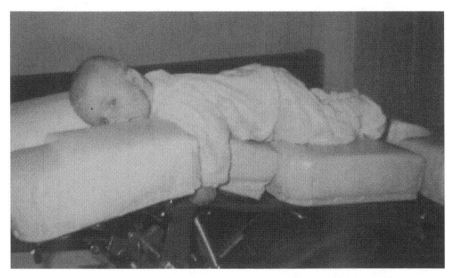

9-month-old Terry Schroeder receiving the miracle of chiropractic care from his father, Dr. Bob Schroeder

had been turned back on. He vividly remembers feeling restored, focused and energized with absolutely no pain. The impetus of that pain-free zone was profound: it was that moment of reckoning where Terry fully understood how much his dad was changing the lives of his patients – every day.

Since that day, Terry continued to feel the impact of many adjustments in his life, but even more satisfyingly, he's been able to witness first-hand the power of the adjust-

Dr. Frederick Schroeder and Dr. BJ Palmer

ments on his patients on a daily basis. Restoring alignment to their lives is inestimably rewarding for a man who loves to help people.

This same course took place in many Schroeder households. Uncles and aunts raised their families with a chiropractic, drug-free lifestyle. Incredibly, the Schroeder family is recognized in the Guinness Book of World Records as the largest chiropractic family in the world. Dr. Frederick Schroeder (Terry's grandfather) was the first in the family to choose this healing career. There are now 74 family members that have earned the degree of Doctor of Chiropractic and have practiced throughout the United States. A photograph, which was featured in a Sports Illustrated article in 1988, displays 35 of the Schroeder chiropractors standing near a giant spine. There are now 12 fourth generation chiropractors in the Schroeder clan. Terry and Lori are very proud to be a part of this family profession. They are humbled by the power of the human body to heal itself – especially when in alignment - and they receive great joy on a daily basis as a result of healing their patients.

Chiropractic is a unique health care science that deals with the relationship between the nervous system and the spine. It also deals with the role of this relationship in the restoration and the maintenance of the physical body. Literally, chiropractic helps people live in alignment. Chiropractic was developed in the United States by D.D. Palmer in 1895, who connected two important ideas: Firstly, the body is a self-developing, healing and maintaining organism. Secondly: the nervous system is vital to how all parts of the body function. Basically, our brain communicates with all body parts, organs, tissues and cells via the nervous system that is housed within the spinal cord. Therefore, if our spine is out of alignment, it may produce a subluxation or fixation that may negatively impact the nerve flow or impede the message from the brain to the intended body part. Consequently, that particular body part or organ may not function at its best until alignment is restored.

The body's amazing, innate ability to heal itself (under the right conditions) means the chiropractor's job is to help create an environment to facilitate this process. The chiropractor's role is to restore proper spinal alignment through vertebral adjustments, thereby freeing the body of nerve interference caused by spinal subluxations (misalignment). Once the body is free of these misalignments and subsequent nerve interference, the central nervous system can then perform its own healing miracles from within. While Chiropractic does not cure or treat disease, it helps the body to heal from within – by being in alignment – and allowing function to occur as close to 100% as possible. This perfect balance allows us to live and perform close to our human potential. It also allows us to live pain free, and that changes people's lives.

Another aspect about his profession that Terry particularly enjoys is educating patients to read their bodies' signals. Subtle changes in the body are forewarnings that it needs attention – long before the chronic pain sets in. It's about developing that mindfulness of tuning in to oneself. People need to be more aware of what is happening in their bodies because being out of alignment or out of balance for periods of time can create weakness in the body which then potentially leads to illness and chronic disease.

There is a paradigm shift that Terry's believes is necessary in our culture: "Most of us believe that if we feel good we are healthy. This is not true. Our bodies are able to hide a myriad of problems by adapting and compensating – so as to allow us to continue functioning daily. But that compensation state is damaging and eventually – it will break down. To truly have optimum health and live in alignment, we must be proactive in our self-care and work to pre-vent disease - before we have symptoms. Unlike medication, which is all about treating the symptoms, chiropractic is preventative: it addresses the causes of poor health and helps restore the body's natural ability to heal itself."

Terry's work has helped shape his perspective too. Seeing so many people in pain has taught him to be more caring, kind and empathetic. The treatment he gives is specifically designed for each patient's unique problem. While moving them out of pain is his first priority, the second equally as important goal is to encourage them to live healthier lives by eating better, exercising more, sleeping more soundly, stressing less, and getting regular adjustments. This will create the optimal health situation for each patient. In that sense, practicing what he preaches is critical. In order to inspire others, Terry has to be the living example of what it looks and feels like to be operating at maxi-mum health.

Terry's and Lori's passion for the topic of healthcare is strongly evident in the seminars they hold regularly and these are just some of their words of wisdom: "Just as doctors have become more active regarding our health care, we, the patients, have become more 'passive'. That's a fundamental problem. Until we start to take the reins again by recognizing that the best doctor in the universe resides inside each of us, we will continue to be dis-empowered and helpless. By not taking our health into our own hands and by continuing to abuse our bodies, we end up paying the heavy price with sickness and chronic disease."

"As a society, we short-change ourselves on quality sleep; eat too much and exercise too little. We sit in cars, sit at work, sit while watching TV, and sit while surfing the web. This sedentary lifestyle promotes decay in our body while conversely, exercise signals the body to wake up, grow and repair. An ideal exercise routine should include aerobic activity for at least 30 to 45 min-utes, 5 to 6 times per week. The key is to involve ourselves in activities that we enjoy – something that has an element of fun. Exercising with a friend or a family member also helps to hold us accountable. Once the healthy effects of an exercise routine begin to show, our motivation increases. Most impor-tantly, a healthy habit would have been formed."

Research tells us that 5-10% of health come from genetics and 90 -95% comes from lifestyle. The choices we make and the good and bad habits we form will determine our health, and ultimately, the length and quality of our lives. Being healthy is a choice that we make.

Terry cannot stress the importance of posture strongly enough: "Posture is of paramount importance. Holding oneself upright with shoulders back, relaxed and in good form, is critically important. Posture is a habit that is developed by repeating movements and patterns over time and in turn, it becomes one of the biggest components to being healthy. Carrying heavy backpacks, slumping at the desk and slouching on the sofa are all destructive habits that will wear the body down over time. Poor postural habits will lead to injuries of many kinds, irrespective of whether we are athletes or not."

"Like a building with a poor foundation, a body with poor posture is less resistant to the strains and stresses we experience over the months, years and decades of life. When the body is properly aligned, it is well balanced, with minimum stress and strain on supporting structures such as bones, ligaments, tendons and muscles. Even internal organs are affected by poor posture. Perfecting our posture requires a lot of attention initially but with practice it becomes second nature. Once again, it is all about body awareness. Good habits build good posture and good posture gives us more energy and fewer aches and pains."

People have a tendency to accept limitations and restrictions and this has always concerned Terry and Lori. "There's a much-used, helpless phrase, 'it is what it is' or 'this is as good as it is going to get' in which people resign themselves to what they perceive to be their unalterable fate." People visit Terry and Lori in pain and may start off by saying, "I've been on disability for over 20 years. The old shoulder injury is something I've learned to live with". Yet, after a few visits, there's a marked improvement in their condition. That instills hope in them, which then changes their perception of themselves.

Much of modern medicine overlooks hope. Without hope, people will give in to what they think is their destiny. Chiropractic and chiropractors provide hope that is vital to resolving any health concern. With chiropractic care, chronic issues are often resolved and people realize that they no longer have to believe in their fate of being permanently disabled. That's a restrictive lie they've bought into. Lives are changed by restoring health and wellbeing to individuals who have lived in pain for years.

Terry emphasizes, "Most people require a road map for living a healthier life. They want the 'how' manual. Coach Mike Krzyzewski, from Duke University, USA, often talks about the necessity for 'standards' in everyone's lives. It doesn't matter if you're part of a team, a family, or a community, there should be a set of non-violable standards that are formed from knowing and defining your goals."

In Terry's and Lori's family, they've created their own set of standards with the goal of living healthy and successful lives. This is a living and evolving agreement that shifts in response to the needs of their family. Standards should always be a call to action or lifestyle that supports the goal. Quality and consistent family time is one of their goals. So, a standard might be an expectation that each member will plan ahead and get their work done in a timely manner so that they can enjoy more fun family times.

While Lori and Terry, as team captains, do most of the job of holding everyone accountable, they do expect their daughters, Leanna and Sheridan, to have an appropriate level of self-discipline. They also insure that the girls are holding them to the same standards. Once again, in order to lead properly, one must first be a good example. The Schroeders have learned how to remind one another gently during times when one of them is forgetting to choose the good habits. These good habits include giving of their best in all things; eating healthfully, finding time for exercising, and getting adequate sleep.

Bad habits don't often come and hit people over the head with a sledgehammer. Instead, they creep into people's lives incrementally until, one day, the person wakes up and realizes that they've been abusing their bodies for 25 years. Whether that is posture or eating the wrong foods, being aware of those subtle changes and making adjustments sooner than later – towards the better goal – is imperative to long-term health and vitality.

People living in the U.S. are particularly prone to the lure of abundance and instant self-gratification, but there's always a price to be paid afterwards. In truth, focusing on others – the family, the team, the company and friends – makes us better, more disciplined people. Getting back on track requires looking at the big picture. Applying self-discipline consistently – whether it feels good or not - is the most empowering habit anyone can develop.

John Naber, a famous American Olympic gold medalist in swimming, has often said, "No deposit, no return". Nobody understands that notion more than Olympic athletes. The deposit (training) they transact is substantial. It's a sacrifice of extensive proportions but each one of them has calculated that the dream is worth the deposit.

Enjoying the benefits of good health involves depositing. Terry and Lori have encountered patients who don't do their part in the transaction. They're advised to exercise and lose weight by following a healthy daily eating plan, but they are not motivated to do the work it takes to get healthy. It's as if they have become complacent in their 'victim' stance, and their health often suffers substantially. They pay a large price for that complacency, and so too do their families and loved ones.

Passion is an interesting character quality. Terry credits his dad for passing on the genetic aptitude for passion. Exercising it was second nature to Terry because it was already imbued in his DNA. Also, having the role model of Dr. Bob Schroeder was the ultimate representation of passion, and living with such an enthused dad brought out the very best in Terry. Dr. Bob invested copious amounts of energy and resilience in the things he wanted from life. He wanted his children to feel secure in a loving family home while reaching for the stars and using their God-given gifts. When Bob saw the passion that Terry felt for water polo, he was 100% behind his son in every respect – encouraging him wholeheartedly, driving him to wherever he needed to be. Bob never did anything with half an engine. It was full throttle all the way. Pat was equally as supportive but in her own, quiet way. Terry is exceptionally thankful that he had parents that gave him such love and support. He remembers only a few of his games - high school, college or national team - that his parents were not there in the stands cheering him on.

But it was Dr. Bob's work as a chiropractor that impacted Terry most profoundly. As patients enthused about how his dad's hands had impacted their lives, it became clear in Terry's heart that after his water polo career, this was where his other passion lay. Both his water polo and chiropractic careers give him to this day an exceptional sense of fulfillment.

The cruel day that changed the Schroeders' life forever - arrived later - when Terry was in his 40s. Dr. Bob Schroeder, who didn't always practice what he preached, became ill because of a stroke, and could no longer work. He had overindulged in rich, unhealthy foods life-long while not exercising enough on a regular basis. The long-term ills of that habit caught up with his body. Terry empathized with his dad and thought about how unimaginably difficult it would be for him to have to give up his passion – chiropractic care – and reinvent himself for the remainder of his life. The reality was he might never be able to work again. The devastation turned out to be as immense as Terry had thought. Dr. Bob loved being a husband and father, but he loved being a chiropractor equally as much.

Bob's illness stoked the fire of passion for chiropractic in Terry even more. It was as if Terry had gathered in Dr. Bob's portion of his love for the profession, and combined it with his own. In 2005, Bob Schroeder passed away. Terry's exceptional closeness to his mentor and dad made the impact of his death a massive blow. Bob was in Terry's life every day. During his Olympic quest, it was Bob who was his biggest cheerleader and encourager. During his Olympic playing days, it was Bob who showed his son how proud he was of him.

Through the years, when Terry was driving home from work, he'd often call his dad as a part of his routine, to catch up and fill him in on the day's news. Bob's routine reliability had become so imprinted in his son that Terry would make his routine calls at the exact same spot on the freeway. Long after Bob's death, he still went through the motions of picking up that phone – to talk to his always-there-for-him dad.

The pain of loss gradually transpired into a great sense of love. Terry credits his dad with passing on so many gifts and life lessons to him, and for that he's forever grateful. His dad continues to be a positive influence in his life. Dr. Bob Schroeder loved serving everyone as a chiropractor and this is what Terry carries with him every day as a chiropractor and as a coach. In serving others, there is a great sense of fulfillment which is enhanced by the challenge to bring out the best in others – whether that means helping another person become a better water polo player, parent, husband or just providing the life-changing chiropractic adjustments on a daily basis.

Chiropractic is a vital part of Terry's Olympic experience. In 1984, during his first Olympic Games as an athlete, there was one official chiropractor on the USA Olympic team staff. Her name was Dr. Eileen Hayworth. By 2008, there were 5 official chiropractors who were a part of the USA Olympic staff. Why? Because the athletes demanded it. Every athlete is looking for any edge they can find, and a skilled chiropractor helps to fine tune the body so that it can function at or near its human potential. When the difference between a gold medal and no medal at all is miniscule, it makes sense for an athlete to get his/her body into proper alignment and make sure the nervous system is working as close to 100% as possible. Terry knows that without regular chiropractic care in his life, he would never have had the opportunity to participate in four Olympic Games as an athlete.

This is the same reason so many professional sports teams and individual athletes seek out regular chiropractic care. They know how much it helps their body stay aligned and functioning at the highest level.

As a coach at Pepperdine University and for the Olympic team, Terry has had the opportunity to introduce many athletes to the positive benefits of chiropractic care and most of his athletes seek regular care. In 2008, when he took over as head coach of the men's national team, just two of the athletes received regular chiropractic care. When he left Team USA in 2012, all of his athletes were receiving regular care – in preparation for high-level competition.

Terry is also proud of the fact that he has personally influenced over 25 people to go to chiropractic school and pursue this wonderful profession. There is no doubt that many more have been influenced towards chiropractic due to Terry's inspiration and success as an Olympian and a chiropractor.

Terry and Lori now call their office 'Live in Alignment Chiropractic and Pilates'. This serves as a daily reminder to do their best to keep their lives in balance. Terry concludes by saying, "there are times and seasons in life when everyone feels like they are a bit out of alignment. This is the time to make some quiet time for relaxation, prayer or meditation to reflect and contemplate where your life is out of balance, and then make the necessary adjustments to realign and balance your life."

Lance, Terry, Tammy, Tucker and Bob Schroeder at the 1992 Barcelona Olympics

1992 USA Olympic Men's Water Polo Team

CHAPTER 12

1992 Barcelona Olympic Games

Spanish Waters

I can't change the direction of the wind, but I can adjust
my sails to always reach my destination
– Jimmy Dean

July 25, 1992: While Terry had officially retired from water polo after the 1988 Olympics, he wrestled with the acknowledgment that a piece of him was missing: that churning desire to compete at the highest level. It was an intrinsic, involuntary need and without it – he was restless. The seismic adrenaline boosts to which Terry had become addicted over the past decade rendered his body chemically deprived, but perhaps even more powerfully, the mental conditioning of his identity being solely that of a star Olympic athlete, left him feeling alienated from his own presence. This would prove to be problematic later.

Despite his days being full with married life, the chiropractic office, coaching at Pepperdine University, and doing water polo color commentary for Turner Broadcasting Station (TBS) alongside Olympic Swimmer John Naber – the flame inside him appeared to be eternal and it would not extinguish itself. It beckoned for more, and returning USA Head Coach, Bill Barnett, must have telepathically read that.

In July 1990, while Terry was commentating at the Goodwill Games in Seattle, Washington, Coach Bill Barnett approached him about coming back to the Olympics, and he even followed Terry back to his home in Agoura Hills, California, imploring him to make the sacrifice and rejoin the team. He felt strongly that the team needed his leadership and play at Center.

It was not a hard sell. After talking it over with Lori for a few weeks, Terry let Bill know that he would love to rejoin the team - but he warned him that his priorities had changed: Lori was the most important person to him; his chiropractic business was his 2nd priority, and water polo was his 3rd. It was a very different picture from 1980 and 1984. But he did promise Bill that when he was at practice, he would give it his all and he would be there for the team in every way possible. Terry's coaching at Pepperdine University had in many ways helped him to become a better player by understanding the game more intricately – but it was nevertheless another commitment and therefore another distraction. Terry knew that this was never an ideal situation when playing water polo at the highest level. Team Manager Barbara Kalbus would later state that "a part-time Terry was better than no Terry at all." Simply stated the team needed Terry and Terry needed the team.

In the 1992 team from the 1988 Olympic squad were:

Terry Schroeder (Captain) - becoming the first ever 4-time Olympian for the USA in the sport of water polo. Manuel Estiarte holds the all-time record for water polo having played in 6 Olympic Games – spanning from 1984 – 2004. In 2016, Tony Azevedo became the first 5-time Olympian for Team USA in the sport of water polo.

Craig Wilson - Best goal tender in the world. By now "Willy" had been playing in Italy and Spain for 4 years and was gaining valuable experience overseas in the professional and highly competitive European Leagues. In the sport of water polo, the goalies tend to have the longest playing lifespan. The reality is that Craig probably could have played in 2-3 more Olympic Games if water polo were a professional sport in the USA.

Doug Kimbell - Center defender returning from the 1988 Olympic team. Doug continued to improve in his game and he became more of an offensive threat from the perimeter in 1992. The daily battles with Terry in practice were epic with both players often going home bruised from their training. In the process, they were making each other better.

Jeff Campbell – the super quiet one who was a water polo junkie. Jeff played the role of a utility player who could transition to almost any position in the pool on offense or defense. It was rare to see Jeff without a water polo ball in his hand.

Chris Duplanty – returning for his second Olympic Games - once again asked to back up Craig Wilson. Chris was perhaps the best back-up goalie in the world. He would stick around for another Olympic Games (1996) and become the team captain and starting goalie.

Mike Evans – returned to his second Olympic Games. Mike would become progressively more deadly with his shooting. He scored more big goals than anyone else on the USA team. An offensive threat every time he had his hands on the ball, he was usually good for 2 goals a game.

Craig Klass – played in his second Games. Craig was a Stanford University center who was converted to a defender for Team USA. His wicked left arm provided a nice weapon on the 4/5 side of the pool. Also, Craig had the size to defend some of the best players in the world.

The first-time Olympians on the 1992 team were:

Kirk Everist – the NCAA player of the year in 1988 at the University of California at Berkeley (CAL) and the fastest swimmer on Team USA. He led his college team in scoring from 1986 -1988. He helped lead CAL to back-to-back NCAA championships in 1987 and1988. Kirk was a "scrappy" player; his speed provided the team with a great counter attack weapon and his movement on offense would help to open up others on the team. In the scrimmages you wanted Kirk on your team. Like Greg Boyer on the 1988 team, Kirk would bump and bruise on his drives and usually the defender would end up bruised or bleeding from unnecessary contact.

Erich Fischer – was an All American at Stanford University who played the game intelligently. Known as "Fish", he was easy going and well liked on the team. Fish was an Attacker who could score from inside or outside. He was a clutch shooter who did not seem to feel the pressure. The bigger the moment the more you could count on Fish. In the 1991 World Cup in Barcelona, Fish would score the game winner to beat Yugoslavia in overtime and secure the world title for Team USA. Erich has two daughters who made it onto the 2016 Rio team.

Chris Humbert – known as "Humbie" was 6 foot 7 inches tall and a big left-handed player of the year at University of California, Berkeley. He won 2 NCAA titles at CAL and was a super-talented center. Perhaps a bit on the crazy side (in a good way), he hung out with Robert Lynn a lot. Once, he and Robert climbed out their hotel window into Lori's and Terry's hotel room in Australia, and challenged them to a tag team wrestling match. They were being absolutely serious. The wrestling match lasted 30 minutes with Terry doing all he could to protect his young wife. On the team bus rides Robert and Chris would sit in the back of the bus and discuss plans to take out the coaches. Although everyone would get a good laugh out of it, the team was a little uneasy that some of these plans might actually come to fruition. Humbie would go on to be a 3-time Olympian in 1992, 1996 and 2000 and be recognized as one of the best players in the world. He also played in Europe for many years and now lives in Greece, married to a beautiful woman he met while playing professionally.

Alex Rousseau – from University of California Los Angeles (UCLA) – was a utility left- hander who could play any position in the pool. He played center at UCLA and had very strong legs. With his stocky build and strong legs he could defend, post-up or set in any international game. He gave the team options and provided an outside threat from the 4/5 side of the pool. Alex had a good feel for the game. He seemed to be able to sense where the ball might bounce on a rebound and usually was in the right spot at the right time.

John Vargas – known as "Varg" was from University of California, Irvine. Small in stature but very smart, he was one of the players that helped to coach the team from the water. He was a great passer and enjoyed setting up teammates. He was the type of player that every team needs. Not looking for his own shot all the time, he was always surveying the pool to find the best opportunity for a teammate. He went on to become Head Water Polo Coach at Stanford University. John would also stay involved with Team USA; in the 2000 Olympic Games in Sydney, he was the head coach.

Charlie Harris – A star player out of the University of Southern California (USC), Charlie was an attacker with size. He outworked many others to make the team. He played a much smaller role on Team USA than he did on his college team, but when he was in the water he played with heart and worked exceptionally hard. Charlie would later become a successful attorney.

Coaches

Bill Barnett – back for a second quadrennial – was determined that the team would not lose because the guys were not in the best possible shape. He conditioned the team like never before. He was a good friend with Coach Jon Urbanocheck and borrowed some pretty tough swim sets to use with Team USA's training. He was more confident this time around. It helped that some family issues that were going on before 1988 had been resolved, and overall, Coach Barnett was in a better place.

Guy Baker – the team's assistant coach joined the staff and gained some valuable experience. He was young but had a good presence on the pool deck. Guy would later turn out to be one of the best coaches in the sport. He led UCLA's men's and women's programs to numerous NCAA titles and would later coach (at different times) the men's national team and the women's national team. As the head coach of the USA woman's team he would help them win two silver medals – 2004 and 2008.

John Tanner: Assistant coach. Coach Barnett would put him in charge of the swimming training. John was hugely into mental imagery and he would attempt to use some imagery during the long and rigorous training that the team did. Most of the team did not go for it and chose to suffer through the sets without appreciating John's mind games. He worked closely with Coach Barnett to develop some very difficult swimming conditioning sets. John is now the Head Water Polo Coach for the women's team at Stanford which is consistently ranked in the top 3 in the country.

Manager Mike Sutton was head coach at Claremont McKenna University and he volunteered to be the team manager and donate hundreds of hours to help the team be successful. He worked hard to keep things in order for the team. Once, he brought a can of "whip ass" to a team meeting. While the idea was great to get the team fired up, the home-labeled can of whipped cream ended up providing a good laugh for everyone.

USA Men's Water Polo in Havana, Cuba with Fidel Castro at the 1991 Pan Am Games

Terry with Barbara Bush, President George H. Bush and Evelyn Ashford.
Project Literacy, Washington D.C. 1991

The team began training camp in Newport Beach in February, 1988 but Terry had a perplexing conflict. He had been invited to go to Cancun to compete in the "Jeep Superstars", a competition designed to pit the best athletes in the world against one another in a multi-event format. He accepted the invitation and while in Cancun, he soon realized that he could actually do pretty well and possibly even win. In fact, after day one of the two-day event, Terry found himself in first place. He won two events: swimming and a pursuit bicycle race. The second day was an ocean kayak race, a basketball-shooting contest, and weightlifting. In the weightlifting (clean and jerk) Terry placed fifth. Feeling a bit over confident in the kayak, he spent some training time teaching Mike Powell how to kayak. Before working with Terry, Mike could only go sideways but after an hour or so, Terry realized that each one of the participants was a great athlete and that Mike Powell was picking up good technique very quickly. Mike Powell would go on to win the kayak race with Terry taking a close second. He would also win the obstacle course race which meant that the overall winner would be determined by the basketball-shooting contest. Each athlete would be paired with a second athlete and those two would go together. This meant that when you shot – sometimes your ball would be knocked out by the opposing player's ball. Terry went prior to Mike and did well. However, Mike Powell earned a huge advantage when he was able to go by himself. He ended up winning the basketball-shooting contest and went on to win the Superstars competition with Terry finishing a close second. Terry was officially one of the best all-around athletes in the world.

The 1992 Barcelona Summer Olympics would turn out to be Terry's favorite games of the three he had participated in as an athlete. Having achieved much more balance in his life, he was able to look upon the challenge with a quite different perspective; since he had been on 4 Olympic teams, he had acquired maturity and experience – giving him a much more adjusted approach. Lori and Terry were planning to start their family and they had a successful chiropractic practice which meant that the Olympics were no longer Terry's singular, do or die focus. Instead, the Games were an asset to an established set of priorities, but deep inside his heart, he still hungered for that elusive gold medal. With that vision strongly intact, Terry sought to get back into peak shape – equipped to perform super humanly.

Doug Kimbell fully expected Terry to join them in 1992, even though he had 'retired'. "Those 2 silver medals plagued Terry – especially the first one in

1984 which the U.S. won jointly with Yugoslavia – but lost on goal differential. I was pretty sure that Terry would be going after that elusive gold in 1992. He was still an exceptionally dominating player – formidable against the best teams in the world. What I respected so much about Terry was that defenders went after him relentlessly in international games, even playing outside the game's rules, and yet Terry never lost control – ever. He was so mentally strong. Besides that he was a great person out of the water – always willing to help others; very giving; very selfless."

The team was also looking forward to the Olympic Games location: Spain during the summer is a salubrious, hard-to-beat attraction that is on most people's bucket list. Barcelona, in particular, is an exciting, cosmopolitan city defined by quirky art, centuries-deep architecture that is sumptuously splendid, imaginative food and a brilliantly vibrant street life. Accomplished musicians fill the night air with the sounds of their mesmerizingly-beautiful classical guitars – and while it may not be famous Spanish guitarist Andrés Segovia performing - his devotees know the rudiments of how to pluck and stroke a guitar like nobody else in the world can. The olive-skinned Spanish are passionate, intense, and immensely proud of the traditions that they have honed and passed down through the generations – for thousands of years. Visitors to Barcelona love to eat out at casual tapas bars or sip sangrias through the warm nights while sitting at sidewalk cafés in places like Las Ramblas – watching the kaleidoscope of street performers.

Barcelona, Spain

Team USA had enjoyed a strong year leading in to the Games - confidently beating all of the great teams in the world. In the 1991 World Cup, they beat the home team, Spain, in the semi-finals, and then came back to beat Yugoslavia in overtime in the final. That victory sealed the World Cup for them. This was an historic win as no USA team had ever won

Traditional Spanish street dancers

the World Cup. Coming into the Olympic Games, this made Team USA the favorite to win the gold. That's always a tough expectation to meet – and the opposing teams always focus on bringing down the favorite team. Team USA swam in with a target on their backs.

But on a personal note, and given the long, in-depth history that Terry had encountered with Yugoslavia, he was saddened to learn that they would have to withdraw from the 1992 Olympics because of the devastating effects of civil war in their region. While they were Terry's adversaries in competition, he had forged many solid friendships with the Yugoslavians on dry land, and he felt their absence as if a piece of something great were missing.

With Yugoslavia out of contention and the USA's record of strong wins, the path to the gold looked realistically achievable. Coach Barnett was so determined that this would be Team USA's year for the top honors that in his earnestness, he over-trained the men. So aware were they of being Bill Bar-

Terry with Yugoslavia's Dubravko (Dudo) Šimenc clamped to him

Terry blocks Russia's Andrei Kovalenko to help USA to an 8-5 win

Game introduction - Terry - Barcelona 1992

nett's over-trained porpoises that the players came up with a t-shirt for themselves that had emblazoned across the front: "TRAIN HARDER NOT SMARTER". Doug Kimbell recalls the priceless moment when they were all wearing their t-shirts, and Coach Barnett walked in, failing to understand that the t-shirts were a sarcastic reference to him. He enthusiastically said, "Nice t-shirts, guys. I want one of them."

Never before had the team done so much swimming fitness training – and the telltale signs of too much physical exertion began to show just before the games. Many of the men arrived in Barcelona fighting low-grade colds and various other fatigue-related maladies. Most were not sleeping well – another sign of overtraining. The human body has a way of signaling when it's being stretched beyond its healthy capabilities. Playing at that level with congested lungs and sinus passages blocked up meant that come game time, many of the players weren't in peak physical form but they were still confident they could win.

Terry's assessment of Barcelona and his part in the eventual outcome was filled with a host of uncertainties: he was the team captain, however, he wasn't able to train with the team full time and so they weren't as closely united as the 1984 and 1988 teams. The team also did not have the history together. Each of the players was an all-star at his respective university but when it came to international experience as a team - they were lacking. A few of the key players had a bit more of the "me" attitude versus the "we" attitude and this was a big concern. Another concern lurking in Terry's mind was that this team had not been tested by adversity. The 1984 team had the 1980 boycott experience to work through together and adversity certainly brings out strengths in people that they never knew they had.

Perhaps this is the reason Yugoslavia took the gold medal in the overtime portion of the1988 Olympics: they had suffered more. Ravaged by their experiences of communism, poverty, hardship and the threat of war, the Yugoslavians seemed to muster up within themselves an immeasurably passionate determination to fight till the death. It was a survival instinct so powerful that it rendered them invincible – immune to implosion. Of course, the Yugoslavians also had Radko Rudić as head coach to prepare them and make sure that they did not forget what it meant to suffer.

Doug Kimbell disagrees with that assessment. He believes that skill sets and other game-related variables play a much larger role in the eventual outcome of the Olympics. "Apart from calls going against a team or an unlucky ball bounce, it really comes down to professionalism. Eastern Europe plays water polo professionally and it shows. If only the USA had the same luxury of circumstances."

But Terry's more personal pressing concern was confronting the excruciatingly painful realization that his body wasn't what it used to be 10 years previously. Whereas before he was an unrelenting machine that could blast forth on full steam for hours, now, at 33, he felt he needed more rest time between games in order to replenish. The hands of time are inordinately cruel to athletes.

Additionally, the over training had worn his body down. One of the biggest challenges for any coach is to properly prepare an entire team. The challenge is that you may not be able to train a 33-year-old the same way that you train a 21-year-old. On one hand, you want the entire team to be working together and doing the same drills, however, each positon and each athlete may require a little different training to reach their peak during an Olympic competition.

As the tournament progressed, Team USA played 3 days in a row before they had a much-needed day off. That was followed by 2 more games in a row, one day off and then the semis and finals. Unfortunately, by the time the semis came, Terry's energy was waning and he wasn't able to strike forward with those explosive movements. Cognizant of the fact that he was relying more on experience and clever maneuvers than on inviolable physical strength brought a lump of anxiety in the pit of his stomach. This was new, unchartered water. For the first time at the Olympics, his over-riding emotion was anxiety instead of the positive anticipation he always felt at previous Olympics. While anticipation charges one to perform better, anxiety does the opposite: it potentially debilitates.

Terry knew instinctively that this would be his last Olympic Games as an athlete. His sympathetic nervous system was bombarded with waves of excitement, joy and pride – but also doubt and anxiety. All these conflicting and powerful elements skewed reality and forced Terry to focus on one play at a time or he knew his performance would implode. His father's lesson of just "doing your best" rang home powerfully in his mind. Even though he no longer felt like superman in the water, he knew he could provide strong leadership and help the team to victory.

But the experience of the 1984 Los Angeles Opening Ceremonies seemed to cast an anti-climactic shadow on each Olympics thereafter. L.A. had been such a force of nature – such an emotionally charged experience

– that it would take 25 rockets and fireworks from another planet to stir up even a fraction of the earth-moving feelings Terry experienced back in 1984. At Seoul, he was anticipating another unique experience but at each subsequent Games, the Opening Ceremony grew less inspiring – more prosaic.

Almost expectedly – the Barcelona Opening Ceremony failed to ignite any passion in the Americans. Choreographing entertainment on that scale is not the Spaniard's gifting and for Terry, the overall experience was mired in lack-luster mud. There were a few nanoseconds of electrical excitement, though, at the actual lighting of the Olympic torch. An archer shot a flaming arrow from 300 meters away to light the torch. That was the resounding climax and it was received appreciatively.

Perhaps, seen from Terry's perspective, there will never be another Olympics anywhere near the scale of inspiration that he experienced back home in L.A. – and maybe it was unfair to compare any others to the power of having the home crowd support, and a Hollywood team who knew how to put on an Oscar-worthy performance. 1984 was an impossible act to beat.

Team USA began their first games on fire - cruising through the preliminary round games, beating Australia 8–4. This game was particularly unique as Terry was matched up against one of the current players he was coaching at

Chris Wybrow, Australian Olympic Men's Water Polo Captain - 1992

Pepperdine. Geoff Clarke was a 6'7" Australian left-hander who was gifted, and although young, he was up for any challenge. Although both of them were centers, the two players would get to guard each other on a few occasions. Not too many coaches have the chance to actually play against one of their athletes in the Olympic Games.

Chris Wybrow, who captained the Australian team in the 1992 Barcelona Games, and who also played in the Olympics in 1984 and 1988, came to know the Americans' strengths well – and in particular, Terry's. Chris' and Terry's histories were vast – both in the water - and out. Not only was Chris the direct counterpart to Terry, captaining the Australian team, but the American and Australian players had always shared a vastly warm camaraderie in-between games. Their priorities and value systems were congruent with their largely laid-back, sunny lifestyles – both sides recognizing that there was life beyond water polo. It helped them to have a healthy perspective and yet they were each fiercely competitive in the water – prepared to do whatever it took to win. After the battles in the pool, the Aussie-American connection was usually sealed with a few cold beers accompanied by the hilarious exchange of stories.

USA team's hotel poolside - Perth, Australia 1987

Terry remembers a particularly memorable trip to Perth, Australia back in 1987, just before the Seoul Olympics. The USA team had traveled there for a pre Olympic tournament and it happened to coincide with the America's Cup Sailing Race. It was just a few months before Terry and Lori's wedding, and so Lori decided it was time to travel with the team. The water polo tournament ended up being canceled – which opened the floodgates to a convivial social time with the Aussies as the trip morphed into a positively-charged social training camp. The Russians were also there, and the out-of-water party began.

Australia's Chris Wybrow, John Fox and Andrew Kerr – in particular – became great friends of Terry's and these are some of his memories: "The tournament was held at a beautiful pool overlooking the ocean, and the teams all stayed in a wonderful 5-star hotel. One day after training, the USA players were all down at the pool relaxing when a large group of Australian Airlines flight attendants joined them." Needless to say, the young ladies boasted some impressive physical attributes, and USA's Greg Boyer wasted no time in rubbing sun tan lotion on a beautiful flight attendant whose microscopic bikini made

Brazilian bikinis look large by comparison. Since this was Lori's first experience traveling with the team, her tentacles shot up perpendicularly, and she decided to set the ground rules straight with her future husband. Without hesitating, she punched Terry in the shoulder – even though he was not the perpetrator of the current crime – and said, "Is this what all your trips are like?"

Terry squirreled out of that corner diplomatically by reasoning that this Australian trip was nothing like the other trips. That unusual incident was brought on because the Australians were so congenial and fun to be around, and the Americans felt so relaxed in their company. It was as unique as kangaroos are to the continent.

The team enjoyed many visits down to the harbor during that trip to support the USA boats in the America's Cup Sailing – and Terry recalls, "Dennis Connors' boat would be blasting a song like *Born in the USA* by Bruce Springsteen, which raised our levels of inspiration markedly."

On the second to last day the teams were invited out onto the water on some private yachts. Terry and Lori ended up with some of the Russian players and together they luxuriated in the splendor of the cerulean water and the general feeling of abundance.

While Terry and Lori were aware that the Russians could knock back quite a few drinks without blinking, it was the unfolding dramatic talk that gave them their first-hand experience of Russians liberating themselves with alcohol. Some of

America's Cup Sailing-Perth Australia 1987

them declared after their 12th drink that it would be a brilliant idea to dive off the boat – and defect from the USSR! As Lori and Terry stared at the shark-infested waters, they hoped against all odds that the idea would not come to pass. To their relief, the Russians dropped the topic of defection and began to dance rhythmically – but this time it was to impress the beautiful women on the yacht, including Lori. Before long, one of the Russians decided to ratchet up his dancing routine by adding headstands - on a moving

Russian gold medalist Yevgeny Sharonov on board yacht with Terry at the America's Cup - Perth Australia 1987

yacht. The rest of the Soviet party decided that headstands were the new move – and a precarious night evolved – saved by the palliative powers of alcohol.

But back to the serious matter at hand – the Barcelona Olympics. Australia would go on to finish 5th in the 1992 Games under Chris' leadership – their best ever Olympic result. Having had over a decade of experience playing against the United States, Chris describes the Aussie-American relationship, as well as the world's perspective on the USA like this:

"In the early 1980s, the Russians called Terry 'the Unsinkable One', and for a good reason. Emotionless and intransigent in the water, Terry always held his center forward position as close to the 2-meter mark as possible. His upper body strength and his legwork technique made him virtually impossible to move – and this put his opponents in a more dangerous position."

"In my opinion, the USA and Australia are similar in that because water polo is not a professional sport in our countries, we have had to rely on fitness, strength and swimming speed. While the Eastern European players have always had more depth and skill in their teams, there's no doubt that the USA and Australia have strong swimming cultures."

"But on top of those strengths, the USA had the benefit of having one of the best center forwards in the world in Terry Schroeder from 1980 to 1992, and one of the best goalkeepers in the world, Craig Wilson. Unfortunately for Australia and myself, they were both representing USA throughout my entire international career. The key positions in water polo are the center forwards and goalkeepers, and for the USA to have world class players in these positions made them a formidable force."

"I vividly remember our game against the USA in the 1992 Barcelona Olympics. One of Australia's tactics was to swim Terry as much as possible in every change of possession and drive him to the 2 meters in our attack, with the plan to exhaust him when it was USA's turn to attack. I directed one of the Australian players to 'swim him' and I recall Terry's emotional response to this comment as the only time I had ever seen any sign of emotion in the years I had played against him. I assume this was a reflection of Terry nearing the end of his career more than anything."

"Out of the water, Terry was and still is an absolute gentleman who was always professional in every sense of the word. My wife and I have caught up personally with Terry and Lori when they were in Australia several years ago, and we have spoken about a fishing trip in Hawai'i together, which will hopefully come to fruition one day. I have the greatest respect for him."

Chris concludes: "Without doubt the best center forwards in water polo in the 1980s were the Russian Georgi Mshvenieradze, Yugoslavia's Igor Milanović and USA's Terry Schroeder."

After the Australian game, the USA team kept it rolling by beating Czechoslovakia 9-3 and France 11-7 before losing to the Unified Team of the Soviet Union. They recovered their dignity fast by beating Germany 7–2 to secure their berth in the semi-finals. Craig Wilson was dominant throughout the preliminary rounds. Once again, he was feeling like the other team was firing "beach balls" his way.

The Spain vs. USA semi-final game is where the tide turned unexpectedly painfully. Before coming out onto the pool deck, goalie Craig Wilson remembers the awkwardness of the inception phases: "We were told to go and wait in the tunnel before entering the pool deck, but unfortunately there was a delay, and Spain was also in the tunnel – waiting. I knew most of the guys on the Spanish team because I had played professional water polo in Spain the previous year, and 4 of the players from our team - Club Barcelona - were on the Spanish national team. We exchanged pleasantries with each other in the tunnel but the tension was palpable and we couldn't wait to get out of there."

When Team USA finally came out onto the pool deck, their small fan base of a paltry 200 supporters began chanting "USA, USA, USA." It took the Spanish fans about a millisecond to figure out what was going on and they responded with organized, soccer-crowd-style force - singing and chanting "España! España!" The home crowd of 10,000 Spanish fans was fully engaged with their tonsils ablaze. It was akin to the atmosphere at a Spanish bullfight with people on their feet shouting "olé" every time a Spanish player broke free on offense.

The strength and the rousing force of that home crowd was so inextricably representative of everything that makes up the Olympics. It's about national

Spain's Manuel Estiarte at the 1992 Barcelona Olympics

pride and patriotic support – but the Spaniards displayed their support so much more demonstratively than the 1988 Koreans, who engaged in polite little claps. The Spanish players' extended national family was on fire with electric passion, and barely a peep could be heard from the American sector. While it was exhilarating to experience an atmosphere of this rousing magnitude, it was also daunting for the Americans.

The two teams battled back and forth and, midway through the 4th quarter, the score was tied 3-3. Despite drawing on everything he had to give physically and emotionally – Terry's recovery was slower – and unlike before where he had the energy to carry teammates whenever they had a weak moment, this time he had nothing left in the tank for the breakout moment of brilliance. The Rock of Gibraltar was in a spot of trouble and he needed his teammates to rally around him.

With just 3 minutes left in the game, USA had a fast break (counter attack) with a good 4 on 3 advantage. Mike Evans, one of their best shooters, had the ball and he had about a body's length lead on his defender, Jordi Sans of Spain. It looked promisingly like a good chance for the USA to score the go-ahead goal. As Mike was approaching the 7-meter area, where he would normally pull up and shoot, something unintentionally happened in the intensity of the action. Nobody could quite ascertain where Jordi was hit, but what Terry is absolutely certain about is that Mike – who was a reliably astute player – would never have intentionally sabotaged his sure-to-score moment of athletic brilliance by purposely hitting his defender in the face. It made no sense to kill off all his effort by drawing a foul – getting excluded – and turning the ball over to Spain for a 3 on 2 advantage going the other way.

Doug Kimbell concurs unreservedly: "with a full body length's lead, it was impossible for Mike to have done something like hit his defender. That was a blatantly incorrect call by the referee against the USA – and it cost us the game."

The referee's reaction was compounded by Jordi Sans' acting performance. The more he writhed in pain and flailed, the more the referee spat into his whistle with equally dramatic effect. He called for a turn over, and Spain swam off with the ball – producing their coup de grâce moment by scoring. The score was 5-4.

With the home crowd about to stage a Spanish Revolution shouting "España! España!", the Americans seemed to lose heart at that crucial point - missing a few other scoring opportunities. Unable to convert, their nightmare unfolded as Spain scored a goal at the end of the game to win 6-4.

Terry with Mike Evans at the 1992 Barcelona Olympics Opening Ceremony

A veritable conquistador stampede broke out in the crowd as the Spaniards celebrated their tough victory in the kind of flourishing way they knew best – with flamenco guitars and bright Spanish skirts ready for action.

Despite being the fastest water polo team in the world at the Barcelona Olympics, USA hardly scored any counter attack goals. They had only themselves to look at while facing the cruel post-game analysis: there were lost opportunities – pure and simple. It was a difficult pill to swallow.

Craig Wilson had a more sympathetic analysis of the end result: "That game could have gone firmly in our favor had Mike scored without the referee blowing up the scoring opportunity. Both the USA and Spain played a brilliant game," he said pragmatically. Beyond that, Craig's opinions on the 1992 U.S. team's complexities are diplomatically couched. "Let's put it this way", he explains, "there were certain factions who had very specific ideas on how to win and how not to lose a game. The complexity lay right there."

Physically spent and emotionally drained, Terry headed back to the Olympic Village with Lori. There would be no gold medal; at best, a bronze medal was the potential consolation. He was in tears and nothing Lori could say was helping. He began to assess whether his comeback was worth all the sacrifices they had made. As the minutes rolled on, his devastation at what had just transpired intensified and he became an inconsolable wreck. At that low precipice moment, Terry and Lori encountered a good friend, Kirk Kilgour, on the way back to the Olympic village. An amazing and special person, he'd coached Volleyball at Pepperdine University from his wheelchair and stepped in for Marv Dunphy when he was at the 1988 Seoul Olympics. Kirk went on to be an NBC color commentator for Olympic Volleyball and he was in Barcelona working for NBC.

The significance of meeting Kirk was a miracle. At the prime of his life, Kirk was one of the best volleyball players in the world. During his time at University of California Los Angeles (UCLA), he participated in their first two NCAA Championships and was a 3-time All American. In 1972 he earned a place on the USA Olympic Volleyball Team. In 1976, he was an enormously accomplished 29-year-old athlete playing professional volleyball in Italy.

On a January day, his volleyball team had some problems erecting the nets for practice and so the team began doing some jump training on a mini trampoline while the problem was being fixed. That kind of training was not out of the ordinary and, in fact, was a part of their drills. When Kirk's turn came, he decided to do a flip on the trampoline, and that's when his life-changing disaster struck. He landed on his head, causing a catastrophic spinal cord injury that made him a quadriplegic. In speeches he delivered after the accident, he said, "I had two choices: I could feel sorry for myself or I could do something positive with my life. I left any feelings of self-pity behind me."

When Lori and Terry met Kirk that night in Barcelona, he was in his wheelchair driving it with his tongue – a routine that he'd mastered in the past 10 years. When Kirk saw Terry, he was so excited because he had not yet heard how the game had gone and was, of course, hoping that Terry had done well. When he asked the question, Terry began to elucidate about a "bad call" from an official that might have cost them the game. As he continued to unleash all of his frustrations about the game, reality suddenly struck like a clay brick on his forehead.

Here he was complaining epically about a game – to an elite athlete who had been struck down in the prime of his life, and was driving around in a wheelchair with his tongue. Terry's personal pity party came to an abrupt end as he felt the lightning strike of real-life perspective.

Kirk's capacity for positivity was particularly astounding. Never once had Terry ever encountered him in anything but a good mood. Adversity had dealt a brutal blow to his life and yet somehow, he found the strength to find a brand new identity and reinvent himself while he creating a new set of goals that had no association with his past. The transition must have been harrowingly difficult, and yet he had decided to be an inspiration to others. The magnitude of his grace and strength was simply mind-boggling. Furthermore. Lori and Terry marveled at all the people's lives he had touched because of his personal tragedy. Had his athletic identity been the sum total of his being, the world would never have encountered the benefits of Kirk's contributions to their lives.

Lori and Terry were so buoyed by this chance encounter that they opted to have dinner with Kirk that night – rather than with the water polo team. It wasn't a case of Terry wanting to ditch his teammates but rather that he knew he needed Kirk's light that evening and the illuminating perspective that accompanied that light. The encounter was also an important reminder of God's consistent presence in Terry's life. Even in his darkest moments, these small miracles appeared. Kirk, Lori and Terry were meant to meet that night and Terry responded admirably: he was not about to play the victim role in front of a wheel-chair-bound athlete who exuded nothing but joy. It was a clarion wake-up call.

That serendipitous meeting with Kirk en route back to the Olympic Village remains to this day one of Terry's most cherished Olympic memories. He recognized that evening that his life's purpose didn't begin and end with water polo. He had an entire journey waiting for him outside that arena: his marriage to a woman he loved deeply; a profession that rewarded him infinitely; the exciting prospect of creating a family, and the extensive latitude that excellent health affords.

Terry's journal records that evening's encounter:

August 8, 1992
It was a night racked with emotions as we lost to Spain 6–4 in the
semis. I am not going to realize my dream of winning a gold medal at
the Olympic Games. The best we can do now is finish third and take
home the bronze. The team is crushed. Our 6 on 5 did not get the job
done. It just was not clicking. We had our chances but could not put
the ball away in the critical times. As for me, I am drained. I feel like
my body is failing me. My recovery between games is not good and I
never really feel fresh. I did the best I could, but my team needed more
from me. I am disappointed in myself and, of course, with the loss. As
I headed back to the village with Lori after the game, I was crying and
feeling pretty down – wondering if I had made the right decision to
come back and play in these Games. I know how much Lori sacrificed
to give me this shot and I hated the thought that I might have let her
down. I love her so! We had given up so much time together for this
shot at the gold and now we may leave here without a medal.

About half way back to the village, we ran into Kirk Kilgour who
was in his wheelchair – driving it with his tongue. Kirk had not heard
about the game yet so excitedly he asked, "How did it go?" My first
sentence was "We got screwed again." Then I woke up... I was com-
plaining to a guy in a wheelchair about how we lost. Yikes! Was
I out of my mind? I felt like an idiot. I had been given this gift of
good health. God has provided me with so much. This opportunity
to compete was amazing. My attitude changed instantly. I felt like
I had much to be thankful for and yes, the loss still hurt, but I began
to process it from a different point of view and I felt like I had to look
ahead to tomorrow and our game against the Unified Team for the
bronze. God's timing is incredible sometimes. I am sure that he placed
Kirk in my path tonight to give me this much-needed wake up call...

The next day, Terry was tested significantly. This was the first time in 3 Olympic
Games that he wasn't in the gold medal final game. That dream was dead in
the water. Heading into the bronze medal game put an immediate dampener on
Team USA's fire, and nothing Terry did or said could ignite that flame again. They
played like disabled penguins and they lost to the Unified Team of the Soviet
Union 8-4. There was a complete absence of spark, flair and hunger to win.

Doug Kimbell describes that disastrous bronze medal game like this: "we were so sure that we were going to make it to the gold medal final that after our semi-final loss against Spain - we were stunned – as if a bolt of lightning had struck us. We dissolved mentally and nothing in that game worked. We were broken and in shock."

The favorites to win the gold were off the podium. As Terry sat with his teammates afterwards, the silence amongst them spoke volumes. Terry played out 18 different scenarios in his head: could he have done more? Passed the ball somewhere else? Talked more to the team? Maybe his quietness didn't produce enough fire in their bellies. The sense of responsibility that he carried was immense and he wasn't the kind of leader to shirk it.

The cold, hard reality of what his body was capable of doing in his 30s was markedly different from his 20-year-old body. He had to rely on shorter bursts in the pool before succumbing to fatigue. But as Terry sat on the pool deck after the game, he reflected on his recent conversation with Kirk Kilgour and a sense of peace flowed through him.

The players reacted differently to the 2 consecutive losses. Having gone into the Games ranked as the favorite to win the gold medal, the 4th place finish was a demolition shock. While Terry escaped inwards and sought his own reflective time with Lori, some of the younger players, led by Chris Humbert, were busting at the seams with emotion and they chose an outlet for their frustration.

On the eve of the final game, they decided to attack the coaches' suite in the Olympic Village with a fire extinguisher. They furtively found their way to Coach Barnett's room and emptied the entire contents of the fire extinguisher under the doorway. What they didn't know is that Coach Barnett wasn't there; instead, assistant coach, John Tanner, was the recipient of their outburst. Five minutes later he emerged from the room completely white with chemicals - save for his eyes - which he had closed during the raid.

He was visibly upset, but what became especially apparent was the team's misfired frustration not finding a healthy place to vent. Their 4th place disappointment was producing a calamitous mental breakdown that Terry sorely regrets. It was not the way he intended to end his Olympic career – with a team whose disarrayed emotions were flailing.

75% of the team chose not to attend the closing ceremonies that night. Mentally spent after the emotional roller coaster of the semi final game and the bronze medal game – they were in no mood to celebrate their loss.

But for Terry, the closing ceremonies turned out to be special. Instead of being cemented in the negativity of their bronze medal loss, his spirit rallied

– determined to make the best of his last few hours. Since this was his last closing ceremonies, he wanted, more than anything, to share the privilege with Lori. After the athletes had all marched into the stadium, Terry climbed up into the stands and brought Lori down onto the stadium floor – where they ran for the final hour – holding American flags aloft. In love and united, they absorbed each nanosecond of the ceremony – knowing that this was the end of a special era that filled their hearts unimaginably fully. They had sacrificed so much to live the

Terry and Lori at the 1992 Barcelona Olympics Closing Ceremonies

dream – and this was their final farewell to the Olympic magnetism.

Neither of them was prepared for what was to come later – when they boarded their flights and returned home to California. Gratitude and positivity were about to be replaced with an ambiguous sense of loss, and a metaphorical dark tunnel was about to test the Schroeder's marriage massively.

Lori, Terry, Bob and Lance Schroeder at the 1992 Barcelona Olympics

Sheridan, Lori, Leanna and Terry

CHAPTER 13

Olympic Farewell

The Turbulence of Change

Man cannot discover new oceans unless he has the
courage to lose sight of the shore
– Andre Gide

10 August 1992: There are few transitions in life that are as radical as that of an Olympian – returning from his last Games as an athlete with a retirement label attached to his new reality. Planning it does not carry a fraction of the tidal wave of feelings that strike when the moment actually arrives. For Terry, 4 Olympics in a row had been his obsession for over 16 years – half of his life. Everything he did every hour of every day revolved around that singular priority, and it consumed his life volubly. Chasing after the gold medal was to Terry the singular focus that obsessed him more than he even realized. His life was out of balance and he was about to find out just how much it was. With no gold medal to chase after, he had to massively redefine himself and find other interests to fill the void that the Olympic Games had left behind.

After returning home to Los Angeles from the 1992 Barcelona Olympic Games, Terry assumed that his other passions in life – his beautiful wife, Lori and his thriving chiropractic business – would replace the Olympics and give him a reason to wake up each day with vigor and purpose. But there was a perplexing shimmer of unforeseen complexities on the horizon: the adrenaline rush was no longer there and for many elite athletes, this rush produces a drug-like strangle hold on them. It did for Terry. He craved it and missed the mental high that it was: the chemicals in the brain that charged him to excel. It was a physical and mental stimulant that he had come to rely upon whenever extraordinary human power was necessary. He thought for sure he would be able to transfer that adrenaline rush into his everyday practice -

after all - he loved his patients and understood that his work as a chiropractor had great value. But there was something missing.

Beyond the adrenaline rush, he craved the competitive nature that the Olympic Games and other high level games provided; that golden moment when a teammate would pass him the ball and he'd seal and control his opponent, turn him and score a goal with seemingly super-human strength. High-level competition brought out the best in him: his strong will to fight and to never give up. Adrenaline and competition had been his allies since he was a young boy. Now there was an emptiness.

Terry's consummate identity was floundering. He found himself back in California in a chaotic daze. Overnight, without any transition period to warm him up to his new reality, there was no reason to wake up in the morning and train. Worse still, there was no structured training whatsoever. There were no goals in any way similar to the ones to which he'd been conditioned for so long. Eating correctly no longer held the same imperative value because it was no longer aligned to peak physical performance. If Terry chomped through a bag of Doritos, so what? The pressure was off. He could drink alcohol, have late nights and indulge in everything he'd limited himself from doing during his Olympic career. It was a blurred bordered, disorganized life he was returning to, and he felt like a fish out of water absent of a rigorous disciplinary schedule.

Most of all, Terry missed the daily camaraderie of the USA Water Polo team family. These were brothers that he truly loved. His teammates were like warriors that would always have his back. He'd built friendships that were based on deep trust, loyalty and love. They'd experienced emotional highs and lows together that bonded them in an incomparably strong way. Beyond that, Terry had always found his relationships with his teammates to be somewhat effortless. Perhaps this was because each one of them was so focused on the same goal, and willing to give up so much of themselves to see that goal happen.

There was very little work involved; they went with the flow of the currents and the simplicity and ease of their interaction set an unrealistic precedent for life. Relationships beyond the Olympics are never that simple, particularly with the opposite sex where there are more intricate nuances that are sometimes complex but deeply satisfying when configured. It is no secret that women and men are different, and therein lies the mystical attraction between them; female and male idiosyncrasies require understanding and empathy – a deeper level of digging than the easy camaraderie of water polo teammates. The true significance of his relationship with Lori would take Terry years to understand.

Saying goodbye to the water polo family left a massive void as Terry returned home to few friendships outside of water polo. The disconnection impacted him profoundly and the transition was substantially worse than he had imagined.

Terry's and Lori's primary goal after the 1992 Olympics was to start the family they so desperately wanted. Their carefully-laid-out plan was to conceive a child naturally and relish the joyful honeymoon that the manufacturing journey promised. These two close-to-nature Californians thought this would be one of their easiest goals to achieve.

After a couple of years of "not being careful," and then returning home from the Olympics and actively trying to conceive, they decided to seek a medical opinion as to why Lori had not yet become pregnant. They were both healthy and in their early 30s, but Lori intuitively felt that something wasn't right. At first everything looked normal on the tests, and being holistic health-care doctors, they preferred to avoid the use of any fertility drugs.

An exploratory laparoscopic surgery revealed that Lori had some scar tissue in her abdomen that was compromising her ability to conceive naturally. Terry's comfort zone had been massively shaken: he had never relied on medicine to achieve wellness. Now it appeared that he and Lori were going to have to go outside their box and rely on the medical profession to help them conceive. Chiropractic had always been the methodology to which he turned and it had always worked before. As much as he tried, there was no adjustment that he could offer Lori that would change her ability to conceive conventionally. Little did Terry and Lori know that they were about to surmount the most daunting hurdle of their lives – a hurdle that exhausted more emotions in them than they cared to discover.

After studying their options, including adoption, Terry and Lori met with several specialists and decided that in-vitro fertilization (IVF) was the route they would take. It was a fairly new process in the 1990s and largely unchartered territory. Adoption was ruled out because they had witnessed one of their relatives adopting – only to have the birth parents want the child back after bonding with the baby had occurred. They also really wanted to have children that were biologically their own. After having a number of long conversations regarding the subject of IVF and with some concerns for Lori's long-term health, they agreed to try 3 cycles and then reevaluate if no pregnancy had been achieved.

Lori did everything possible to give each shot at conception the best possible chance. She took care of her body fastidiously so that each embryo would have the best possible environment. She stuck to a rigorous clockwork regime in the cycle of the IVF process with the healthiest consumption of food and a daily exercise program. She took more downtime than usual to minimize her stress levels and she slept 7-8 hours every night.

The hormones she had to take during the IVF cycle made her feel pregnant and so emotions ran high as she and Terry would feel hopeful and elated - only to frequently find out she wasn't actually pregnant. With each attempt they would ride that same roller-coaster feeling and then just as quickly - their emotions would crash as they watched Lori's hormone levels plummet, signaling that the cycle had failed. Finances were being stretched, more emotions were being invested and before they knew it, they were well beyond the 3 attempts to which they had originally agreed.

During each IVF cycle, the daily injections Lori gave herself produced their own set of hormonal changes that brought physical and emotional discomforts. All of that was bearable if the outcome bore fruit. That was not to be. After each fertilization attempt failed, Terry's and Lori's pain manifested itself in different ways. Terry became withdrawn and depressed with a sense of complete failure. Lori became that much more determined to conquer the obstacles and to bring their DNA, their energy and their love into the world.

Bob Schroeder, Terry's rock of Gibraltar during his sports career, turned out to be less than supportive to his son during this trying time. Impatient about having grandchildren, he'd inadvertently make insensitive comments to Terry about needing a manual on how to conceive a child. He didn't understand the new medical technology of in-vitro and in any case, he was stalwartly anti any medical intervention.

Terry never had a true heart-to-heart talk with his dad about this subject – perhaps because he did to know how to communicate these intimate family matters to him. Most of their conversations had revolved around sports – something they were instinctively comfortable doing. Moreover, Bob had conceived his 3 children with ease, so his lack of understanding translated into what came across as careless comments. The inferred blame was always placed on Terry and Lori – whom he was sure were not doing things correctly. There were many awkward moments where father and son hit the disconnect button and fumbled before changing the subject.

In a similar vein, Terry had never witnessed the ideal relationship between his own parents when it came to marital communication, so he was fumbling for role models when it came to knowing how to communicate to Lori how he was drowning. This was a new coral reef; unexplored, un-navigated and definitely dark and scary.

Preparing for the longed-for pregnancy announcement day, waiting in hope, and then finding out that it had all come to nought – happened more times than they wished to count. With each failed attempt, Lori was determined to figure out what she could have done differently. She persevered with fortitude and resolve while Terry floundered because he couldn't fix the problem nor control the outcome. What should have been so natural became foreign, turbulent territory to him.

The Olympics – it turned out – was easier. In water polo there seemed to be a direct correlation between effort and results. Plans were laid, effort was exerted, and goals were usually achieved. Terry had never faced this type of failure and it was wearing him down. Creating a family was anything but predictable; none of the logical steps were working. At age 33, Terry's feeling of loss and subsequent isolation produced a distance between himself, God and Lori that he would come to regret more than anything else in his life. He was radically off track – living out of alignment – and spiraling out of control. The void by then was so large that his chiropractic business and his Pepperdine University water polo coaching could not come close to filling the magnitude of the hole.

The failed IV attempts were mounting and even though one cannot put a price on a life, the medical bills produced their own set of financial stresses. Terry's heart was not in the right place and his depression grew. His negative self-image was exacerbated by fridge-raiding evenings. When he was down, he turned to the ice-cream bucket and the pounds packed their way onto his formerly chiseled torso.

With no goal to work towards he found exercising futile. He couldn't make the conversion from exercising for the team's sake to exercising because it was a healthy choice for Terry Schroeder. The lack of exercise and the extensive change in his eating habits fed into the downward spiral of depression and lethargy. The set of unclear goals produced a hazy mist in front of the once rigorously motivated athlete. The goal of having a baby wasn't making sense: despite doing everything they were supposed to do to give each Schroeder embryo a fighting chance - a dead end was the consistent result. A sense of failure, worthlessness and purposelessness were invading and testing Terry's and Lori's marriage dangerously.

The preparation and recovery for each implantation meant that the IVF procedure could only be performed once every 3 months and, during treatment, Lori needed a great deal of emotional and physical support. Terry continued to struggle with the idea that western medicine might produce what he - as a man - could not. He was also deeply worried about his wife and her future health. Because IVF was new, they did not know the long-term effects of the drugs on a woman and Lori was carrying with her the knowledge that everything could have negative consequences down the line. But she was undeterred.

Lori's sister, Robin, spent much time emotionally supporting Lori. After 5 failed in-vitro attempts – one of which resulted in a potentially fatal ectopic pregnancy - Robin volunteered to have Lori and Terry's embryo implanted into her uteruses as their surrogate, increasing their chances of having a baby. She already had 2 healthy young children so she knew that she was more than capable of carrying a pregnancy to term. With each new cycle, the best 4-5 embryos were implanted in both Robin's and Lori's uterus. Terry was concerned about having an entire team of babies but the couple was desperate after so many failed attempts. The truth is that a "team" would have been welcomed by the Schroeders. Unfortunately, 3 attempts with both sisters being implanted with multiple embryos all failed even though that there were many grade "A" embryos.

Terry's super reliable ability to remain calm under pressure, and to let his rationality lead the way, started to slip, and that frightened him more than anything else. His ability to rise above during a storm in his water polo career had kept him at the top. But in this game of procreating life – he was sinking to the bottom of the pool. He began to doubt himself and in self-pity, questioned God for not helping them, and the associated anger put a strain on his once-strong faith.

Adding to his personal struggles was a feeling that he was an outsider to the process of creating his own family. He couldn't take on the task of preparing his body to carry a child, and his role had become mechanical and dramatically unromantic: dinner dates became dates with the doctor in a sterilized office. His role was reduced to producing a sperm sample in a sterile cup - occasionally in a public restroom. On one occasion, he handed the sample to the doctor who jokingly said "I hope I don't confuse this sample with the black Schroeder couple's sample". Of course, he was joking but the recognition of having little control over the entire process was wearing Terry down.

By his own admission, Terry allowed the deep connection Lori had with her sister to fuel his sense of isolation. He felt that Robin had become his wife's hero, and that the job was taken away from him because he couldn't fulfill it. It was an unforeseen chasm in their intimacy. Many of the doctors' visits were far away and since Terry had to man the business, Lori would try to reduce his stress levels and protect him by saying that Robin could accompany her. Given Terry's deep-rooted sense of inadequacy, he understood it to be a dismissal and he did not communicate those feelings to Lori. He felt that he was a third wheel in the process and the canyon between Terry and Lori grew wider. Perplexing to him was the fact that he knew how to make a water polo team strong - by being a leader and communicating well – thereby conveying feelings and desires and building trust, respect and love. He was adept at bonding with his water polo teammates and yet he was struggling to create that same emotional intimacy with his wife.

Sisters Lori and Robin

Terry wrote in his journal:

October 20, 1993
Lori and I continue to struggle with trying to have a baby. This whole
process has been so difficult. I am glad that Lori has been so grounded
and disciplined through it all. I think I would have thrown in the
towel at this point and looked for an easier way. It has left me feeling
weaker and has lowered my self-esteem even more. After all, I have
always been the rock – strong emotionally and physically and now I
am cracking. I am sure that I am living with some depression. I am
still trying to get over my "loss" after retiring and not doing a very
good job of communicating that loss to anyone. I feel like I am hold-
ing a lot inside. Lori seems to be bonding closer with her sister Robin
and that has pulled us further apart. I feel jealous towards Robin but
instead of talking to Lori about it, I am acting out. I don't like who
I am right now but I cannot pull out. It is hard for me to fully love
Lori when I am not loving myself very much. I know that I should be
thanking Robin for all of her help with what we are going through but
I am acting selfishly. This has to get better soon. If only the IVF could
work and we have a baby - then maybe I can get on a better path…
Thank God for Lori's strength!

At Terry's most vulnerable point, he was attracted to people who affirmed him as a man. There were plenty of women who were willing to affirm him without respecting the boundaries of Terry and Lori's marriage - perhaps due to their own pain and suffering. The potential for having an affair was created because of Terry's sense of inadequacy. He knew that he was entering into dark and dangerous waters, but he was so far from God and so dissatisfied with himself at this point – that he acted out against his far better judgment. So began Terry's affair with another woman and while it occurred, instead of being more fulfilled, he spiraled down further. Yet like a drug, the affair was addicting because it was helping Terry escape his reality. Being mired in self-pity and depression, he made choices that were implosive, and to this day, he takes full responsibility for those damaging mistakes.

Terry was on a rebellious and anarchistic road as he tried to navigate the duel life that he had created. Circumstances took charge of him and instead of confronting his demons, he ran away from them and continued to spin. At a time when Lori needed his support more than ever, he was not there for her. Months went by and instead of getting better, things became substantially worse. Guilt-ridden, in pain, and fully cognizant of this massive mistake that threatened to take his family down, Terry arrived at a point where he wanted the affair to end. He covered the tracks of his double life more sloppily in the hopes that someone would reel him in and address the situation.

December 17, 1993
I am emotionally spent. I am feeling drained. Lori and I are more disconnected than ever. It hurts me because I know it is my fault. I am searching for my happiness in the wrong places. I am not sure that our marriage is going to make it. It is certainly not because I don't love Lori. She is the best thing that ever happened to me. I am just falling apart. Not dealing with life very well and not talking to anyone about my struggle. Instead, I'm internalizing it and feeling more and more depressed. It has been a downward spiral. At least work is an outlet. I enjoy the day-to-day work and seeing people respond to chiropractic. Thankfully, I have that going. I make myself put on a smile at work and act like everything is good. But I am not focused and happy inside. I am in a fog. Only my ability to put on a different hat and be in the moment at work has saved our practice. It is my escape right now.

Although, heavily involved in an affair, Terry deeply longed for what was right. He yearned to end his unjust relationship and make things right with Lori. He was stuck in a bad place, unable to go back in time, and worried about the repercussion from all sides. Unfortunately, he did not have the tools to reverse this path on his own, and he did not seek help from a professional.

The conflicting feelings Terry experienced watching Lori and Robin in partnership superseded recognizing that Robin was putting her life on hold – with 2 young children of her own – so that the sister and brother-in-law she loved could have a family. He tried to be a part of the process in little ways: making dinner for them, cleaning up the house, running errands, making brownies, and tending to them when they were on bed-rest for the first 48 hours after implantation. But all these actions were couched in feelings of guilt, immense inadequacy and a rhetorical sense of impotence.

Meanwhile, Lori, unaware of Terry's ongoing affair, continued to try to create a family. After 13 in-vitro fertilizations there was nothing to show. There had been 2 viable pregnancies; one that failed early on and the other was a life-threatening ectopic pregnancy. There were 5 frozen eggs left and at their last appointment, Lori and Robin were informed that of the 5, only one looked viable – the last embryo. With heartfelt consideration and knowing that Robin had the better chance for a successful implantation and carrying the pregnancy to term, Lori chose to have the last embryo implanted into her sister. Robin, Lori and Codi (Robin's 18-month-old daughter) held hands in the clinic and prayed for a miracle.

A miracle did happen. Robin became pregnant with Leanna Schroeder. It was a rough road with the worst morning sickness imaginable. Robin would fly in from Texas with her 2 young children for doctors' appointments - and Lori nursed her through the morning sickness. Robin and husband Chuck were making the ultimate sacrifice while Terry battled his own demons and found it difficult to express his gratitude. He was fast losing his battle with adversity and was a physical and emotional wreck.

Leanna was born on October 14, 1994 with huge blue eyes that peered at the world in anticipation. Terry held her in his arms for the first time and that first night, he cried while his heart ruptured with guilt as he prayed for guidance and forgiveness from God.

Months after Leanna's birth, Terry finally tried to end the affair but then had to deal with a scorned and angry woman. As a result, Lori, who had suspected

Lori with baby Leanna

something was going on, finally found out about the affair. Even though they had a baby at home, she asked Terry to move out – to figure out what it was that he really wanted for his life. It took courage and indescribable strength to ask the man who was the love of her life – to leave. She knew she had no other choice. Lori had not married the man that Terry was disintegrating into. In truth, she had not recognized who he had become since his retirement.

Terry moved into the home of a long-time friend,

Charles Hollingsworth, who lived in Ventura. This meant lots of driving time to and from work in Thousand Oaks, California. It also meant that Terry had vast quantities of alone time. In the darkness 3 truths were revealed: (1) The affair was over and he could never go back there. (2) He missed Lori terribly and wanted a chance to prove that he could be the man she married. (3) He was missing some critical days with his new daughter, Leanna.

About a month into his time in Ventura, while he was trying to win his way back into his family's life, Lori encouraged him to be honest with his closest friends. Terry had not shared the ugly truth with many. Obviously, he was embarrassed as to what he had become but he summoned the strength to call one of his closest friends and it turned out to be one of the best decisions of his life. Ken Bastian was like a brother to him. Through all his years as a competitive athlete, Ken had been there for Terry and they'd shared their triumphs and their heartaches. An elite athlete himself, Ken was also a politician – but he had suffered the greatest tragedy of his life when he lost the love of his life to a tragic accident. Shortly thereafter, he became the Head Schoolmaster at All Saints Episcopal School in Lubbock, Texas, and he dedicated his life to helping others. The school children followed him like he was the Pied Piper.

Witnessing Ken's impact and purpose in life, Terry recognized that he wanted the quality of character that Ken possessed. It was about service to others and giving of oneself unselfishly. Despite the tragedy in Ken's life, he applied with equanimity the lessons that life's hardships had doled out. He never complained about life's fairness or the struggles he had; instead he turned his energies towards others and gave of himself - unreservedly.

Nobody in Terry's circle understood the pain he was experiencing - retiring as a professional athlete and then transitioning into life – more than Ken. He too had to re-invent himself after his athletic career. He guided Terry through every phase of his transition from a mistake-ridden few years to becoming the amended husband and father he longed to be. Lori and Ken encouraged Terry to turn back towards God. Highly remorseful and repentant, Terry became determined to get his life back into alignment.

While doing this, he discovered the true definition of unconditional love. Lori never gave up on Terry and simply asked him to be the man she already knew existed – a good, decent, honest man. No matter how much he had hurt her, Lori's capacity for forgiveness was overwhelmingly powerful. Terry sought to soak up her love and build up his inner strength through God's grace.

However, there was healing that needed to happen, and Lori was not in a hurry to have Terry back in the house full-time. He needed to prove to her that it was she he really wanted – lifelong. Somehow, Terry had to show her that being a husband and father was going to satisfy him. She knew that unless he put the Olympics to rest, their marriage would never stand a chance. She also knew that Terry had some substantial depression to deal with. She encouraged him to seek counseling individually and together as a couple. This was not always easy, but in the six months or so of counseling, many demons were exorcised.

Terry finally summoned up the courage to tell his dad about his affair and Bob came close to hitting his son. Emotion swelled up in him as he lambasted Terry for jeopardizing the relationship with the woman who was the best thing that ever happened to him. Bob was furious and deeply disappointed with his son and Terry reacted measurably – deeply shaken by the force of his dad's reaction.

It was the tidal wave of forces that would ultimately help lead Terry out of his quagmire. It was also a turning point in Bob's relationship with his daughter-in-law wherein a rekindled warmth emerged towards her. Having been a victim to his own father's marital indiscretions while growing up in New York, Bob knew how acutely painful it was to have a philandering father who abandoned his family in favor of another woman. He desperately didn't want Terry to make the same mistakes. Lori and Leanna deserved more than the life Bob's father had meted out to him. Because of those difficult years growing up in New York, Bob knew only too well that the pain of desertion would affect Lori and Leanna lifelong.

On one significant evening, while Terry was driving home from work back to Charles' home, he was struck by a force that he can only imagine was from God. Out of nowhere, his conscience burst with the pain of guilt and remorse, and he cried so much while driving that he had to pull over to the side of the Californian 101 freeway because he couldn't see where he was going as the tears cascaded down in torrents. For 45 minutes the tears flowed down his cheeks. He missed Lori and Leanna indescribably, and he longed to return home – to where he belonged. It was a climactic evening of experiencing more emotions than he knew anyone could feel. It was as if God was tapping him on the shoulder and giving him the reality check he so desperately needed.

With renewed energy and focus on becoming a better man, over time Terry came to realize that being an Olympian paled in comparison to the elation he felt at being a committed husband and father. Those two roles began to marinate his senses like nothing else had. He woke up to a revitalized reason for rising up in the morning. Once again there was purpose and passion in his life, and he was determined to ask for Lori's absolute forgiveness so that he could have one more chance at being a better man.

After being out of his home for 6 months, Lori agreed to give Terry a second chance and invited him back home. He understood how fortunate he was to have a loving and forgiving wife who would give him another chance. This was a time of healing – of rebuilding trust and love. He stepped back – making a herculean effort to be understanding and loving when Lori was having a tough time. He realized that he had broken a sacred bond and that God's grace and Lori's forgiveness would heal their relationship if he stayed the course and became the man he knew he wanted to be.

During this pivotal transition time in Terry's and Lori's life, Ken Bastian was a tremendously valuable boulder of support. Ken navigated Terry out of his dark days when he couldn't see the wood for the trees. His own example of leading a productive, meaningful life was a constant source of inspiration to Terry. His sage advice helped Terry to see the bigger picture after his Olympic retirement: that a beautiful wife who loved him unconditionally, a beautiful daughter who needed her dad present, and a promising chiropractic career could make Terry exceptionally happy. Ken knew how to balance life according to an all-encompassing picture. Ken was also a man of faith and his closeness to God inspired Terry to become a better Christian.

On November 6, 1998, Terry received a call that shook his world to the core. Ken Bastian had been killed instantly in a head-on car collision. Next to his father, Ken was the best man Terry had ever known. He had always been there and he lit Terry's life in so many positive ways. Most of all, Terry learned from Ken that a life of service would ultimately be the ingredient that fulfilled him the most. The soft-spoken, humble Ken Bastian would forever be a guiding beacon in Terry's life – even after his untimely, tragic death.

Five years after Leanna was born, and with a great deal of healing and growth together as a couple, Lori and Terry decided it was time to try to conceive a second child.

But the Schroeders experienced another set of challenges bringing their second daughter, Sheridan, into the world. They made the decision to have Lori carry the baby through in vitro fertilization – which they attempted 3 times. During the process it was discovered that the condition of Lori's fallopian tube could negatively affect the outcome, so she underwent another surgery. This time, however, things went radically awry. During the procedure, an artery was accidentally nicked but the doctors missed it during surgery. In recovery, Lori knew something was drastically wrong and even told the nurses something was amiss. The nursing staff downplayed Lori's concerns and only gave her more Demerol for the pain, hoping she would feel better. The nurses thought that if she would just get up and move (which is a usual request after most surgeries), she'd begin to feel better and could relieve herself and then be released.

At the nurse's request, Lori stood up, passed out and flipped over the hospital bed. Only then did she have the nurses' full attention. Lori was in trouble; she spiked a fever, started bloating and she was throwing up blood. She was bleeding internally. By 02h00, Lori had lost almost half of her blood supply and the general surgeon was contacted and he immediately wanted to open her up. Fortunately, Lori's IVF doctor was close by, and he put her back in surgery instantly for a 3-hour procedure where he found and repaired the bleed. After two transfusions and 4 days in ICU, the decision was clear: surrogacy was their only choice for their second child.

Providence provided the answer as God led the Schroeders to a special woman, Stacy, who had been a surrogate before. She had two children of her own and loved being pregnant. In her first experience as a surrogate, the couple whose twins she was carrying, did not even participate in the process much at all; in fact the couple had not even come to the birth of their own children. Instead, they had chosen to go out to dinner and see their babies first thing the following morning. Disappointed with this process, Stacy was open to try it again if the circumstances were right and the couple whose baby she would carry was going to be involved and show their love through the process. When the Schroeders recognized that the surrogate mother's values aligned with theirs, they made the decision to proceed.

It turned out to be a great match. Sheridan Schroeder was carried by a loving woman who knew the value of her birth to her parents. She entered the world healthily and to the greatest sense of gratitude from Terry and Lori. Auntie Stacy, as she is known, is still very much involved in Sheridan's life.

Looking back, Terry realized that Lori's critical condition in the interests of conceiving a second child was a stark reminder of the fragility of life. He wrestled with the thought that losing her would be more devastating than anything on this earth. He felt an even greater love for her, and was determined to nurture her and take care of her to the best of his ability.

Blessed with two beautiful daughters, Leanna and Sheridan - Terry held their new baby, Sheridan, in his hands and he bowed his head in prayer and thanked God and Lori for giving him a beautiful family. In all his years of being a competitive athlete at the highest level, Terry recognized that he had never met anyone as committed, persistent and determined as his own wife, and she has continued to be a source of inspiration. Without Lori's unrelenting desire and willingness to get up after being knocked down by adversity – he would never have the family he has today and the incredible opportunity to be a father. It humbles him like nothing else ever has.

Lori with baby Sheridan

Sheridan and Leanna with Buddy

Terry Schroeder coaching at Pepperdine University

CHAPTER 14

Coaching at Pepperdine University

A New Perspective in a Familiar Pool

Success is peace of mind, which is a direct result of self-satisfaction
in knowing you made the effort to do your best to become the best
that you are capable of becoming
– John Wooden

July 1986 – Terry and Lori had recently become engaged and were chart-
ing their future together. The strategic questions they pondered revolved
around where they would eventually settle, and the best location for their
chiropractic business. The decision carried the weight of encompassing Terry's water polo commitments as he prepared for the 1988 Olympic Games.

A phone call from the President of Pepperdine University, Dr. Howard White,
would provide answers and give the couple some direction. Dr. White was interested in hiring Terry as the head coach for Pepperdine's water polo team. The position was open in the fall with the season beginning in September. Terry and Lori
discussed their options assiduously, and concluded unreservedly that Terry should
take the job. It would keep him close to the pool for training purposes and provide
some income as they began their practice. The plan was to coach for a few years;
complete Terry's Olympic playing days at the Seoul Games while building up the
practice – all in preparation for the transition into full-time Chiropractic.

Terry quickly discovered that coaching provided him with substantially
more than an income, and Pepperdine was the perfect fit since he was
returning to his college pool as an alumnus. Imperative to his success was the
recognition he enjoyed as one of the best players in the world. This provided
instant respect from the athletes he coached – an ideal platform from which
to work. This so-called 'temporary' job that Terry accepted turned into a
passion literally overnight. Refreshingly unexpected was the deep sense of

fulfillment he felt while working constructively with his team. Within weeks Terry began to build relationships that have fed him substantially – relationships with his athletes that have formed a core part of his sense of purpose.

There is an unparalleled joy in seeing a team come together and improve. Beyond that, coaching helped Terry to understand the intricacies of the game at a much deeper level.

The direct derivative of coaching and helping others to learn the game made Terry an all-round better player.

Particularly satisfying when coaching effectively is helping players to find their own path to greatness. This is done by unlocking their potential and bringing out the best in each one of his athletes. That is the heart of true coaching. Then, as individual players improve, the responsibility lies within the coach to energize the team into seeing the value of uniting – each person sacrificing for each other and for the benefit of the team. As the players understand that by helping each other to be successful - they in turn help themselves – a team can experience greater success than they ever imagined. Spectacular results emerge and for Terry – there is nothing more fulfilling than facilitating a team coming together as a consolidated family.

One of Terry's strong character traits is his humility, and resultantly, he has always made of point of having mentors in his life; strong people who have achieved much in their respective fields and from whom Terry has sought counsel and guidance so that he could become a better man and a better coach.

The handful of mentors who have played a significant role in Terry's life have given him clarity on how to move through to the next step in life's extensive journey. He's been dexterously careful about choosing people who aren't just gifted athletes or businessmen – but people who accomplish success in their respective fields with vast quantities of integrity. In that light, Terry has always been amazed at the people whom God has brought into his life at strategically important crossroads. There were never any accidental meetings. People came into his life when he most needed them, and their friendship, trustworthiness and influence have honed him into the man he is today.

After retiring from playing water polo at the conclusion of the 1992 Olympics, Terry's personal life crisis hit rock bottom. David Holder, the parent of one of the water polo athletes he was coaching at Pepperdine, was one of those critical people who steered him to healing waters. David Holder was a hugely successful businessman who had been through personal struggles similar to Terry's. A man of strong faith, he offered Terry sound pearls of wisdom. He listened while being exceptionally open about his own history. He shared with Terry the steps that he had found most critical in healing the wounds in his own life, and he reminded Terry to pray for guidance while reconnecting with God and the 'big picture'.

During a time when Terry was overpowered by fear and debilitating doubt about how he was going to 'fix' his life, David gave him hope and assurance while his example of success achieved through a life of integrity inspired Terry to make life-long changes that would steer him back on track.

Included in that esteemed group of mentors to whom Terry is forever grateful are Ken Bastian, Monte Nitzkowski, Ken Lindgren, Pete Cutino, Steve Heaston, Rick Rowland and his high school coach Mike Irwin. To this day, the loss of Ken Bastian has left a significant hole in Terry's heart. He was a stalwart confidante; a wise and trustworthy friend to whom Terry went for counsel and refuge.

Perhaps one of the greatest mentors and influencers on Terry's coaching career is John Wooden. Terry spent many hours reading many of Coach Wooden's books that were full of hidden gems for being successful as a man and as a coach. When Terry took over the national team in 2007 as head coach he had the opportunity to talk with Coach Wooden with the privilege of one-on-one interaction for 3 hours. After this meeting Terry shared with Lori that he wanted to leave a legacy in coaching like Coach Wooden has where the relationships he shares with his players are nothing short of exceptional. When Terry asked Coach Wooden about leadership, he replied that one of the greatest attributes of a leader is to listen. Another aspect that Coach Wooden emphasized was to lead by example. He believed in teaching life lessons through sport, and he stressed to Terry that faith, love and balance are the keys to a healthy, happy life. He also told Terry that the love he showed his family and friends sets the example for his players to follow.

One of Terry's associate coaches once told him that the best coaches in the world watch other coaches - and then incorporate their best techniques into their

Ken Bastian congratulates Terry after his Pepperdine Water Polo team wins the 1997 National Championship (NCAA)

own repertoire. This has proved to be a favorite past time for Terry through the years: to watch and analyze coaches who excel in their profession. The international experience of playing and coaching at the highest level has provided Terry the opportunity to observe and learn from some of the best in the world: Ratko Rudić from Croatia, Dénes Kemény from Hungary, and Dejan Udovičić from Serbia - to name a few.

While watching how foreign coaches conduct workouts and interact with their team, there is often a language barrier, so while Terry may not understand the words, the coach's demeanor, actions and drills show him a great deal. While sponging in the best techniques that the world's coaches utilize, he has found it actually liberating to have the freedom to be inspired - or to improve by merely watching how other skilled people live, work and play.

At Pepperdine University, where Terry still resides, he has had years of opportunity to watch and acutely observe Marv Dunphy run his practices. Marv Dunphy is a renowned volleyball player and coach who holds a career record at Pepperdine of 589-254 (.699). He has led Pepperdine to 5 National Collegiate Athletic Association (NCAA) Championships, was head coach for the USA team that won the gold medal in the 1988 Olympic Games, and he was inducted into the Volleyball Hall of Fame in 1994. Terry has always respected Marv as one of the best volleyball coaches in the world. He's watched him interact with his players and analyzed the adept manner in which he phrases things. Through the years, Marv has made a remarkably positive impact on Terry's growth as a coach.

Understanding the wide variations in goals is also critical to being a successful coach. In Terry's case, he played water polo because he wanted to become an Olympic champion and the talents he possessed made the goal realistic. A quick reality check occurred in Terry's early coaching days at Pepperdine University when he realized that each team member had quite different goals: only a select few wanted to make the Olympic dream come true while others had far less ambitious goals. And then, there were those who played for the pure fun and enjoyment of the game. There's nothing wrong with that.

But what is critical is that each player agrees that in order for him to be a participating member of the team, he has to play a specific role. For some that might mean being a cheerleader during games and helping to keep the positivity buoyed on the bench. For others that might mean being the one that is counted on to score in the critical moments of the game or to shut down the opposing team's best player. Regardless of each role, a healthy team must share a common team goal. Without that unity in direction, things disintegrate.

Being an effective coach necessitates understanding that everyone's perspective is vital, and it's up to the coach to meet the needs of each individual. Terry worked exceptionally hard at helping each man on his team set and achieve his individual goal, but he was also determined to inspire each person to want to reach his potential. As a coach, Terry would often tell his players that too many athletes shortchange themselves by not pushing themselves to become the best that they can be. The psychology behind that is interesting. Many people don't set lofty goals because they are afraid of not meeting the challenge and failing. Terry understood that but he also knew that failure is a part of learning and growing, and so it is a vital part of coaching.

As a coach, he also learned that in between the winning and losing of games, players were building character and becoming better men so Terry consciously adjusted his goals to include being a better example of the qualities that defined strength of character. At its core, coaching is about inspiring, motivating and teaching young men to become the best people possible - not just the most accomplished athletes.

One of the best parts about coaching at the college level is that Terry spends more time with his athletes than anyone else – including their parents. That gives him a huge opportunity to be a positive influencer in their lives, and to help them understand and learn the valuable life lessons that sport provides. It is one of Terry's primary goals to help each athlete leave his program with the skills to become a better man, a better husband and a better father. Even if they don't take up those roles, he hopes that they emerge better people all round.

As the years at Pepperdine have passed, coaching has become an indispensable passion – an unanticipated, fulfilling and deeply satisfying component of Terry's life.

He has grown as much as the athletes by recognizing that the attainment of excellence comes with multiple levels of refinement. Having the privilege of guiding and mentoring young athletes to reach their potential in every sphere – not just athletically – has fed him immeasurably and given him a purpose that is profoundly rewarding.

There are numerous stories from coaching that Terry will always treasure and many of the best stories come from some of the mediocre players. Will Cain came to Pepperdine from Texas with limited high-level competition in his background. He barely made the traveling team and for the most part sat the bench. On one occasion, Pepperdine enjoyed a comfortable lead against league rival University of California Santa Barbara. What made it extra special is that the game was being played at UCSB, which usually has a very hostile crowd, and this day was no different.

In the 4th quarter, with Pepperdine leading by 4 goals, Terry put Will into the game and watched him rise to the occasion stupendously: within seconds he scored one of the few goals in his career at Pepperdine. Immediately, Will turned to the bench and with a huge smile on his face and in celebration, he gave the "hook 'em horns" sign with his hand. It was an appropriate Texas gesture and the picture still brings a smile to Terry's face.

Another special Pepperdine player was Bob Nutcher. "Nutch", as he was called, quit in his junior year because he was unhappy with his playing time. One night, about a week after his departure, Terry was swimming in the Pepperdine pool after practice. Unbeknown to him, Bob had decided to enjoy a swim that evening too. As they were doing laps, they almost collided as they both focused on the rhythm of their strokes. The near-collision led to a meeting in coach's office where Terry was able to have that important heart-to-heart chat with Bob, and encourage him to come back to the team and finish out his career at Pepperdine. It was that once-in-a-lifetime opportunity that Terry didn't want Bob to lose, and he emphasized that.

Bob returned to the team the next day and after working hard to get himself back into shape, he played some impressive minutes in big games in the rest of his junior and senior year. Bob had come back revitalized to give water polo his best shot and to this day, he thanks Terry for talking him out of quitting and for the opportunity to come back and play.

One of the most outstanding players ever recruited to Pepperdine during Terry's extensive coaching history there was a 6-foot-7-inch Australian left-hander with boatloads of talent - Geoff Clark. Like Terry, Geoff had huge dreams: he wanted to make the Olympic team, playing for his home country, Australia. After Terry had coached Geoff, he went on to achieve that goal and, as fate would have it, Terry ended up playing against Geoff in the 1992 Barcelona Olympics when the USA met Australia in the preliminary rounds. A coach having the opportunity to play at Olympic level against someone he's shaped and developed - was a peculiarly satisfying experience for Terry – and a memory he cherishes.

But the story about Geoff at Pepperdine is more extensive – and illustrates the depths of a coach's responsibilities – that is if a coach wants to extend his sphere of influence past just the athletic prowess. No doubt Geoff's priority was water polo, but he also came to Pepperdine to earn a degree. In his first semester he was red-shirted but Terry wasn't concerned about his absence from the game. Geoff was so talented that he could forego workouts for weeks, jump back in the pool and accelerate his way to peak form in virtually no time. Beyond that, Terry figured that a break from heavy competition would give Geoff an opportunity to concentrate his energies on his studies. However, that hope didn't transpire. At the end of the first semester, Geoff's Grade Point Average (GPA) was rock bottom.

Terry learned that Geoff's weakness was his lack of goals outside of water polo. The incongruence between his achievements in water polo and other spheres was perplexing to Terry: the whole point of coming over to the USA and Pepperdine was that he wanted to experience playing the top college players in the country in order to improve his skills.

Terry soon deduced that what Geoff lacked was balance. Recognizing that achieving balance was critical to Geoff's overall success in life, he called him in for a meeting. What transpired was illuminatingly educational for Terry. It turns out that Geoff's only concept of the American collegiate system was what he had seen in the movie *Animal House* from his home in Australia. For those not familiar with this classical story, mayhem is the central tenant of the story. Chaos and disorder amidst rampant self-serving students with little impulse control – are the central themes in Animal House. Clearly, Terry knew that he needed to assist Geoff in giving him a more accurate perspective on American college life.

Since he was a long way away from his parents, Geoff was receptive to his coach taking on some of the parental responsibilities, and Terry and he wasted no time in structuring some goals for all facets of his life. Terry's reasoning was this: that if Geoff took charge of his life by exercising self discipline extensively, not only would he excel at water polo, but he'd earn a degree that would empower him and open doors for him in life.

Geoff responded magnificently. By the time he graduated from Pepperdine, his GPA was up to 3.75; he achieved his dream goal of becoming an Olympian for his home country, and he fell in love with a straight 'A' pre-med student whom he married. Admittedly, this may have helped him a bit with his study habits! Geoff went on to become the District Attorney in San Antonio, Texas, but later, he joined his Medical Doctor wife in the medical field. It still amazes Terry how Geoff turned his life around with structured self-discipline.

Terry's experience with Geoff and so many other Pepperdine students enriched him – and continues to positively impact his life today. He attributes his ability to really be able to enjoy the 1992 Olympics from having gained a much healthier 'big picture' perspective through the experience of coaching his charges – and – from being mentored by people he respected and admired greatly.

Perspective plays a key role in a person's ability to take ownership of his or her actions. As a player, Terry had kept his emotions rigidly under control – and that iceman demeanor made him impenetrable. In the 2-meter man position, that emotionless front was like a suit of armor and it worked in Terry's favor irrefutably. He could take a beating from his opponent and never show that it was affecting him. This frustrated the man marking him to no end - and the psychological victory was more than often - his. It also assisted Terry in focusing on the game and the scoreboard – instead of on a referee who may have made a bad call or a team player who made a costly error.

While that icicle demeanor was part of Terry's Swedish genetic package, it certainly didn't come from his dad. Bob Schroeder vented his emotions often and loudly – and Terry learned that the best way to defuse the flying emotions in the house was to remain steadfastly calm in the storm. He transferred that homegrown skill into the water polo pool, and while his opponents worked themselves into a frenzy of flailing emotions, he remained unfazed and per-fectly intact. That made the person who was harassing him even more furious!

As a water polo coach, though, Terry's story changed – perhaps because he no longer had the advantage of being in the water where he could burn off his emotions – with physical exertion. Now that he was coaching, all that energy had nowhere to go. At first, he had moments of doling out con-sequences by yelling loudly at players from the pool deck. The very thing he swore he'd never do – he was doing: losing his composure and letting his frustration show. The frustration emanated from that initial feeling of being disconnected from the game; standing above the water – unable to dive in and do what he felt was needed. The frustration was compounded by his soft-spoken nature and the poor acoustics around the pool. Many times when Terry called out an instruction to his players – they couldn't really hear him properly and so they didn't respond. To someone who is trained to react in split seconds to a team's need in the water – the empty chasm that the mis-fired communication produced was enough to change Terry's temperament.

Another geographical change also raised Terry's blood pressure. No lon-ger in the pool, he was able to survey everything that was going on with the players from the same bird's eye vantage point as the referees. It thus came as a shock to him that despite the elevated vantage point, the referees sometimes made blatantly incorrect calls - and Terry's patience was severely tested. For the first time in his extensive water polo career, the Rock of Gibraltar was showing the world that he had emotions – lots of them. On two different occasions while coaching at Pepperdine, he showed his displea-sure so enthusiastically that he was red carded and kicked off the deck. While some coaches regard this as a trademark of efficacy, Terry holds no pride in either of those two occasions.

In 1994, shortly after Leanna's birth when she was just 3 weeks old, Pepperdine played against University of California San Diego (UCSD) in a night game. Like most new dads, Terry was severely sleep deprived – not a good mixture at such an important game. While all games count and are important in the college season, this one was particularly pertinent because it carried the weight of deciding if Pepperdine would make it into the NCAA Championships at the end of the year. But there was another reason that particular game was so under the microscope: the team was being observed by a man who was considering donating money for an endowment fund for men's water polo at Pepperdine.

Things started precariously when Terry overheard comments being thrown around by the San Diego officials - comments that didn't sit well with him. Randy Burgess, who is now a friend of his, was one of the officials, and Terry felt that several bad calls had been made against the Pepperdine team. Sleep deprived, fatigued and with his emotions on edge – Terry was a bomb ready to explode: When the Pepperdine goalie had the ball with 15 seconds left to play (and Pepperdine was up by one goal), official Randy called a turnover that almost cost them the game.

Vehemently in disagreement with the call, Terry came undone – ran down the pool deck and grabbed Randy by the shirt and picked him up off the ground while he let rip a few choice words – 5 inches away from Randy's face. It's a moment he regrets significantly. The truth was that his team played carelessly towards the end of the game – and Terry's outburst did not do his professional reputation any good. The incident also almost cost him his coaching job and possibly cost Pepperdine a huge monetary donation.

Thankfully, Randy let it go, and he forgave Terry while not pressing the issue with the league. It was a valuable lesson learned about controlling one's emotions and accepting responsibility. That night in San Diego changed Terry's coaching style forever. This was not the man he wanted to be and he never intended to let it happen again. In Terry's mind, anger was not the right competitive motivator; rather, it was a deflection of responsibility.

Since that watershed night, Terry has learned to respect the officials with the understanding that water polo is one of the most difficult sports to referee because so much of the game happens below the surface. He has become the modicum of calm while coaching – always focused on the result. He's also learned to be realistic about the things he can and can't control. Coach Schroeder has raised his level of compassion for the players while remaining placid under pressure. He has also let players learn their own lessons at times because at the end of the day, they're in charge and therefore they have to take responsibility for their actions. As a result, when Terry does become angry – rare as it is – his players really do come to the surface and take note. His emotions have far more impact when displayed sparingly.

This principle was clearly evident at a game at CAL in Northern California. After being ahead at half time, the players engaged in a futile blame game. Terry saw the worst instigator in action, so he reached over the edge of the pool, grabbed him by the water polo cap and pulled him out of the water to eye level – yelling "That's enough!" Stunned silence ensued – a sign that the team had clearly understood the message. It was a timely display in leadership: a time when yelling was necessary to rise above the chaos and help to reestablish the focus of the team.

This coaching style has carried Terry well throughout his tenure as head coach of Team USA. While the USA was playing Australia, one of the veteran players on the team made a mistake – but he compounded the error by letting the guy on the other team just swim away with the ball and eventually score at the other end. He was so fixated on his first error that he complicated matters by making a second error. His intransigent perspective was that someone else on the team should have stepped in to cover for him – and that inability to get out of his own way – gave the opposition a scoring chance.

Terry immediately took that player out of the game because he was not taking responsibility for himself, and Terry's disenchantment was voiced in no uncertain terms: "That was your mistake and it cost us a goal. It did not need to, but when you stopped playing and tried to see who else was at fault, you only compounded the mistake and it turned out worse!" Not being a coached who yelled, the volume and intensity of Terry's admonishment had a definitive impact on the entire team that day. One of the biggest tools a coach has for molding his players is the bench.

This particular player spent some time on the bench – like a 'time out' for children – and that consequence gave him an opportunity to evaluate what had been happening during the game. It's imperative that athletes be given the space and the solitude to figure out the pros and cons of their actions. Responsibility leads to self-respect and better team chemistry. Athletes are far more likely to reach their potential because a coach gave them the guidance and then the space to figure out their personal responsibility on their own. When all the players accept their own responsibility and the blame game is not a factor - the team has a greater chance of being successful.

When it comes to the topic of team chemistry, Terry says unequivocally: "Team chemistry is a critical component of a team's success, but it revolves around trust. Without trust for one another, individuals cannot sustain a relationship and the team suffers as a consequence. On any team, some of the players may have trust issues – perhaps having been burned in a prior relationship with a teammate or a loved one. But the bottom line is that in order to be trusted, you must first trust others. You must be willing to put yourself out there and risk vulnerability in order to build the trust factor on a team. A truly great and united team is formed out of mutual respect and the shared experiences of the group. Trust grows as the individual players respect the differences of their teammates, learn to take responsibility for their own actions, rise to the occasion in critical moments of a game, and finally give of themselves to the shared vision."

Terry's journal entry on this date:

November 20th 1997
Many of the lessons that I learned as a player are being magnified this year as I coach. Our team is doing well – very well as we prepare to head into the MPSF (Mountain Pacific Sports Federation) tourna-ment – we are the top-rated team in the country. We have a legiti-mate shot at winning the national title. Perhaps that makes it easier for me to be calm and confident. However, I feel I have learned to use that same calmness in coaching that helped me when I was striving to be a better player. I also feel like I have done a better job this year of owning up to my mistakes and giving credit where credit is due.

As far as mistakes go, we all make them and when the leader is not afraid to admit that he has made a mistake, then the athletes begin to feel that this is how they should act too. I can tell that the team is feeling empowered and more of the guys are beginning to use praise more often in practice and in games. It's become contagious this year and the team is moving to a new plane. The winning is helping too. But in my opinion, giving credit and accepting blame (when appropri-ate) is helping the team come together as much as anything. We will see how far it takes us this year at Pepperdine.

Pepperdine would go on to win their first National Championship (NCAA) a few weeks later. The victory tasted exceptionally sweet – especially in light of the fact that big schools like Stanford University, UCLA, USC and CAL usually harness the best players in the country. This time a strong vision, hard work, talent and cohesive play made the Pepperdine team the best in the country.

The Pepperdine team has their last confab with Coach Schroeder in overtime at the 1997 Championship Game which they won a few minutes later

Pepperdine University wins the National Championship 1997 (NCAA)

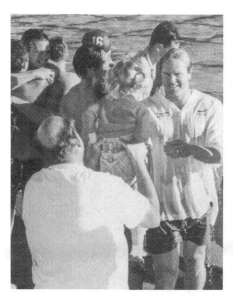

Leanna is handed to her victorious
dad by Charles Hollingsworth at the
clinching of Pepperdine University's
1997 National Champsionship title

Charles Hollingsworth celebrates
Pepperdine's 1997 Championship title
by jumping into the pool

Jack Kocur was one of the team captains on the 1997 championship team. After the championship game, he looked completely spent, having given everything to the team and to the victory. As Terry soaked up the moment and celebrated with his team, he noticed that Jack was still alone, hanging onto the side of the pool, so he moved towards him and noticed that he looked pale and was shivering. As he asked him what was going on, Jack replied, "I can't get myself out of the pool." Every ounce of energy was in the pool. He had given everything he had and could not even pull himself from the water.

When they announced the Most Valuable Player (MVP) for the tournament, they singled out 3 players: Jeremy Pope, Alan Herrmann and Merrill Moses. Throughout the season, Jack had scored numerous game-winning goals and even though he did not score in the championship game – he had played an integral role on the team and he was a true champion. Jack would later go on to become a very successful coach and is currently the assistant coach of the USA team at the 2016 Rio Olympic Games.

Also part of that team was Brain McAlister, who, when his name was announced before every game, he would thump his fist to his chest – indicating that he was going to play with heart! That gesture was infectious. One

Alan Herrmann playing for Pepperdine University - 1997
against University of Southern California (USC)

by one, each player adopted the same gesture and committed himself to play
with heart and give everything he had to help the team win.

One of the key Pepperdine members of the victorious 1997 NCAA
Champions, Alan Herrmann, describes that period of his water polo career
as life defining. He sums it up like this: "Being part of the Pepperdine 1997
championship team was one of the greatest times in my life. Terry showed
us how to be a family inside and outside the pool. Even our extended families united. Pepperdine University became our core strength because we
received incredible support from everyone at the university and we felt the
energy of the community behind us."

More specifically, Alan describes the 1997 team like this: "We weren't
necessarily the best players in the country, but we were passionate about
playing water polo, and Coach Terry assembled and drove that passion within
us. He was the best father figure to us and through him we discovered the
best parts about ourselves because he knew how to bring out those attributes. He advised us to set aside our egos and to put our energies into our
teammates so that we could become a cohesive family that really cared about
each other. He also asked us to let him coach us to the best of his ability – and

because we respected him so much – we became 100% committed to being coachable. That's critical. It also helped that Terry was such a brilliant player himself. He got in the water with us and showed us what to do. You had to live it to know what an exceptionally special time in our lives this period was. Merrill Moses, the current Olympic 2016 USA men's goalie was part of our team and we have all remained close to this day."

As for Terry specifically, Alan describes him like this: "Terry is the most incredible leader I've ever encountered. He leads by example and is a man of his word. He's genuine, motivating, inspiring, compassionate, strategic, technical, calm and excited only when necessary."

On the topic of Terry's impact on his and the team's lives, Alan says, "Everything I am today as a man is because of what Terry taught me. I owe him a debt of gratitude for my successes in life. He taught us how to visualize; to play like champions, to conduct ourselves with integrity. We all benefitted from his mentorship and everything we learned transcended beyond the pool into our professional and social lives. We are all substantially better people for having had Terry in our lives."

The next year in 1998, Terry worried about the Pepperdine team. Complacency after a victorious 1997 – had set in – and Terry knew the price of complacency. Hailed as the pre-season favorite team, by the time they were 60% of the way through their games, their record was 6-9 and they were ranked 5th in the country. Terry knew that something had to shake them out of their inertia, so he called on the much-respected, Marv Dunphy, who had amongst his substantial coaching credits an illustrious gold medal in USA Men's Volleyball from the 1988 Seoul Olympics.

Of all the pertinent information Marv delivered to the team that day, perhaps the words that shifted all of them out of complacency were these: "Either you are getting better, or you are getting worse." He paused strategically and then asked, "Which are you doing?" It became abundantly clear to the team that they had been resting on their laurels and they needed to jump-start their engines in order to move forward. So powerful were Marv's words to them that day that each member of the team reminded each other of those words almost every day after the visit. When they were scrimmaging or practicing or running drills, a new awareness was rising as they asked each other, "Are you/we getting better or getting worse?"

With a renewed attitude, the team's performance ratcheted up markedly and they became unstoppable – with a winning streak against many of the best teams in the country. By the end of the regular season, they had moved up to being ranked 3rd in the country – giving them a lot more momentum at the conference tournament - the Mountain Pacific Sports Federation (MPSF) Tournament – which consisted of the 8 top teams in the country.

Their first round opponent was University of California Irvine (UC Irvine) – a team that had the distinction of having the top scorer in the country, Ryan Bailey[1], who played the 2-meter position. Ryan was scoring goals like a machine that year and by Pepperdine's game time against UC Irvine, Ryan was 3 goals shy of scoring 100 goals for the year.

The team's game strategy was two-fold: of course most importantly they wanted to win but from a tactical perspective and fitting in with how they would win the game, they wanted to prevent Ryan from scoring his 100th goal on their time. They followed their game plan well - shutting Ryan out and moving into the semi-final round against UCLA (University of California Los Angeles) - another team on a hot streak. The tight game ended in Pepperdine's victory: 9-8.

Only one team stood between them and a trip to the NCAA finals and that team was Stanford University. The game was a battle – compounded by the fact that they were up against a hot shooting team with a player named Layne Beaubien[2]. Stanford ended up winning the game 10–9 with Layne scoring 4 goals -- all from outside shots. The Pepperdine players had played their hearts out but fell slightly short – and there is never any shame in that. Having been mediocre most of the year, they had become one of the two best teams in the country.

Marv's words, "Either you are getting better or you are getting worse", have stayed with Terry ever since. He uses those words to motivate himself in every aspect of his life. Complacency and going through life on tepid cruise control are not what Terry expects of himself, his family or water polo teams. No doubt Bob Schroeder's words of wisdom about doing one's best also echo through strongly in those temporary moments of placidity.

Through Terry's extensive coaching career at Pepperdine University, he has had some of the country's top players in his teams. The 2008, 2012 and 2016 Olympic goalie, Merrill Mosses, is one of his star protégés. Also spawned out of the Pepperdine pool is the powerfully talented Jesse Smith who represented the U.S. in the 2008, 2012 and 2016 Olympics.

Merrill Moses gave this voice of praise for Terry: "Coach Schroeder has had a huge impact on my life and has made me the man I am today. He is the person who believed in me as a walk-on freshman in college. He gave me a shot even though I was considered a 'nobody' in the water polo world coming

---

1. Ryan Bailey...2004, 2008, 2012 Olympics 2. Layne Beaubien would later participate in the 2004, 2008 and 2012 Olympic Games.

out of high school. Without his guidance and leadership, I don't think I would have been as successful in water polo and in the classroom in college. He is the coach who called me to come back and play with the national team after being the last cut in the 2004 Olympics. Without his leadership and belief I would not be a 3-time Olympian and silver medalist. I also have the privilege of going full circle with Coach Schroeder and being his assistant coach at Pepperdine University. It is such a pleasure to be working beside a great human being who has so much knowledge in all aspects of water polo and life. He is such a genuine person that has become a father figure to me and I will be forever grateful for everything he has taught me and done for me."

Terry feels mutually honored to have coached alongside many of his past players at Pepperdine including Jim McMillan, Jack Kocur and Alex Rodriguez. His assistant coaches now are Merrill Moses and Mike Tragitt - both past players for whom he has incredible respect. It is a joy for Terry to work with young coaches that are passionate and driven to be successful. He has felt special bonds with each of these coaches and the relationship he shares with Merrill and Mike is extraordinary. It's the reciprocity between them that creates the extraordinary part: while mentoring them, they give back to Terry so many affirming gifts and a perspective that has made him grow.

Unlike many of his coaching peers, Terry does not believe in ever humiliating his players – publically or privately. Instead, he concentrates on building people up versus tearing them down with criticism. His methodology extends to the same expectation in the behavior of his athletes. Instead of allowing them to suffocate their teammates with negativity and criticism, he insists that the team forms relationships with each other that will take them to the top. He says with resounding conviction, "when you elect to become part of a team, the success of the unit depends on each person sacrificing a part of himself and becoming accountable to the team. This means that all of the choices that the individuals make – both good and bad – have an impact on the team."

"In the course of a game, there are opportunities to praise your teammates for making a good pass or shot; for making a steal and for helping on defense. Unfortunately, oftentimes all we focus on is what goes wrong. When a player looks to blame others with comments like, "Hey bad pass!" or "Why didn't you help me?" the trust begins to erode. Bad feelings arise and an unhealthy undercurrent begins to develop on the team. This can tear even a great team apart."

"As I matured as a player, I learned this valuable lesson; my ability to act differently and diffuse a situation by accepting responsibility was invaluable.

It is a sign of mature athletes who know that they have made that same mistake that a teammate just did and can look at the offender and say, 'Let's move on and focus on the next play'."

Terry Schroeder coaches his charges at Pepperdine University

Terry continues, "Blame often comes from feeling that success is out of reach, but that perspective will eat away at the foundation of every team where that behavior exists."

When Terry would later take on the responsibility as Olympic head coach for the 2008 Beijing team, he instinctively knew that one of his first major tasks with the team was to free them from the blame game. Without that monumental mental shift, he knew that the team wouldn't stand a chance in the Olympics. They moved towards trust and compassion for each other – and the results were miraculously transformative.

In Terry's view, there are two types of successful coaching styles that he has witnessed - one is fear based - and one is centered in love. He has tried to focus on love. Terry believes that the most meaningful aspect of his coaching career has been the relationships that he has formed with his players and coaching staff.

Forever grateful to Pepperdine for the opportunity he has had to positively influence the young men he works with every day, Terry hopes that coaching will continue to be an integral part of his life for years to come.

The 2008 USA Men's Olympic Water Polo Team becomes a tightly bonded family

CHAPTER 15

Preparing for Beijing

Swimming Harmoniously

Teamwork begins by building trust, and the only way to do that is
to overcome our need for invulnerability
– Patrick Lenciono

December 15, 2007: After USA Men's Water Polo finished a disappointing 7th place in the 2004 Athens Olympic Games, Ratko Rudić, the illustrious head coach of USA Men's Water Polo, made the decision to resign his position and return to his native Croatia. Widely respected as one of the best coaches in the world, Ratko had been with this veteran team since 2000, and Tony Azevedo, the 2008, 2012 and 2016 USA Men's Water Polo captain, describes their 4 years with Ratko as the most intense training they'd ever endured. He came from the school of hard knocks in Eastern Europe and only the toughest players survived Ratko's 'take no prisoners' intensity. Ratko's modus operandi was that he felt Team USA needed to learn to suffer in order to be hungry for success,

and the training he put them through was sheer sufferance. The team's Olympic history since their last medal in 1988 had been disappointing. After a 4th place finish in 1992 (Terry's final Games as an athlete), the team had finished 7th in 1996, 6th in 2000 and 7th in 2004.

Following Ratko's departure, USA Men's Water Polo was thrust into muddy turmoil

Ratko Rudić leaves the USA to take up the
Head Coach position in Croatia

as coaches were brought on and fired with machine-gun rapidity. In 2005, head coach Guy Baker led the team into the World Championships in Montreal, Canada. After finishing second in their bracket to Serbia-Montenegro, they fell to Italy and Germany before finally beating Cuba for 11th place. This was the worst finish in USA Water Polo history and led to a coaching change.

Tony's father, Ricardo Azevedo, was elected head coach. He brought on Terry as assistant coach in 2006. During this period, most of the players opted to go over to Europe to play professionally from December to May – and then they would regroup back in the USA during the summers. This allowed them to play in many more high-level games while earning an income and experiencing another country and culture. It also worked with the USA training schedule as most of the competitions were during the summer months when the entire team was together. With no major competitions in 2006, time flew by and 2007 meant World Championships and the Pan American Games that were both opportunities to qualify for the Beijing Olympics.

In March 2007, the team headed to Melbourne, Australia for the World Championships. They kicked off promisingly with two convincing victories: 9-3 over Australia and 14–4 versus South Africa. Their final game in-group play was against Croatia, the eventual champions and one of the strongest teams in the world, and they lost to them10-8.

The all-important cross over game would be against Germany. This game would determine if they would advance 1st through 8th or 9th through 16th in the tournament. Unfortunately, the team played poorly and ended up on the short side of a 6-3 loss. The inability to score on their 6 on 5 was the downfall. Although USA won their final two games against Canada and Australia, their 9th place finish was not enough to save Ricardo's job. His firing took place just 5 weeks before the Pan American Games in Rio - Team USA's best chance to qualify for the 2008 Olympic Games.

Tony and the team were left to coach themselves virtually solitarily while USA Water Polo figured out who to invite to fill the void of head coach. The term 'critical timing' is a vast understatement here. Firing a head coach 5 weeks before the Olympic qualifiers must go down in history as one of the riskiest moves ever.

USA Water Polo's C.E.O., Chris Ramsey, called Terry to offer him the job of head coach. This was a lifetime goal that Terry had dreamed about – to return to haloed Olympic ground with the honor of coaching the USA team. The Olympics were in his bloodstream and he missed every facet about them: the opening ceremonies, the sense of enormous pride at representing your country, and the competitive element that brought out super-human characteristics in almost everyone who participated.

However, Terry had dreamed that the offer might come when Leanna and Sheridan were a bit older. In 2007 they were only 13 and 6 years old – an age range where they needed their parents' full, undivided attention. In his role as assistant coach, he was able to balance family time and work. Head coach took on an entirely new set of responsibilities and expectations. This would take some lengthy discussions with Lori to find out how this proposal would impact their family and change their lives.

Chris was determined to have Terry give him the answer he wanted, and so he embarked on the 3-hour drive up from Orange County, California to the Schroeders' residence at Lake Sherwood where he assured Terry and Lori that USA Water Polo would take care of both of them unremittingly through the process. There was nothing to worry about, so he said.

Terry and Lori analyzed it pragmatically as a highly-pressurized 14 months – because that's all the time they had left to the 2008 Beijing Olympics. With that short time frame, they figured that they could make the substantial sacrifices that the 14 months would entail. Lori would have to take on double parenting duties while Terry was away extensively, but once the summer vacation started, the girls could join their dad in Beijing. Their chiropractic business would be greatly affected, but it wasn't 5 years; it was 14 months, and Terry's magnetic pull towards the Olympics was a force he couldn't deny. This was the moment and he knew he had what it took to elevate the team. Lori knew how important this offer was to her husband, and she selflessly supported him, knowing that it would fulfill him.

Since time was of the essence, Terry dove into the pressure chamber to begin a massive amount of work. At this moment, the Pan Am Games was their biggest and most important tournament because it was the team's best chance at qualifying for Beijing. Winning the Pan Ams would mean beating Canada and Brazil rather than some of the highly-ranked European teams. If they failed, there was still one last Olympic qualifier in January of 2008, but that would be a highly undesirable situation with many of the European teams also fighting for their lives.

Just 4 weeks to go before the Pan Am Games, the team was understandably confused and nervous. Given the distance between Terry's work place and the team's practice base in Orange County, California, it was impossible for Terry to make the journey to the team every day. The rumors about practices moving closer to Terry's work place added fuel to the team's nervous embers. With all the coaching changes, uncertainty and confusion was all they had known for 5 years and their skittishness was undeniable.

For that reason, before any workouts took place, the senior members of the team, led by Layne Beaubien and Ryan Bailey, decided to confront the uncertainty by questioning Terry on his plans for the team. They conducted an interview of their coach – even though essentially they had no choice. The decision to hire Terry had been made.

After conveying his strategy to Layne and Ryan, Terry knew unflinchingly that the responsibility lay with him to earn their trust – incrementally – and he was up for the challenge. At one of their first meetings together, he introduced the idea "Let's get back to the Podium" in Beijing. It was about earning a medal. In the meeting room were banners of all the USA Olympic Water Polo medal-winning teams in history. Sadly, there were few, and the last medal was in 1988. Terry felt it would have been too much of a long shot and incredulous at the time to say, "Let's win a gold medal". But he had the conviction they could medal, and his task was to convince the team that they could do it too. This was to be Tony's and Ryan's 3rd Olympics; they'd suffered through 3 coaching changes in 3 years and the Olympic Games were now one year away. They had reason to be jaded and skeptical.

The first day on the pool deck with his new team was weighed down with tension but Terry's mathematical brain turned to analyzing the team's emotions. They had learned to suffer under Ratko – and he carefully deduced that the key element that could change them significantly for the better – was to have them become an imperviously united team. That was Terry's primary mission. Having been successful in his past captaincy and coaching roles at helping a group of men with assertive and varying personalities become a strong family, he was confident in his abilities to do the same with the USA team. He never doubted their ability; they had all the medal-worthy physical criteria intact and they were hungry to win. Mentally, though, they were exhausted, having consumed so much change and disappointment over the past quadrennial.

Terry progressed with vigor knowing that he could change the men's outlook; he had a track record both as an athlete and coach where he led the mental offensive. He knew that he could infuse new mental vitality into this team of talented, veteran players. The timing was also favorable with a team that was hungry for success.

Training went as well as could be expected for that first month but it was time to be tested. On the way to Rio, the team stopped in Washington

DC for outfitting and meetings with the United States Olympic Committee (USOC). The stopover was for a few days so Terry harnessed the opportunity to take them to the Lincoln Memorial and address them on the steps looking out over the reflecting pool and the National Mall. He gave an emotional speech to the team about what it meant to be an American, the opportunity they had to represent their country, and the history of Lincoln and his many failures before he succeeded and became one of the country's greatest Presidents. The sensitivity in their eyes indicated that they had absorbed his message - or at least he hoped.

The demonstration of leadership strength surfaced the following night. With just a few days to go before the Pan Am Games began, some members of the team stayed out late and drank too many beers. Tony Azevedo and Merrill Moses were the worst offenders. When Terry questioned them about their actions, they weren't forthcoming with the truth and this disappointed Terry enormously – especially since they had just discussed the opportunity that this team had in front of them. Realizing that this was contrary to any teambuilding, Terry knew he had to respond firmly and set the precedent that this pattern of behavior could not be tolerated. In fact, it was destructive.

He suspended Tony and Merrill for the first game at the Pan Am Games. Since an Olympic berth was riding on the games, this was a difficult decision to make – shutting out two of their best players especially since this first game would be against host Brazil. Terry looks back on the incident and has no regrets. Establishing discipline up front was imperative not only to his reputation and credibility as a head coach, but also to the team's ultimate success.

The disciplinary measure didn't harm the outcome: USA beat Brazil 12-6 in this first game and would roll through the competition before coming back and beating Brazil 9–2 in the gold medal final with Merrill and Tony playing substantial roles. With the win at the Pan Am Games, the team was a step closer to their goal. They had qualified for the prize and they could now focus on the Olympics.

When Terry had been brought on as assistant coach with Ricardo, he asked Merrill Moses from Pepperdine University, to come out of retirement and to consider joining the team. Merrill dropped everything unhesitatingly, hopped on board and became a valuable component on the team. As the goalie, he was the key to playing a defensive style of water polo. The 9-2 victory over Brazil in the final was the inception of what would become the trademark style of this team. The team wholeheartedly adopted the methodology of winning by playing great defense.

Shortly after the Pan Am Games, Terry and Chris Ramsey met with high-level administrators from the USOC to determine the kind of support for the athletes during the Olympic year. Typically, the level of support is based on whether or not the USOC believes that the team has a legitimate shot at earning a medal. The potential medal-winning teams are always favored with substantially more money distributed to those athletes.

The athletes who are left out in the cold with little financial help invariably find themselves in a quandary: with their full Olympic training schedule they are not able to work and this is hugely problematic. During these meetings, the USOC essentially told Terry and Chris that based on their record over the previous 8 years - they were not being considered medal contenders - and therefore they would not qualify for the higher level of athlete support.

This was a blow that was going to be difficult to surmount, and it would almost certainly prohibit any of the men being able to train full time for the Olympic year. With no other choice, Terry set about immediate fund raising to help balance the budget - another responsibility that his plate was barely able to absorb.

Despite a weak American economy, Terry's reputation preceded him, and many generous supporters rallied to donate funds to the team's journey. The added funds allowed the team to train full-time in Thousand Oaks, California – close to Terry's work and family. The community also adopted the team and many of the team members stayed with host families while they trained - allowing them to save funds while they trained for the Olympics.

As Olympic team training began in late December 2007, the first thing Terry worked at extinguishing in the team was the climate of blame that resulted in friction, and he intended to work on replacing it with self-respect, responsibility and discipline. After reading the inspiring book, "The Lone Survivor" by Marcus Luttrell, about the survival of a U.S. Navy SEAL in Afghanistan, Terry embarked on an innovative experiment that evolved into something uniquely special.

The U.S. Navy SEALs are famous worldwide. Pushed to their limits physically and mentally, their crucial strength is their teamwork. It was Terry's decision to take Team USA to the SEALs so that they could experience first-hand what it was like to be a member of this elite squad.

They joined them at the SEAL's training base on Coronado Island, California. Their instructor for the day was Special Warfare Operator 1st Class (SEAL) Lieutenant JG Andy Stumpf. He was injured in battle after he

USA Navy SEALs

climbed back into a strike zone to save a fellow SEAL who had been injured and trapped behind enemy lines. His sense of team was so strong that he risked his own life to save a teammate. The SEALs team has to operate at the highest levels of cooperation. Lives are on the line if there's miscommunication or if anybody puts himself before the team.

Lieutenant Stumpf explained that being a team can't be taught. It comes from experiencing adversity together, and it's the ultimate act of selflessness. The purpose of achieving a united goal is the team's priority – and anyone who isn't focused on that priority needs to leave. He reiterated that the momentum that leads to greatness comes from sacrificing, sticking together and paying attention to detail.

Before beginning the physical workout, Lieutenant Stumpf advised Terry to stay with him on land because, as he put it, "this is going to get ugly – but besides that – it's a better teambuilding experience if you don't participate. It should just be the guys".

After watching the team progress through 4.5 hours of punishment - in and out of the water – Terry admitted that he was relieved to have opted out. The first thing that Andy did was to have the team lock arms and march out into the 58-degree-fahrenheit Pacific Ocean on a cold December day. Their instructions were to keep the chain intact - in other words, to not let go of their teammates. After they had gone out to chest-deep water, he instructed them to float face-up, arms interlocked, and he kept them in the water for about 20 minutes as the waves crashed over their heads. The team had to rely on each other to stay afloat and survive.

Everything was timed to take the men to the edge of hypothermia, and then Andy would get them out of the water to do some dry land drills including doing burpees and rolling around in the sand. At one point he asked them to cover every inch of their bodies with sand. When nobody did it, everyone was punished by running up sand dunes.

Andy challenged Tony's leadership with some exacting exercises, ultimately helping him to understand his critical role in the team's dynamics. When the men were hot and sweaty, it was time to get back in the water again and hold the chain - each time a little shorter - timing them again to take them to the edge of hypothermia. The SEAL's Obstacle Course was another significant challenge and by the end of the day, the men were more beaten up than they had ever been. Some of them nursed bruised ribs from hitting logs they were supposed to clear while jumping over, but to their credit, they finished together – cheering each other on in the process. Nobody had given up. They were literally coming together as a team right there before Terry's eyes. The evidence of those key strengths made Terry proud, and he felt even more convinced that his team had the resilience to take themselves to the top of the podium.

Team USA's Captain, Tony Azevedo

At the day's conclusion, two common themes emanated from the debriefing:

1. Pay attention to detail: every time the guys did not listen to instructions they were punished.
2. Stick together: when they tried to work alone they were also punished.

Andy also shared with the men his story. The SEALs have a motto or creed: never leave a teammate behind. Andy was shot while on an al Qaeda ferreting mission in Afghanistan, and so was his partner. He had escaped to a safe place but his partner was still in danger, so Andy risked his life and went back to find his friend and shepherd him to safety. It was an impactful story about sacrificing for your teammate, and it was exactly the penetrating impression that Terry wanted the team to hear. The men listened – transfixed - as Andy gave them a first-hand account of the harrowing events. Obviously, the SEAL's version of teamwork was a life and death situation – incomparable to the Olympics – but the central notion of becoming a teammate of distinction hit home markedly.

The impact of the SEAL visit was measurable. For weeks after that, the players kept relaying to Terry how valuable they had found the experience – siting it as the best team-building exercise they'd ever had. The caveat at the end, though, was, "please don't make us to it again!" The land training had proved to be the most difficult aspect of the SEAL visit; the men were more akin to the life of dolphins rather than land animals, and their beaten-up bodies and heavily-stiff legs were apparent for the next week of water training.

Terry's next task was to insure that Team USA practiced and played against the first-tier-ranked teams during the run-up to the Olympic Games. He deduced that the only way he was going to return them back to the podium was to have them play as many games and scrimmages against the most powerful teams in the world. This meant that having Hungary, Serbia, Montenegro, Italy, Spain and Croatia on Team USA's training schedule for 2008 was imperative. It was also a tenuous situation because being clobbered by them repeatedly would be confidence shattering – but winning against them was the self-doubt elixir that USA so desperately needed.

The strategic plan worked as Terry procured training time with Serbia, Croatia and Hungary on USA's training schedule. In February they traveled to Serbia for 9 days training, and in May, they hosted Croatia in California for 8 days. By June, barely a month away from the Olympics, they were invited to train with the Hungarians for 5 days. This was undeniable proof that these teams respected the USA squad, or they would have dodged the common training. Their time was too valuable to waste against 2nd-tier teams – so the invites to train were an assurance that Team USA was a respected opponent.

The more complex task forward was to convince each member of the USA team that they were in the elite teams' league. Unless they internalized the recognition individually, their confidence would wane in the debris of self-doubt and the chance for success would be slim.

In February, the plan began shakily when the training with the Serbs became a mental battle. The Serbian players arrived at the pool confidently and dominantly, and Team USA failed to challenge them in the water. The Serbs responded with a kind of unbridled arrogance that was disconcerting.

For 7 nights the USA team was dispatched easily with lopsided scores. The Serbs won 14-6, 13-5, 13-6, 15-8, 12-6 and 13-7 before showing up for the final game - straight from 'happy hour' where half of them were at various stages of inebriation. Despite their compromised, drunken states, they beat a completely sober American team 12-5. The loss stung like salt on a wound. More alarmingly, Terry knew that the Americans had added another verb to their mental burdens: they feared the Serbs, and he was determined to eliminate that emotion. Respect was healthy; fear was crippling.

Over the next few weeks Terry and the coaching staff spent hours going over game film. Looking for any positive from the trip, Terry focused in on the fact that in each game or scrimmage, Team USA had drawn double the number of ejections than the Serbians had. Even though they had been beaten convincingly, they had played well enough to earn twice the exclusions.

Terry was resolutely sure that if Team USA perfected their 6 on 5 opportunities, they could invert the scores against the Serbs. The 6 on 5 situation was always the measure of how well a team was performing together. Beyond that, what Terry was trying to psychologically inculcate into his athletes was that building on and celebrating small successes was critical. There was hope – even in defeat – and they had to focus on the affirming possibilities ahead.

Back home, the team began to have dinner together once a week. These dinners were sponsored by a German friend of Terry's, Abby Franke, who had played in the German national league back in his day. Abby had done well as a local baker and he wanted to support the team in any way that he could. These dinners proved to be hugely valuable as the team spent a few extra hours each week outside the pool together - decompressing while building their relationships on a wholly different plain.

Peter Hudnut and Jeff Powers at
Team-building dinners

Layne Beaubien and Tim Hutten at
Team-building dinners

Merrill Moses, Jesse Smith and Adam Wright

Peter Varellas and Robert Lynn

Ryan Bailey, Tony Azevedo, Merrill Moses

Photos this page by Curtis Dahl

Patriotic supporters of the 2008 Olympics - Robin, Lori, Sheridan, Leanna, Codi, Jesse, Shannon, Mc Kenzie and Reef

After two months of training back home and trying to focus on the positives, there was a different vibe in the pool. By May, the team was preparing to host Croatia for a 3-game series at home. This was a significant turning point for the men: a new sense of confidence started to seep into their consciousness – replacing the debilitating disbelief they had felt previously. For the first time, the team was operating with a bit of a swag – a real sense of "maybe we really are a great team". Incrementally they put the pieces of hopefulness together: they had been together for a long time - many since they were on the junior team - and maybe now was the time to prove it in the pool against the number one team in the world.

Terry's journal records this important progress:

May 9th, 2008
Wow! What a fun game. We beat Croatia, the reigning World Cham-
pion, on a televised game. Coach Ratko was really ticked off. It was a
great crowd and a very impressive win. We were down by a couple of
goals and then things just seemed to click. We began to work together
as a team. Tony took over as our leader and scored a few huge goals

but more importantly, he made his teammates better. We won 8–5. The reality is becoming clearer: we can do this. We can beat anyone and we can get back to the podium in 3 months. The team is coming together and I can sense the belief is beginning to take hold in our hearts....

Terry's team would win 2 out of 3 games against Croatia in this crucial series. Besides the 3 official games the teams played in California, they trained each day for 10 days. The team's frame of mind was distinctly more optimistic than the one in Serbia just 3 months earlier. With new conviction they reasoned that if they played their style of defensive water polo together while perfecting their 6 on 5 power play – they could actually beat the best teams in the world and win a medal at the Olympics. The timing couldn't have been better, and Terry wasted no time in elevating them to the next level where trust, respect and love amongst them would seal their chances of success.

In the exhaustive lead-up journey to the Olympics, people need reminders along the way because human foibles creep into situations all too easily – even when the game plan seems to be on track. As the Olympics approached, with fatigue becoming a factor, Terry noticed that a few of his players were starting to feel entitled when it came to special services and luxury amenities. He also noticed a concerning aspect of selfishness etch its negative way back with some players being blatantly impatient with their teammates – thinking only of how that teammate's actions helped or hindered their own dream. It was time to address those foibles.

In an effort to bring balance and perspective back to the team, Terry invited Nick Vujicic to speak to them. Nick's story is an amazing one: born with no limbs whatsoever, this legless, armless man has not let any of those limitations faze him or stop him from pursuing his dreams. His visit happened to coincide with a big team cut that was about to occur: several players were going to be told that they were not going to the Olympics, and Terry knew that they would be devastated. During this difficult period, it was time to prepare both the eventual Olympians and the cut players about a life that had plenty in store for them. Nick's speech was about gaining a balanced perspective.

When he arrived, his little torso was hoisted onto a table so that all of the players could see and hear him. At one point, he purposely fell down and he would not let anyone help him back into a vertical position. Instead, with his head on the table he asked, "What happens when you fall down?" While they were all pondering the answer to that question, Nick used his head and a Bible to bring himself upright again.

That action was incredibly powerful to watch. While he was pulling himself up, neck muscles straining as he did it, he talked about the importance of standing up after you fall down. He acknowledged that the road of life can be difficult, hurtful and that people may not be prepared for the bumps – but that picking oneself up isn't an option. It's an imperative.

Nick also asked some difficult questions like, "What is life's purpose?" and "Why are you here?" Spending a few hours with Nick and experiencing his faith and positive attitude helped every member of the team refocus as they realized how fortunate they were. Those were powerful messages not only for the men who would go on to the Olympics, but for those who would not see their dream come true in 2008. Nick provided perspective about the opportunities and goals that were still in front of them.

Nick's enthusiasm was irrepressible. A few weeks later he insisted on getting into the water with the USA team at one of their practices. What a sight! He really wanted to score a goal, but clearly he couldn't throw the ball. So the players used their arms to lift Nick up so that he could "head" the ball into the goal.

He also received a chance to shine when he challenged the guys to an underwater breath-holding contest. Nick beat every one of them! While the water polo players generally have great lung capacity, Nick explained that while his lungs are the same size as theirs, without arms and legs, the oxygen in his lungs lasted longer as there was less tissue that needed to be oxygenated in his body. Everyone enjoyed the extra time they spent with Nick. He gave them such a valuable lesson in opening their eyes to the "bigger picture".

After legless, armless Nick's visit, Terry noticed a refreshing attitude adjustment on the team. There was less complaining and more expressions of gratitude forthcoming. It has always been Terry's fervent belief that gratitude is immensely beneficial in relationships – and that includes teammates. He says, "we all get so caught up in the details of our problems; perspective is a combination of having goals while always remembering our blessings. As much as I wanted this team to win an Olympic medal, what I wanted more for them was for each player to see water polo as a part of their journey – not the culmination of it. The goal of winning had to be considered within the context of the bigger picture. Remembering to be grateful, to say 'please' and 'thank you' meant that they had enough room in their hearts to accommodate the sentiments that would ultimately make them happier people. That was my goal for them".

Terry noticed - gratefully - that the players were growing, maturing and acquiring a much healthier perspective. It's not an exaggeration to say that every-one's life was changing for the better. They weren't just a group of men work-ing together. They were uniting into a caring family with greater respect for one another's similarities and differences. It was a far cry from the tenor that Terry had witnessed in 2007 where the team had a reputation for being aloof and self-ish. All of those things were changing as Terry watched the metamorphosis of a team that was giving him every reason to be proud.

People in the community would make it a point to tell him how respectful they had found the team members or Terry would hear a story about how some of the guys spent a few moments with someone else's child, impacting that family forever. The men were shifting their attitude with each other and with people outside of their circle - and people were noticing. Fear, anger and anxiety were in the past; the team was moving forward - allowing respect, love and trust to be their guiding principles. In watching them, Terry was constantly reminded to let those qualities be the guiding lights in his own life. The truth of the matter was that he was learning valuable lessons from his players too.

Being an effective communicator became another one of the key strengths to Team USA's Beijing success. Terry wanted the players to feel like they knew what was expected of them, and he wanted them to be equally as clear in their expression with the coaching staff. He felt it was critical that each player understand his role on the team. Many of the players were the superstars on their teams in college or club, and now they were being asked to play a different role - perhaps very different - to help the USA team to suc-cess. The team was not yet finalized so players were developing and improv-ing while their roles were changing - in some cases slightly, and in others more drastically - right up to when the final cuts were being made.

Each player took advantage of those individual meetings to the best of their ability – absorbing the information they were given on a meaningful level. These meetings also gave the players a chance to voice their thoughts and concerns. Terry's contention is this: "goals, skill, desire, perspective and work ethic are all components of success. Equally important is a person's willingness to listen to their heart as well as their head. When the head and the heart are communicat-ing effectively; when that personal awareness and accountability are in sync, our actions are more likely to earn the trust of others."

Being an excellent team player isn't just a theory; it's the end result that comes from being tested. Being prepared to sacrifice everything for the sake of the team – is a rare gift. It's about unquestionable trust that someone is going to "have your back" when the moment is critical. Building on trust requires that people overcome their own invulnerability, and become comfortable with being vulnerable. That's when teamwork is ignited at its fantastical best.

The only way that this is developed is by being tested at the highest level as much as possible. Even though the games and scrimmages against the world's best teams had accomplished much in this area, the true test was in the day-to-day practice. Could they challenge each other to be better everyday - thereby imitating the high-level competition that they desperately needed in order to succeed? To really be successful in Beijing the individual team members had to be willing to push their teammates to the point of breaking - on a daily basis. This meant working harder than they had ever worked before. The team responded well - and critical trust and respect were being built every day in practice.

The final strengthening of the bonds experience - before the final 13 cut for the team was made - took place at Indian Paint Bush Ranch near Lake George in Colorado, USA. After 5 days of intense training at the Olympic Training Center in Colorado Springs, Terry decided that some down time together would be valuable. During that infinitely restorative experience, there were many highlights, chief of which was everyone hiking into a beautiful meadow where teepee tents had been erected for the group. The setting was deeply impactful.

After a scrumptious dinner was appreciatively consumed, the coaches built a campfire for the team to sit around and talk if they wished. One by one, the players gravitated around the glowing fire – sitting and relaxing for probably the most unpressurized few hours of the previous 4 years. With their elevated moods made warmer by the fire, they shared their hearts and souls through the evening as the crackling wood popped amongst the embers and the stars shone brightly. Each teammate learned something significantly important about how each other really ticked, and the evening became a very special solidification of everyone coming to understand each other in ways that would make them better teammates and ultimately better people.

After the Coloradoan experience, the men were transformed in the water. They were on fire for each other and it showed in every part of their game. Taking complete ownership of everything they did, they began to excel consistently. Shifting the responsibility and casting blame on others was a fruitless impediment that was left behind in the past.

For Terry, this change in the team was a healing mechanism for him too: for years he'd lamented the loss of the gold medal in the 1984 Olympics – blaming it on biased referees who held the U.S. in disdain. Along with the team, he finally realized that there were missed opportunities, and it all came down to personal accountability. They blew opportunities with their 6 on 5 and they played to protect the lead – rather than to win the game. There was no one else to blame for the 1984 silver medal disappointment. This new acceptance of the situation had the added benefit of allowing Terry to once again take charge of his life – instead of ceding control to a Spanish referee whom part of the USA staff had overheard saying, "Screw the Americans" after the gold medal game.

That promising transformation was none more evident than in the final weeks before August 2008. There was no way that a cohesive, trusting and highly functioning team could exist when everyone was worried about the risky consequences of a mistake or about who would or wouldn't own their own mistakes. By stepping up to the plate, apologizing and being accountable while knowing when to correct a behavior, each member of the team earned the respect of the other. The new maturity was highly supportive, and with it came an increase in the team's overall confidence. It was a liberating new freedom that paid dividends.

In late June 2008, Terry was preparing to make the final cuts for Beijing. Fifteen men were on the team, and two more had to be cut. The final roster in Beijing would have only 13 players. Given the enormous sacrifices every-one had made up to this point, it was an irrevocably tough decision. All 15 men were exceptionally talented, had great commitment to the team, had shown outstanding self-discipline; they were in the best condition of their life and each person was extremely coachable. Every player thus far deserved to be an Olympian. The final selections really came down to - who could fill the roles that the team needed the most.

The final team would consist of two goalies, two centers, two defenders, two 1-2 side attackers, two 4-5 side attackers and 3 utility players. Making the final selections was a process that Terry wrestled with for weeks and it was pain-fully stressful for him as a coach. He lost sleep at night and his heart hurt. Noth-ing about this was easy, especially as he understood deeply that each player had given so much to be a part of the team. It was the most difficult part of coaching at this level. The original 27 men were down to the final choice of 13.

In order to be completely fair to everyone, Terry made the cuts a team process. Holding individual meetings with each player, he posed this primary question to each: "If you were to be cut, how would you like that to play out?" The answers he received helped to ease the pain but, in truth, nothing would ever obscure the heartbreak he felt in releasing the final two Olympic hopefuls and finalizing his Olympic team. Before letting anyone go, the team had all the men sign a banner that traveled with them to Beijing and served as inspiration to the guys who weren't cut: who had the privilege of being able to realize their dream. It was the final realization that in order for them to be where they were, many had sacrificed and given a large part of their life to the team. It cast a new light on the responsibility of making the team.

One last training trip was planned to Hungary. Terry and the other coaches decided that they would bring the remaining 15 players and make the final decision at the end of the trip. He felt that this would give all the players, but especially the ones on the bubble to be cut, one last chance to prove their worth. In the middle of the training with Hungary, USA Water Polo CEO Chris Ramsey visited with the team after a scrimmage with the Hungarian team and said, "You're a 2nd-tier team that stands no chance of winning a medal at the Beijing Olympics. Afterwards, all of you will be replaced with younger, better players."

Tony Azevedo responded: "Our team had a ton of experience; we worked harder than anyone in the world, but more than anything, we were a TEAM! All of the years' struggles and hardships had made us into an unbreakable team. We had a win or die mentality that was impenetrably strong. Stats and glory never mattered to us more than actually winning. We went into every game the underdog, but no matter what happened, we would end the game with 13 players and 3 coaches having given every ounce of energy that was humanly possible to win the game. Going into the Beijing Olympics, you could say that we had a chip on our shoulders, and we were determined to prove the cynics wrong."

The team played with extra intensity and fire for the remainder of the trip in Hungary and were on an even plain with the powerful Hungarians. D Day for the final cuts arrived and in an emotional meeting, the coaches agreed that the two players to be cut were John Mann and Brian Alexander. No one celebrated. This group was united and cutting anyone at this point – hurt everyone. John was a center and a very strong player but he was young and lacked the international experience. He was bigger and stronger than JW Krumpholz but he lacked the speed that JW brought to the team.

Brian was an attacker with an amazing shot. His teammates called him "Thor" because he was built like a Greek god. He could do everything well but Terry just could not find the right role for Brian. Both players were crushed by the decision. Later that night John reacted poorly and threw all of his USA gear out of his hotel window. Brian was calmer with the decision although there was no doubt that he experienced a deep pain. Their huge sacrifices had come to nought and there were no words to make this any easier for either player. Terry walked alone for hours along the banks of the Danube River feeling the pain of his cut warriors.

The final 2008 Beijing Olympic team was a blend of veteran players who had extensive experience mixed in with a few younger players who brought a new level of vitality and enthusiasm.

The men were united in their goal of getting back to the podium, and each team member knew his role and responsibility based on his strengths and weaknesses. All the communication between the coaches and players was open and honest. They were not about to settle for mediocrity; the pursuit of excellence was their mission. Their commitment was based on rock solid values – not emotions. Being adaptable to the needs of the team and being able to roll with the punches was also a strength that they had mastered. Selflessness was their core value – "What can you do for the team" verses "What can the team do for me". Caring and being service orientated was another critical component, as was accepting responsibility for their actions. Finally, all of these essential ingredients were wrapped up with self-discipline – an asset that builds dependability, trust and success. They set out to accomplish their goal of getting back to the podium with conviction.

USA team unity at the Beijing Olympics 2008

2008 USA Olympic Silver Medalists at the Beijing Olympics

The Arrival of the 2008 Beijing Olympics

A Glorious Current

The will to win, the desire to succeed, the urge to reach
your full potential... these are the keys that will
unlock the door to personal excellence
– Confucius

8 August 2008: Leading up to the 2008 Beijing Olympics there was worldwide concern about human rights abuses in China. *Human Rights Watch* noted that the Chinese government had smothered the voices of those who spoke out publicly about the need for greater tolerance and for more human rights in the country.

The Chinese government responded by announcing that protesters were free to protest at the 2008 Olympics in a designated park in Beijing but that they had to apply for a special protest permit – making it assiduously difficult for watchdogs, investigators and dissidents. Washington Post journalists discovered that this was the Chinese government's calculated way of making protestors beholden to them so that they could watch them with an iron fist.

The extensive list of grievances against the Chinese government extended to the 2008 Tibetan unrest that involved the Dalai Lamar and the Tibetan monks. Tibetan exile groups claimed that the Chinese exerted a brutal crackdown on them, and the western media speculated that the violence might affect attendance at the Beijing Olympics. However, that did not come to pass even though the tension in Beijing was palpable.

Beijing had its hands full with scrutiny in other areas too – notably the levels of air pollution. The last thing that healthy, elite athletes needed was to contaminate their lungs with toxic air – and Beijing's promises during the Olympic bid about taking care of the problem failed to live up to expectations.

Some athletes reported feeling nauseous and disoriented as they breathed in the thick, polluted Beijing air.

That was behind the scenes. On stage, in front of billions of people worldwide who watched the Beijing 2008 Opening Ceremonies on television, the Chinese put on a spectacular performance that demonstrated absolute precision excellency. Not a single person was out of synchronization in a show that mesmerized the world.

Basketball player Yao Ming led the People's Republic of China's Olympic athletes in the Parade of Nations, but few, no matter their nationality, had dry eyes when 9-year-old Lin Hao, a young survivor of the school that collapsed in the recent Sichuan earthquake disaster, came on stage to hold the massive hands of 7-foot-6 inch Yao Ming. It was an emotionally moving vision because of Lin Hao's survival story.

Yao Ming and 9-year-old earthquake survivor Lin Hao carry the Chinese flag at the 2008 Beijing Opening Ceremonies

Just prior to the Opening Ceremonies, Lin Hao was buried underneath the rubble of the earthquake in China that registered 7.9 on the Richter scale. When he emerged, instead of finding safety for himself, he went back to save two of his classmates. When asked why he risked his life to save the others, he said, "I was the hall monitor. It was my job to look after my classmates." The massive healing power of the Olympics captured even the cynics' imaginations when Lin-Hao was hoisted onto the shoulders of Yao Ming to watch the Olympic torch being lit. Beijing pulled it off spectacularly and the torch stood watch over the duration of the Games with its enormous symbolization. This time there were no screw-ups; no birds of peace accidentally getting barbecued by flames. This was Chinese distinction.

Mirroring the vast imperfection of life, the start of the 2008 Olympics was marred by a tragedy that hit close to home. The USA Men's Volleyball team – of which Pepperdine University's Marv Dunphy was an assistant coach – suffered an unfathomable loss. While touring Beijing with a Chinese tour guide, the father-in-law of the Olympic Men's Indoor Volleyball head coach, Hugh McCutcheon, was murdered by a mentally unstable Chinese man wielding a knife while they were touring an ancient tower. As isolated and incongruous as the incident was, it was a shocking reminder of how the course of fate can change lives in an instant. Despite the emotional impact of the incident, the team went on to win the gold medal two weeks later - a remarkable feat given their circumstances.

Team USA Men's Water Polo arrived in Beijing prepared and hungry for a chance to prove themselves or as their captain Tony Azevedo put it – to do or die. Their motto, "let's get back to the podium", was emblazoned in each one of their hearts. The team members stood as follows:

Tony Azevedo – Stanford Graduate and team captain, Tony was regarded as one of the best players in the world. Known as the "Golden Boy" he was an attacker who was playing in his 3rd Olympic Games. Opposition teams focused on double teaming Tony and taking him out of the game - and yet - he was still always amongst the tournament leaders in scoring. Before Terry became coach, Tony had won many individual scoring titles in big tournaments but the team had not placed highly in those tournaments. Terry and Tony entered into some invigorating discussions about what it meant to be an exceptional captain and leader, and Tony rose to

Team USA's Captain, Tony Azevedo - committed

the occasion. In Beijing, he made everyone around him better and that is the real test of a captain. He scored when he needed to; he made some incredible assists and said all the right things during meetings to lead the team. Terry particularly appreciates that Tony gave him a chance after his father was let go. That was a tough spot for Tony to be in, but he responded with maturity and won Terry's respect wholeheartedly. Tony was the young rising superstar when Terry was near the end of his playing career and Terry had the opportunity to play with Tony at some club tournaments during this period of time. Everyone knew Tony was one of the best individual players in the world but his leadership and performance in Beijing cemented Tony's position as one of the greats of the game. He was the consummate real deal.

Ryan Bailey – "Big Bails" or the "Machine" - played the center position and was from the University of California Irvine (UCI). The team's big man in the middle, he was a critical player in the team's success in Beijing. Also playing in his 3rd Olympic Games, Ryan provided a presence in the middle that made everything else work on offense. In 2004, Ryan had been the starting center and his overall stats were not great. He had only scored a few goals, earned a handful of exclusions and had been called on too many counter (offensive) fouls. Ryan had played professionally all over the world and had done well but Terry knew he needed more out of Ryan in order for the team to reach its goal and get back to the podium. Initially, Ryan also seemed to doubt that Terry could help them win a medal. However, as the positive energy built and the team enjoyed

Ryan Bailey - Team USA's hugely strong Center

success, Ryan bought in. The two men worked on technique extensively since it was Terry's belief that if Ryan could augment his undeniable brute strength with finesse and other technical skills, he would become an even more formidable player. For a big man, Ryan had unbelievable hands and the 1-2 combination of he and Tony was almost unstoppable. A hugely powerful center presence, Ryan led the team in offense. His ability to get position-forced opponents to drop onto him - which would then open up others for scoring opportunities – was immensely valuable. He also did a fantastic job on defense in critical moments. He drew exclusions, scored goals and although he did not say a lot, when he did talk to his teammates, everyone listened. Ryan became one of the best centers in the world.

Adam Wright – "Chuck" or "Riles" was a graduate from the University of California Los Angeles (UCLA). He was an attacker and could play both sides of the pool. Adam was the closest thing to having a coach in the water. He was a true student of the game and studied opponents more than anyone else. He was a veteran of the 2004 Olympic Games in Athens. When you looked at him, he didn't resemble the typical water polo player; not the most muscular or tallest guy, he nevertheless managed to outmaneuver anyone who doubted him. He was strong in the water and he knew how to use his body with good fundamentals to be highly successful at any position. Occasionally, he would even go in and post up an opposing player. He scored big goals, made huge assists and provided leadership to the team. He was an all-around valuable player who may have played as many minutes as anyone on the team in the Beijing Olympics. The team was better when Adam was in the water. In the biggest moments, Adam wanted to be in the water, and his presence helped the team immensely.

Adam Wright

Merrill Moses – known as "Moshie" was the first person that Terry called to come back to the team when he learned that he had been offered the assistant coach position in 2006. He had been cut from the team in 2004 and had quit playing to enter a lucrative career as a mortgage banker. Without hesitating, Merrill jumped back on board with the confidence and readiness upon which Terry knew he could always count. Having already played for him at Pepperdine University, Merrill was a critical force that helped lead the Pepperdine team to a national championship in 1997. Unremittingly consistent, confident, and some would say even 'cocky', Terry found that Merrill always backed up what he said he was going to do with action. Hungry and determined to prove himself on the international scene, Merrill worked hard to become the team's starting goalie. Terry will never forget the words that Merrill uttered during an important college game against University of California Los Angeles (UCLA). Terry had asked him if he had any preference who shot after UCLA had earned an exclusion and called for a time out for their 6 on 5. Merrill replied, "Coach, I don't care. I am going to block it no matter where they shoot from." He went on to do just that! In 2008, Merrill went on to become one of the world's best goalies – voted to the All-World team after the Olympics. The team's success in Beijing can be attributed to Merrill leading a team defense that was the best in the pool. Merrill was Mr. Clutch – the bigger the game - the more he would step up.

Jesse Smith – Pepperdine University center defender, Jesse had the skills to be the best player in the world. He was as strong as a bull and he could crush anyone with his powerful legs. No center enjoyed playing against Jesse, including Terry who used to get in the water with him at Pepperdine and play with the guys at practice. Jesse was the reason that Terry decided to quit playing! He had always felt he could beat anyone one-on-one with his leg strength – until Jesse came along. Making it look incredibly easy and

Goalkeeper Merrill Moses and Jesse Smith defend Team USA

using his leg strength, Jesse can push almost any center out of the strike zone and his hands would be up out of the water. He was undoubtedly one of the most powerful defenders in the world and he was also a very skilled attacker and shooter. Jesse was a complex individual. He could be super friendly and cordial, and then in the next moment he could be withdrawn and seemingly angry at the world. Every player and every coach on the team knew that Jesse could be a valuable asset when he was on. However, he tended to be inconsistent. Terry had dealt with this same issue when Jesse was at Pepperdine. When he wanted to be - he was the best player in the pool. He played a few games where he absolutely dominated, and then he had other games where he just seemed to be out of it. Jesse was the puzzle that Terry was determined to figure out; he could be phenomenal if he just got out of his own way. His abilities were awesome and his leg strength was unmatched.

Peter Varellas - "V ray"– was a left-handed attacker and a Stanford graduate. Smart, fast and extraordinarily talented, he was the only lefty to make the final Olympic team. Peter's role was vital, especially on the 6 on 5. The 6 spot (where a lefty plays) runs the 6 on 5. Peter did a superb job of helping the team to have a highly successful extra man. He scored some huge goals, made some beautiful assists and led the team on the counter attack with his speed and great swimming ability. He always displayed a mature, steady perspective and it was difficult to rattle him. From a coach/player perspective, Terry appreciated some

of the conversations he shared with this respectful player. The Varellas family adopted Lori and the girls on Terry's first tournament as the head coach. They were in Rio de Janeiro and the girls were stuck in a dumpy apartment in a less-than-safe area. The Varellas family invited the girls over to their Sheraton Hotel to hang out, eat some good food, and feel safe. This allowed Terry to focus on his role as coach and not worry about the safety of his family.

Peter Varellas

Photo by Curtis Dahl

Peter Hudnut - "Nut" or "Nutter Butter" was one of the team's center defenders. One of those paradoxes, he was a total gentleman outside the pool, but inside, he could be as mean as anyone. Peter was a center at Harvard-Westlake High School where his dad was Head Master. Terry had recruiting him heavily out of high school and felt he could have really helped him develop as a center but was not upset when Peter chose Stanford University. Definitely part of the "glue" that held the team together, Peter was a powerful and positive influence on the 2008 team. A 2-meter defender, he would go in and battle anyone. Often the voice of reason, Terry respected and supported Peter

Peter Hudnut

enormously. A fighter at heart – he would do anything and play any position or role to help the team win. His career was full of adversity. He bounced back from numerous injuries including a broken back and shoulder surgery and reinvented himself by learning to be a center defender. All through high school and college, and even early in his international career, Peter was a center. On the USA team, he learned to play a critical role as a much needed center defender and he filled that role to perfection.

Jeff Powers – "Pow Pow" was a star player out of UC Irvine. Jeff stood at 6 foot 7 inches tall and was one of the team's utility players, adept at playing any and all positions in the pool. His long, untanned frame led to another nickname "The White Whip." He could throw the ball harder than anyone on the team. He played whatever position Terry asked him to play. Against certain teams he was asked to be a center; with other teams he was asked to play center defender or attacker. So versatile was Jeff that his role often changed as the game progressed. He might start the game at center and then finish the game as a defender. During the Games he had some amazing shots/plays but none greater than the goal he scored in the 3rd quarter of the semi-final game in Beijing against Serbia - to break their backs. Jeff was instrumental in getting his team to the gold medal final.

Jeff Powers, Layne Beaubien and Merrill Moses - Beijing 2008 Olympics

Layne Beaubien – another Stanford graduate was a utility player known as "Beubs." Another very cerebral player, he was a great shooter on the perimeter. He scored many huge goals on the 6 on 5 for the team in Beijing. He was also a very skilled defender and perhaps the best center defender on the team's 5-man defense. His leadership and wisdom were greatly appreciated on the team. A veteran of the 2004 Olympic team, initially, Layne may have doubted that Terry was the right person to coach the team. He and some of the other veterans 'interviewed' Terry to make sure that he had a plan and was ready to lead the team (after Ricardo was let go). In the end, Layne became a big supporter. His buy-in and that of the other veteran players was critical to Terry's ability to be a successful leader.

Tim Hutten – The "Ice Man" was another University of Irvine (UCI) player who played center defender. He was also a post up player who had the strength to get deep on an opponent. One of the youngsters in the team, he was coming off a year at Irvine where he had won the Pete Cutino Award for being the

Tim Hutten

best collegiate player. Young, tough and energetic, he guarded well and posted up when the team needed help at set. He was also a big scoring threat from the perimeter. Tim was quiet but part of that might have been just being a youngster on a team of veterans. He was ultra polite but could be mean and tough when he needed to be. His nickname came from his calm demeanor and poker face even when fully engaged in battle with his opponent.

Rick Merlo - out of the University of California at Irvine, "Merl" was a utility player who was as tough as nails. Though he played the fewest minutes in Beijing of any player with the exception of Brandon (back-up goalie), he made some huge goals and made the most of his time. He played well on defense. A sharp shooter on the perimeter, Rick definitely earned his place in the team. He came in off of the bench and usually provided a spark - a vital role on the team. Rick was also super coachable and was willing to play whatever role he was asked to play to be a part of the team. He would go in and bang with the toughest of opponents and usually came out on top.

JW Krumpholz – "Dubs" was from the University of California (USC) and played center. At just 6 foot tall, JW was a long shot to make the team as a center. He was dominating the game in the college system – leading USC to multiple national championships. The question was - could he hold his own against the huge international guards? He made the team because he proved to Terry along the way that he could, indeed, handle guards much bigger than he. Fast and with great technique, he pushed the older guys to be better. He had a great Olympics and ended up with great stats for the minutes he played. In fact, for minutes played, his stats were as good as anyone's. As one of the younger players, he brought energy and challenged the older players to be better. Dubs also scored some big goals from the post position on the 6 on 5. He played the role he was given in 2008 perfectly and exceeded all expectations most admirably.

JW Krumpholz , Rick Merlo, Peter Hudnut, Jeff Powers - Beijing 2008 Olympics

Brandon Brooks – "Brooksie" was the back-up goalie (although he was the starter for Team USA in 2004). The 6-foot-6 inch University of Los Angeles (UCLA) athlete was super talented in many sports, including basketball. Terry was confident in Brandon's ability and experience to step in and play if something happened to Merrill. His role as a back-up goalie was something he managed superbly. While it may have killed him to sit on the bench and cheer for the team, he never once complained or had a poor attitude. He was a great team player and he longed to be part of a successful USA team. He had strong relationships with the other players and provided some outstanding leadership from a different perspective. Brandon was a joy to coach.

Robert Lynn was Terry's assistant coach. He had played with Terry on the national team in the late 80s and early 90s. In Terry's opinion, he should have made the Olympic team as a player in 1992. He was an amazing shooter/ attacker who played his college days at University of Southern California (USC). After the disappointment of not making the team in 1992, Robert went to Europe and played professionally where he became known as "Crazy Bob". He would do anything it took to help his team win including fight. No one wanted to mess with him. While playing Premier League in the U.S. in the late 90s he had his two front teeth knocked out by Peter Hudnut. This look also helped with the Crazy Bob persona. He finally made the U.S. Olympic team in 2000 but the team had a disappointing finish. He went back to Europe and played professionally for many more years before retiring to coach. Having played for some of the best coaches in Europe, and the world for that matter, Bob learned the game at a very deep level. His knowledge of the game and especially of European water polo would be invaluable for the success of the team in 2008.

Ryan Brown was the second assistant coach and goalie coach. He had played for University of Pacific (UOP) as a goalie. Reliable and loyal, Ryan spent endless hours with the goalies working on conditioning as well as technique. He also became a close friend to Terry - someone that Terry could go to and discuss anything at any time. This was very important because there are many lonely moments as the head coach to an Olympic team. Ryan did a great job of preparing the goalies to be ready in Beijing. Merrill and Brandon were two of the best at the Olympic Games, and Ryan deserves a great deal of credit.

Rick McKee – the team leader - had been involved with the game of water polo for many years as a coach. He joined USA Water Polo as a team leader after Ricardo was let go. Rick did endless hours of work behind the scenes - working with the coaches to prepare the travel/training schedule - and then following through with all the details to make each trip successful. Rick did a ton for the team and was often the liaison between USA Water Polo and the team. He was a good Christian man and Terry and Rick would often pray together on trips. His faith and friendship helped to keep Terry balanced.

The team arrived in Beijing almost 3 weeks prior to the Games and earlier than any other water polo team. The thought process was that there would be plenty of pool time available and they could train hard while they were acclimating and becoming familiar with their surroundings. One of the real advantages that Team USA had was that the USOC (United States Olympic Committee) had rented out Beijing Normal University and all of its facilities for the duration of the Olympic Games. This meant that the USA team would always have a pool and they did not have to worry about scheduling or perhaps taking an hour-long bus trip for a 90-minute practice. It also meant that the team could eat a home-cooked "American" meal at Beijing Normal daily.

USA team unity at the Beijing Olympics 2008

The USOC had also brought in chefs from home and while training at the university any USA team could eat breakfast, lunch or dinner there. The meals were so full of quality that they made the village food look like fast-food junk. Terry realized how important this was to his team and scheduled practice times around either lunch or dinner to give the team a break from the village food. There were also trainers, doctors and chiropractors available at Beijing Normal. A few of the other teams figured this out and made Beijing

Normal University their training base. USA Basketball trained there often and Terry's team enjoyed some casual moments with them on the court. Adam Wright even challenged Kobe Bryant to a game of HORSE! Adam lost badly when Kobe did a slam dunk directly over his head by jumping over him. This established a relationship with the basketball players.

A few days later at the opening ceremonies, all the athletes were staged at the fencing arena that was about a half-mile walk to the Bird's Nest where the opening ceremonies were to take place on 8/8/08. The Chinese were a bit superstitious about the number 8 being lucky so the Games were also to begin at 8 p.m.. In the staging area, athletes from each country were lined up with their respective countrymen. Terry's team found its way close to the USA men's basketball players who included Kobe Bryant, Carmelo Anthony, LeBron James, Dwyane Wade and company.

As Team USA marched out of the fencing arena and made their way towards the Bird's Nest, they stayed close to the basketball superstars. Terry found himself

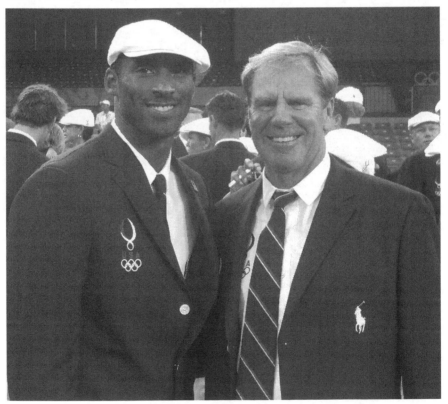

USA basketball giant Kobe Bryant with Terry Schroeder - Beijing 2008 Olympics

marching out directly next to Kobe, and as they came outside and were directed into the corridor that would lead to the Opening Ceremonies, a crowd of thousands of Chinese nationals had gathered to cheer on the athletes. These were mostly volunteers who could not get into the Ceremonies and there were only ropes that separated the crowd from cheering fans that were at least 50 deep in numbers. As the crowd recognized Kobe they began to chant KOBE KOBE KOBE. It was loud and crazy. By then Kobe was enjoying a conversation with Terry about water polo and the two athletes continued to walk alongside each other with Terry feeling like Kobe was his body guard! With each corner turned, the crowd would erupt and go crazy for the basketball icon. It's a moment Terry will never forget.

With the Games officially opened, it was time for Team USA to prove itself in the water. Game one was to be against up-and-coming host country China. They recently had made a huge effort to improve their game in all sports and they had greatly improved in water polo. They were big, physically strong and could swim well. They only lacked experience. As his team

Terry Schroeder with President George H. Bush - Beijing 2008 Olympics

Terry Schroeder with Laura Bush - Beijing 2008 Olympics

warmed up, Terry began to feel a pressure that he had never experienced before. Uncharacteristically, he began to doubt and question himself. Had he prepared the team properly? Were they ready? It was 30 minutes before game time and he was sweating profusely. He needed a quiet place to settle down and he found that peace in the team's unoccupied locker room. Getting down on his knees he prayed to God. It was a prayer of surrender and his words were: "God, this belongs to you. You are in charge. Give me the peace and strength to realize that and to allow your outcome to happen." With a renewed sense of calm, he headed to the team bench and never experienced that same sense of pressure again.

The Olympics is unquestionably an emotional experience. Nothing amplified that more poignantly than when Terry looked into the faces of each team member as they lined up. Ryan Bailey had lost his father unexpect-edly and shockingly 8 months before the Olympics, and since he was playing water polo in Serbia at the time of his death, he did not have time to grieve. When fathers and sons are close – particularly when they've shared a love for the same sport – their loss is felt sorely and deeply at a grand occasion like the Olympics. Terry immediately noticed tears streaming down Ryan's face as he stood on the pool deck, and knew instinctively what Ryan was feeling because Terry, too, had lost his father in 2005. This was the first time that both men were at the Olympics without their dads. The piercing sentiment is, "if only they could have been here with us". For two men who never showed their emotions in public, this was a watershed moment – one that they discussed after the game in sensitive detail. Terry simply said to Ryan: "Your dad is right here with you, and he is so proud of you".

With the commencement of the game against China, Terry was mentally at

The strength of Ryan Bailey

peace and ready to enjoy the moment. Team USA would dominate the game and despite some opening game jitters, they came out on top with a score of 8-4. Tony led the way with 5 goals followed by 2 from Layne. Merrill played solidly in the goal and the team defense in front of him looked impressive. The games were underway and with one win sealed, the team looked forward to a day off to prepare for Italy.

Twelve teams qualified for the water polo competition and there were two brackets of 6 teams each. On the USA side was China, Italy, Serbia, Croatia and Germany. This was also the order of the games. The bracket was set up to play a game and then have a day off. So for 10 days each team would play every other day. The winner of each bracket was awarded hugely by advancing directly to the semi-finals while the teams that finished 2nd and 3rd in each bracket would play in the quarter-finals for the right to play in the medal round.

The second game against Italy was a battle. Both teams played their hearts out. It was close all the way and in the end, Italy had a chance to tie the game on a 6 on 5 man advantage. The USA made the critical stop and won the game 12-11. It was a high-scoring game that really came down to a battle of 6 on 5 and 5 on 6. Jeff Powers finished with 3 big goals to lead the team in scoring and Tony added a pair. On reflection, Terry feels that this was a critical match. The team had beaten one of the top-ranked teams by winning the battle of 6 on 5 and 5 on 6. It provided great confidence moving forward with the rest of the tournament.

Next up was Serbia. The Serbs were loaded with talent and this would be the first time back in the pool against them since the debacle in February when the Serbian team had dismantled Team USA. The game began with a good pace for the American squad in a defensive battle. Unfortunately, Terry's team once again struggled with their 6 on 5 against the big Serbian men - struggling to find the shooting angles around the wide circumferences of the Serbian defenders. The final score was 4-2. Peter Varellas scored the only two goals for USA. Merrill had played exceptionally well in the goal, and the defense in front of him played well enough to win. In the post game meeting, Terry emphasized how the team had closed the gap between themselves and the Serbs and he let the team know that he was confident that if they had another chance to play them, the outcome would be different. Optimism was crucial and there was no time to wallow in defeat.

The next opponent was reigning world champion, Croatia. Their coach, Ratko Rudić, had been the head coach for Team USA from 2001 - 2004. Whatever people's private opinions may be about Ratko, he is widely respected for achieving so much with the teams he has coached. After a successful series with the Croatians in California a few months earlier, the team felt confident that they matched up well with Croatia. Once again, Merrill and the defense played exceptionally well, and Tony provided enough offense with 3 goals to help the team to a huge 7-5 win. At an appropriate moment after the game, Terry found Ratko in the locker room, and was quick to give him a great deal of sincere credit for what was happening with Team USA. This was a big win for them and it set up an enormous final game of the bracket play. Terry was elated with his team. Their 6 on 5 had come alive in this game and winning that battle of 6 on 5 and 5 on 6 against the best team in the world – was a significant feat. More importantly, they were playing together with confidence.

Everything was on the line in the final game of bracket play against Germany. The USA's team record of 3 - 1 put them in a tie for first place with Croatia and Serbia. By the time the USA played Germany they knew what they had to do. A win against Germany would assure Terry's team of the top spot in the bracket and place them in the semi-finals. It would also mean an extra day off to watch the 2nd and 3rd place teams play, rest and prepare for the semi finals. A tie would mean that the team would play in the quarter-final game, and a loss would result in a 4th place finish in bracket play, and then playing in the 5 - 8th place division. Germany was also a higher-ranked team prior to the Games but at this point that did not matter at all.

Team USA approached the game confidently knowing that their defense was proving to be a winning formula. Another heart stopper of a game would ensue. With time running down, Germany scored a goal that would have tied the game. However, because the shooter was inside the 5-meter foul line, and he had shot the ball after being fouled, the goal was disallowed. It was a nerve-wracking close call. Germany even threw an extra player in the pool at the last minute to give Terry's team a penalty throw. Their strategy was that if the Americans missed on a highly-pressurized penalty throw, then they would get the ball back and have another opportunity to tie the game.

A tie meant that the Germans would advance, so they were playing as if their lives depended on that critical few minutes. After a time-out call by Team USA to discuss their options, assistant coach Ryan Brown consulted with Terry about the rules which stated that he could refuse the penalty. Terry decided not to accept the penalty throw and instead, take the ball and run out the clock for an 8-7 win. Jeff Powers and Adam Wright both scored two goals to lead the team. Adam Wright had one of the best games of his life - making some keys steals and assisting on 3 other goals. Unbelievably, Team USA was in the semi-finals and their pent-up emotions found new freedom in the water after the game. So close to realizing their dream of getting back to the podium was the first major rush they experienced. With the win against Germany, the team also earned an extra two-day break – an important time to relax and restore as they prepared for their semi-final game.

Another unusual tactic that Terry adopted during the Games was to let the team spend valuable time with their families who had traveled to support them. He trusted his team members to make good choices while unwinding with their loved ones – and to stay off their feet as much as possible. His trust was well placed. This also gave Terry time to be with Lori and his girls so that they were able to celebrate Sheridan's 7th birthday on August 10th at the Hilton Hotel where they were staying.

Leanna, Sheridan and Lori Schroeder supporting Terry - Beijing 2008 Olympics

Blonde-haired, blue-eyed Leanna and Sheridan were a sensational hit in China. Everywhere Terry traveled with his family, they were constantly stopped – not to ask for the successful coach of a winning team's autograph – but to have their pictures taken with the two cute Californian blondies. While walking around Beijing, not one of the local nationals gave a hoot about Terry; it was all about his girls and his dry sense of humor absorbed this new reality wittingly.

Serbia would go on to win its quarter-final game, thereby setting up a rematch with Team USA in the semi-finals. Team USA had never beaten Serbia in a major competition since it had become a country following the ravaging Yugoslavian civil wars in the 1990s. The odds were heavily stacked against the USA as they went into the game as the definitive underdogs. In preparation for this game, the coaching staff spent hours going over game film. In particular, they were looking for holes in the 5 on 6 defense that Serbia was playing. They were fairly sure that Serbia would play the same type of game that they were good at – being hugely physical - with a lot of holding and grabbing. In fact, the Serbians were so confident in their 5-man defense that they were not afraid to take the exclusion and give their opponent 6 on 5 opportunities.

One thing was for certain, Team USA would have its opportunities - they just had to find a way to score when they were a man up. The game strategy was to play confidently and look for the quick opportunity; they would try to beat the Serbians' defense on the extra man situation before they had time to fully set up. The plan worked to perfection and Terry's team jumped out to an early lead with some great 6 on 5 goals.

Merrill Moses had a huge game against Serbia in the semi-final and USA's defense frustrated the Serbs immensely. Another tactic that worked effectively was to have some of the key Serbian players "break" by swimming them out of their normal positions. Aleksander Šapić, Serbia's alpha male in the game at the time, was substantially frustrated by the Americans' tactic and did not play well. Merrill shut him down on some key shots and the team forced him to swim out of position more times than he cared to count. It was as if Šapić's machine-like power seemed to dismantle as the Americans cornered him into disarray.

In the 3rd quarter with the Americans building confidence and beginning to smell an upset, Jeff Powers made an incredibly athletic move and scored a highlight-type goal to put the USA team up by 4 goals, and essentially break the Serbians' backs. The Americans would go on to win 10-5, their first-ever win against the Serbians. Tony led the team with 3 goals, and Layne and Big Bails added 2 each. The euphoric relief Team USA felt was inconceivable. The hundreds of hours spent working on their 6 on 5 play had just paid off magnificently, and there is nothing more affirming than hard work paying off

Terry Schroeder coaching at the 2008 Beijing Olympics

to that degree in the biggest of moments.

The tactical game plans the USA team applied permeated in all their games – not just against Serbia. They focused on playing great team defense and keeping the pace of the game in their favor. They knew they would get their opportunities on offense if they were patient. On the extra man, they ran pretty much one rotation and had some variations depending on how teams reacted to their movements. They became especially adept at this one 6 on 5 rotation during the Beijing Olympics and it produced significant success in each of their games.

Terry's opinion is summed up like this: "Nothing shows up more clearly whether a team is in sync or out of sync than the 6 on 5 or 5 or 6 situation. The team has to be working together in complete harmony; it is a true measure of how well everyone is working together. If one team member is having an off day, or someone feels like he has to be the hero and take a forced shot – it becomes painfully evident as the unity crumbles in that vital moment. But to watch a team whose unity is impermeably strong – is a beautiful sight best illustrated in a 6 on 5."

The USA ended up scoring 70% of their 6 on 5 opportunities in that game. When the final whistle was blown with the scoreboard reading 10-5, the faces caught on camera of Team USA were mirrors of complete elation. August 22, 2008 will go down as one of the finest days of their water polo lives. They outwitted a demolition team and the shock on the Serbians' faces painted the picture of the completely unexpected toppling of the giants. Tony's "do or die" plan with

Head Coach Schroeder and Assistant Coach Lynn celebrate from the bench

his teammates meant that the eagles had landed – back on the podium - and Terry couldn't have been more proud of his brilliantly performing underdogs.

Tony's role as superb captain cannot be emphasized enough. He inspired his teammates to reach deep inside of themselves – to find that elusive piece of untapped potential – and let it loose at the crucial moments. Each man on the team played with extraordinary flair. For the spectators,

Terry Schroeder celebrating one of his team's victories at the 2008 Beijing Olympics

those Olympic moments where athletes display superhuman talents beyond anyone's imagination – provide the thrilling experiences that make the Olympic Games what they are. That semi-final win against Serbia is one of the finest team wins for a USA team. All the players from the most veteran to the youngest player on the team contributed to the victory. Merrill Moses' part as a dominating goalie was inestimably valuable but he certainly could not have done what he did without the defense playing as well as they did in front of him.

From Terry's perspective, his conclusion is voiced like this: "We became a family and everyone felt that. The confidence and belief that this team had heading into the Games was huge. I was honored to be a part of this team."

For the first time in 20 years, USA Men's Water Polo had made it into an Olympic Gold Medal Final Game. The last time they had made it this far was when Terry was captain of the 1988 team in Seoul, and the last time the USA won a gold medal in the sport was in 1904. Just from a podium perspective, it had been a long, dry 20 years of disappointment with lost dreams and frustrated misses permeating USA Men's Water Polo. At last, the accomplishment of achieving their dream: To Get Back to the Podium – was in the bag. They were now in a position to win that gold medal. Barely able to sleep the night before the big game, the 13 men arrived at Beijing's Ying Tung Natatorium for the Gold Medal Final against Hungary – the powerhouse.

To put this into perspective – Hungary was on the confident pedestal of coming off two consecutive Olympic Gold Medal wins in the 2000 and 2004 Olympics. Everybody feared them, and they had that upper hand of psychological dominance. Terry had often contended that genetically, Hungarians were born to play water polo. They also had the advantage of learning to play the game at a very young age and it was their national sport.

Terry's journal recounted the day of the gold medal final:

August 24, 2008, Beijing Olympics
It's Gold Medal Sunday in Beijing! Our last day as an Olympic Team against Hungary. It is ours to win. I believe that we will get a fair game and have our opportunities. We have to score 6 on 5. Our percentages 6 on 5 or 5 on 6 have been good, and that is one of the big reasons we are in the championship game.

We did our warm-up in the Olympic Village pool and so did Hungary. They seemed to be very confident; they smiled and were laughing together. They were surprised that we had made it so far, and yet, I am sure that they are happy to be playing the USA; after all, they anticipated having to play one of the higher-ranked teams like Serbia and they had the perception that a team like that would be more difficult to beat than us. After watching us play the day before, I do think they had to have a little respect for us, perhaps even fear us a little. We earned the respect of the water polo world with our efforts in these games; I couldn't help but feel a sense of pride about that. Many of the other coaches kind of blew me off prior to the start of the Games, and now almost every one of them has made it a point to come over and say, "Congratulations." They looked me in the eye and said, "Great job." They have seen what a different team we changed into from only two years prior, and they understand the coaching effort it took to arrive at this place.

At our pre game team meeting we discussed many tactics that we needed to use in order to win the gold medal game, as well as all that we had accomplished to earn the right to play in Beijing. The challenges those guys had to beat ranged from internal team conflict to shaking off a negative U.S. water polo image that saturated the world. When the Games began, even the key people at the U.S.O.C. didn't believe we were good enough to accomplish anything significant but we dealt with our adversities and forged ahead to be noticed as worthy of our spot at the Olympics.

At the end of today, we will either be the best or second best team in the world! If we can just keep playing with the focus, drive and skill with which we have been playing so far, we can actually take this game. I told the guys, "This is our opportunity! Don't be satisfied with the silver. Fight on every possession – win every battle. Give 100% of yourselves – mentally, physically and emotionally". As I remembered back to my friend Igor Milanović in 1988 telling me that Yugoslavia simply wanted the gold more than we did, I said to the guys, 'Fight for the gold! Don't let Hungary want it more than us. You are the best water polo team in the world. Believe it and play like you know it."

The final Gold Medal game of USA against Hungary geared up to an antici-patory explosion point. Team USA felt confident in their abilities because their dynamic defensive play throughout the Olympics had outsmarted all their opponents. Statistically they had been holding teams to just 6 goals per game. They needed to play one more game with this same style and intensity.

The tempo of the game started badly for Team USA. Dauntingly quickly, it turned into a shoot-out and this gave the Hungarians the advantage. While they were shooting the lights out, Team USA responded by matching them point for point. Hungary would forge ahead and Team USA would catch up. At half time, the score was 9-8 to Hungary. While there was hardly any dif-ference in the score, the Hungarians were still loaded with great shooters who appeared to be super-humanly inviolable.

Early in the 3rd quarter, Team USA was tied with Hungary. It seemed at that moment that the gold medal was in sight. However, during that last half of the game, Team USA's 6 on 5 failed. After going 5 for 5 in the first half, they were 0 and 6 in the second half. Eventually, the pace of the game – which the Hungarians had set early on - caught up with the Americans. Ideally, Team USA needed to play at their pace, and this would have set the tempo of the game. The Hungarians took control like only they can – and Team USA went into reactionary mode. Their adversaries were simply too good that night. The final score was 14-10 to Hungary.

Even though hindsight is always rich, Terry has often wondered if he made a mistake by creating the mantra – Back to the Podium. If that was the ultimate team goal – they'd already achieved it. They had won the silver medal merely by beating Serbia. Had the team settled with that achievement? Maybe they weren't as hun-gry for that gold medal aspiration as they were for just the podium medal aspiration?

Terry muses, "As crazy as it seems, we may not have been quite as focused on winning the gold. We may have relaxed just a bit and let down our guard - and

Team USA defending at the Beijing 2008 Olympics

that is all it takes. Merrill was not quite himself. Our defense was not playing as well in front of him either. Putting Brandon in was an attempt to make a change and spark the team. Brandon had played in 2004 so he had experience and he was hungry to prove himself. Merrill had brought us to this point so it was a difficult decision to pull him; however, looking back, it was the right move. Brandon made some big saves, but it simply wasn't enough. In the end, I believe that Hungary was more experienced in this type of pressurized gold-medal-at-stake situation. While we were newbies to the gold medal game, the Hungarians had become veritable experts with countless gold medals – but particularly so for this group - who had already notched away 2 gold medals in the last two Olympics. We were playing against a veteran group whose experience had made them experts in the gold medal games."

Terry continues: "Winning the silver was my 3rd experience of 'we just missed the gold,' and it's a bitter sweet sensation. Bronze medal winners celebrate their victory, but silver medalists lose the gold. It's a confusing paradox. There is not much sense of victory in that, unfortunately. However, as far as America was concerned, we were winners – and in the big picture, we were. I was so proud of the team and all that they had accomplished. As I watched Team USA stand on the second tier of the podium, I cried like a proud parent, excited for them and at the same time, sad that they didn't get the gold that they had worked so hard for, and which I knew they wanted so badly."

Terry's journal entry after the ceremony reads:

August 27, 2008
Another silver medal; my heart is a little heavy, though I could not be more
proud of the team. Having been in their shoes, I know first hand what the
guys are going through....they fought hard, but not hard enough to be gold
medal winners -- it stings deeply. But after the game I felt it was my job
to emphasize what went well and the accomplishments we achieved as a
team. My locker room talk to the guys after the gold medal game was
simple. "Yes it hurts now and that is what made us good. We have learned
to be winners; we had become used to winning, we expected to win, and
so losing hurts. However, as time passes, each of you will realize what an
amazing accomplishment this has been and you will be proud of yourself
and of each other. I am proud of each of you and I feel honored to have been
your coach. Thank you for allowing me to share this journey with you."

With that, another Games was over. Reflecting back, it has been
an incredible journey, filled with success really. Yes, at times I had my
doubts. There were times where it felt as though I was walking through
a mine field, and it could all have blown up if I, or anyone, had taken
one wrong step. Despite that, we grew together and we experienced
some small successes and we built on those. We learned to appreciate
each other and our differences. This is what respect is all about. We
learned to trust each other and care for each other. Yes, it may sound
mushy, but we learned to love each other and, ultimately, it is this love
that carried us to the Games together. We could not have accomplished
all that we did without this love. I certainly felt it for each of the guys.

Coaches do not receive a medal at the Olympics, but I feel like I got
one anyway because honestly, my medal is the relationship with each
one of these guys and the life memory that we have created together. I
am a blessed man to have shared this journey with this special group.

The Beijing 2008 Olympics would turn out to be one of the best experiences
of the entire team's lives. It entered into the realm of surreal accomplishments as the naysayers watched the USA men dismantle their supposedly
indestructible opponents, game by game. All the critical elements that bring
out the best in a team have to work synergistically at the right time and at the
right place. It's impossible to orchestrate all those moving parts like a machine
because some of it revolves around heart and passion – and those things can't

be ordered to switch on. But for this special group of 13 players who were unified tightly, the opportune moments played right into their hungry hearts and the team chemistry kicked in when they needed it most - producing those "wow" moments that pumped up everyone's adrenaline levels during the crucial 16 days.

Terry was able to relive all the elements that made him respect everything he loved about the Olympics. All the flood of emotions and layers of excitement that he had felt in 1984 and 1988 cascaded back like a waterfall as he returned to realize his Olympic dream as head coach. With brave hearts and gargantuan fortitude, every person on Terry's team excelled in their role, and as the days marched on, Terry couldn't have been more elated at the herculean effort that each team member made.

The Beijing Olympics ended in a way that felt right for the team. Instead of attending the closing ceremonies, all they wanted to do was spend time with their family and friends who had flown all the way to China to support them. So the team – together with the people who mattered most to them - headed over to the USA House in Beijing to celebrate their Back to the Podium accomplishment. With tears welling in his eyes, Terry said to the men he'd come to love, "As long as you live, you are an Olympic Medalist; no one can ever take that from you. This is something you share for the rest of your lives. I am so proud of each one of you. You are a very special group of men. "

Adam Wright recounts the success he and his fellow teammates' shared in Beijing in these words: "Terry Schroeder has the unique and rare ability to bring a collection of people together and make them function as a united team - in oneness with each other. When Terry took over our USA National team in 2007, we were in a very bad place. We had been through so much over the span of 5 years, and Terry – who was our 4th coach in a 5-year span - was thrust into a very difficult position of trying to quickly repair our team. Despite being a dedicated group, we were in a bad mental state. Terry had less than a year to put the pieces back together in order for us to have a chance to be successful, and he started at the foundation of re-establishing relationships within our group. He also knew how critical it was to establish trust again between the players and the staff. It is hard to put a finger on how he was able to do this but I would say the following characteristics in Terry made it happen: Compassion: he is the most caring person and he wants to get to the core of each person so that he can establish a relationship. Even keeled: I am not sure how Terry never lost his composure while coaching us over a 6-year period (into London 2012). Never once did he lose his emotional control. This is something that I truly look back at with awe. He would never make something bigger than it needed to be. Within a team, there are always going to be issues, and sometimes those issues are blown up. Terry controlled this from happening, which I know was critical to our success. Love: he truly cares for his friends and his friends are his athletes. On a personal level, Terry has been there for me in tough times as he has been down the same road we all have. It is not easy to adjust to a mainstream life after an Olympic career. Your world comes to a crashing end, and he was there to help and mentor all of us. As a coach, I try to remember those things Terry did to put us in a position to be successful. Those invaluable lessons have made me a much better person."

After International Olympic Committee President Jacques Rogge declared the Beijing Olympics one of the most "truly exceptional Games" – Team USA's 13 men agreed – albeit tiredly - as they boarded the United Airlines airbus the next day, and flew home to California and a welcome they will forever cherish.

Terry felt a warmth deep in his soul as her returned home to spend more time with family. The task of "getting back to the podium" had been completed and he knew that his work had paid off. It was a dream completed - and yet there was a little voice in his head reminding him that Team USA was so close - and just maybe - that gold medal could be earned in 2012. His Olympic journey was not yet over.

Lori, Sheridan, Leanna and Terry Schroeder - 2015

Mermaids Sheridan & Leanna- Hawai'i 2016

CHAPTER 17

The Healing Waters of Family and
the Maui Mermaids

Love is that condition in which the happiness of
another person is essential to your own
– Robert Heinlein

In March 2017, Terry and Lori celebrate their 30-year marriage anniversary. They feel genuinely blessed to have experienced such a full life together with two beautiful daughters, and if there's one piece of wisdom they've acquired through this process, it is that parenting is humbling. Leanna and Sheridan have taught them essential lessons about life, and without that experience, they would not be the progressively honed adults they are. It is their fervent hope that the girls will continue to fill their lives with growth in the most unexpected places.

Parenting has brought Terry and Lori some of the greatest joy in their lives but as with anything miraculous, there is also heartache and pain. The challenges lie in trying to balance family time with work and play while creating healthy boundaries in the juggling act of being a parent and a friend.

One of the most difficult challenges is providing enough support so that their children can be successful while not over-indulging them so that they lose all initiative and maintain the chains of dependence. Raising children successfully is about balancing discipline and giving them strong flippers to be able to swim off on their own one day. While mom and dad need to nurture their own relationship by creating date nights, it is also imperative that children know that their parents are there for them – always.

The parenting odyssey requires constant communication, something the Schroeder family has learned well, and the journey, although far from perfect, continues with their all-in passion.

Terry's and Lori's childhood experiences shaped them multi-dimensionally, and they've tried to reconfigure the type of home they want to provide for their girls. Terry's sun-flecked, water-saturated upbringing in Santa Barbara, California was the ideal island-like launch pad to the success he enjoyed in aquatics. His parents loved him unremittingly, devoting most of their time and energy to their three children, often placing their own relationship behind their parental duties.

Terry is sure that his parents loved each other but they floundered in their ability to show each other that love. Date nights were rare for mom and dad Schroeder as they seemed to devote all of their spare energy to ferrying Terry, Lance and Tammy to their various activities. Unlike his father, Frederick, Bob's all-encompassing mission was to provide a stable home for his children and consequently, Terry witnessed little affection between his parents.

Bob Schroeder was always the unquestionable head of the household. A passionate man who wore his heart on his sleeve, he sometimes let emotions overrule him and his outbursts were tornado-like. Terry and Lance experienced their father's wrath on more occasions than they cared to remember when Pat – who had reached her maternal limits on controlling their rambunctious boyhood mischief – would report to Bob that the boys had misbehaved. When he returned home from a fully-charged day healing patients, his benevolent resources were fully tapped out. Upon receiving Pat's news, he'd explode into a belt-whipping tirade as he set about punishing Terry and Lance. When they knew that they were in trouble, both boys would prepare for dad's homecoming by putting on a second pair of underwear to soften the blow.

Once, on a road trip to Las Vegas, with Terry and Lance sitting next to each other beside Grandma in the back seat of their family station wagon, predictably, they grew bored and decided to start a wrestling match in the backseat. Having been told to stop one too many times, Bob pulled the car over to the side of the freeway, yanked the boys out, and ordered them to pull their pants down so that he could whip them resoundingly with his belt. The corporal punishment upset Grandma, who pleaded with her son-in-law to stop spanking her grandsons! It was like a horror film version of *National Lampoon* as motorists charged past the Schroeder station wagon – witnessing two young boys being disciplined with their pants pulled down to their knees. Today, Bob may well have ended up being charged for his choices in discipline but in the 1960s, punishing children in this manner was not uncommon.

While the *National Lampoon* family travels now elicit a chuckle from Terry, they were also some of his most difficult memories of his dad. While

Bob was capable of great love and affection towards his children, he was also capable of leaving physical and emotional scars that Terry and Lance handled differently. Terry tended to take on the responsibility as older brother while Lance stoically dug in his heels – determined to show his dad that he could never break him.

Years later after Bob's death, Lance would communicate to Terry that he felt he had been abused physically and mentally. This was perplexing to Terry who had usually reasoned that both he and Lance had mostly deserved what they had received. These differing perceptions are interesting when dissecting siblings' feelings. Most of the time, Terry gave Bob the benefit of the doubt by earnestly believing that he was doing the best he could as a parent - teaching his sons to respect their elders while behaving 'properly'.

In those early years when Bob's voice was raised – either to the boys or to Pat – Terry desperately sought peace. He became an expert at tactics that brought down the temperature in the room and returned the pressure chamber to a state of normalcy. The mission of being the family's peacemaker has stayed with Terry all through his adult life, and Pat was an admirable model of that approach. Her gentleness and her calm demeanor won Terry's respect and he became determined to emulate his mom's humble spirit. Drama and emotional outbursts produce a disturbing visceral response in Terry, and he instinctively drives towards dispersing the conflict – dispelling the drama that was an unhappy part of his boyhood.

This in large part explains Terry's unshakeable disposition in the water polo pool. Many opponents tried to rattle Terry and break his laser-sharp focus but they picked the wrong audience in Schro. Immune to outbursts of anger, aggression and histrionics, Terry always swam away from them like a calm, unidirectional submarine – impervious to what he perceived as unnecessary energy wasted. A coach once said about Terry, "you could hit him on the head with a 2 X 4 and he would still remain focused on the scoreboard." His Swedish genes, combined with his boyhood experience, melded him into an implacably calm water polo machine.

In keeping with his gargantuan, passionate personality, Bob's impact on Terry was immense. He never did anything in half measures and wanted his son to succeed from an early age. Oftentimes in those fledgling years, his own ambitions for Terry superseded what Terry wanted and he often pushed his son beyond his comfort zone. The 06h00 swimming training at the YMCA was brutal, but in retrospect, Terry is grateful for the swimming speed and endurance he developed and the discipline that those days imbued in him. Perhaps

Bob knew better and Terry needed to be pushed during those early years. In actuality, he was helping Terry build the foundation for success later in his life.

In time, Terry would come to develop his own goals and ambitions, and once he did that, Bob and Pat supported him in every way. It was during his school years at San Marcos High in Santa Barbara when Terry really became focused on making it to the Olympic Games in water polo. Once his own internal combustion engine was on fire, Bob realized his role from thereon could change. He no longer needed to push his son at each juncture. What Terry needed more than anything at this stage was encouragement, love and support.

Over the years, fellow athletes and coaches have come to study the Schroeder discipline and intensity. Alex Rodriguez, an assistant coach at Pepperdine University, who had a reassuringly positive impact on Terry, said to him one day, "It must be really difficult to live with you because you have such high expectations of yourself and everyone around you. It is exhausting trying to keep up with you."

Once Terry stopped to analyze what Alex had said, he had a light-bulb moment: Lori had probably been trying – for years - to figure out a way of deftly communicating with her husband that his intensity and his expectations of her were immoderate. Occasionally, Lori would have enjoyed a break from the daily, pursuit-of-perfection goals. Only once in a blue moon could she convince her Olympic-driven man to unplug, watch a movie, and munch popcorn with her – without feeling guilty. Because of Alex's words and Lori's communication skills, Terry learned that he needed to tone down his all-encompassing drive. He also learned that he needed to figure out how to be more content with downtime and quiet time spent with his wife and family. Recognizing that there is so much more to life than achievement, he could still focus on becoming a better version of himself without making others feel badly about themselves.

As time has progressed, Terry has learned that everyone has his or her own personal definition of high expectations. While he still tries to help those around him achieve greater success in their own lives, particularly in his role as a water polo coach and in his capacity as a chiropractor, he no longer tries to insert his numbers into the equation.

When it comes to parenting Leanna and Sheridan, Terry and Lori have stood resolutely united in the recognition that it's unfair to impose their goals and aspirations onto their girls. While they encourage and support their daughters' choices, they've tried to find the balance between pushing and encouraging their daughters towards success. Children will often choose to take the easy way out and they need a gentle push from a parent at times. Terry feels certain that without his dad pushing him, he would have never achieved half of what he did. But ideally, it is not about Terry's or Lori's ambitions for their children. It's about empowering Leanna and Sheridan, and setting an admirable example so that they are equipped to make good choices.

When Bob passed away in 2005, the pain Terry felt was palpable. His dad had been his rock, a solidly reliable force in his life, and his passing made him realize that as the eldest Schroeder son, it was his turn to take up the leadership position in the family – to step up into the vacuum that Bob left - and embrace his role as a father, husband, brother and son.

At the age of 12, Leanna was alone with her dad when he received the news that his father had passed away. Lori was out of town visiting her sister, so Terry had no one to hold him. Leanna saw her father sobbing, came to him, and just held onto him with a giant hug. Her mature words melted right into Terry's heart as she said: "Grandpa is in heaven now dad. It is going to be OK. I love you." Those words from his 12-year-old daughter were exceptionally comforting and he will never forget that day. Leanna's strength has always been imbedded in her resolutely unshakeable faith – the depths of which have often left her parents emotionally moved.

Just as all children learn from their parents' behavior, Terry was determined to continue his father's legacy by being a dedicated, world-class chiropractor and a devoted family man; but he was determined to improve on the balance between being a loving husband and a supportive father.

While Terry witnessed a less-than-perfect relationship between his parents, Lori also witnessed a great deal of brokenness in her family. When she was only 3 years old, she experienced how divorce broke a family apart. Once again, both parents were doing the best they could but they fumbled without the right healing tools - falling short in a divided family. Lori's dad, Bill, was orphaned at the age of 8, and learned to survive and thrive on his own. He had no concept of stable family life and although he has been married 3 times, he raised 3 daughters virtually single-handedly while running a successful business. Being the family's only means of income, he rarely went to watch Lori play sports or witness her accomplishments. Regardless, he was the only rock Lori knew during those early years when a broken family was her norm. Bill has now been married to Susan for 37 years – but that stability in marriage only occurred when Lori was 19 and past her formative years.

Childhood histories create lessons, and for Terry and Lori, their fervent pact at the beginning of their marriage was to do a better job of nurturing their own love with parenting. Their honeymoon in Turtle Island, Fiji was a promising foundation to the shaping of their marriage. When they finally had Leanna and Sheridan, they always wanted their daughters to witness how much they loved each other. Both Lori and Terry felt strongly that it was healthy to grow up in a home where physical affection was natural, and where showing appreciation for one another with affirming gestures, hugs, kisses and kindness – were the tenements for love to grow and flourish.

Most importantly, there is little tolerance for yelling or shouting in the Schroeder home. The goal is always to resolve issues by communicating clearly with one another – long before tempers have room to flair. Of course the perfection of this model doesn't always happen, but the intention of choosing a better route than an anger flair-up is always a priority.

Being honest at all times is an unsaid expectation, and communicating in a kind and solution-oriented manner is always the objective. Terry will be the first to admit that he has not always been the best parent at this. There are times when he has come home physically and emotionally drained from the

Sheridan and Leanna, the Maui Mermaids - New Year 2016

Lori and Terry in Maui

Terry and Lori on Lori's
50th birthday celebration

Lori and dad Bill Bell on her 50th birthday

office or coaching his athletes - and the girls have tested his patience. A deep breath and the images of his dad losing his temper usually help to reel him in.

Terry and Lori have earnestly tried to be parents who earn respectability and trust from their children by setting the example with the life they live. There is nothing worse than a parent saying one thing while his actions contradict those words. The clear chain of love and command in the Schroeder home is God first, Terry and Lori second, and the children, a very important third.

The most important rule that Terry and Lori have tried to live by as parents is the golden rule: Do unto others as you would have them do onto you. They constantly re-center themselves towards that ideal at all times.

The fascinating topic of DNA replication is most certainly evident and on display in Leanna and Sheridan. Leanna is much like Lori in temperament, and Sheridan takes after Terry – but the similarity from both parents in the girls' athletic abilities is undeniable. Leanna is a gifted beach volleyball player enjoying the challenge of being a part of Pepperdine's nationally-ranked team, while Sheridan is in her sophomore year of high school and playing libero on the team's indoor volleyball team.

Terry and Lori have never pressurized the girls to take up water polo. If anything, they've dissuaded them from that path because they know how hard it would be to have constant comparisons made to their father. They are determined to let Leanna and Sheridan be their own people while encouraging them to follow their passion. If the girls had taken up water polo, Terry believes that it would have been much more difficult for him to just be a fan rather than try to be too much of a coach. This has been an interesting dilemma for Terry; his knowledge of what it takes to be successful in sports is clearly almost unmatched - having played and coached in 6 Olympic Games - and it is excruciatingly difficult for him not to want to coach his girls. He has learned over the years to be gentle with his daughters while trying to be a good listener - and to give feedback mostly when asked. While this has helped to keep the relationships with his daughters healthy, he wonders if he has not pushed them towards their potential as much as he could have.

Terry is often asked if he wants his girls to represent the USA in the Olympic Games like he did. It is a difficult question for him. On one hand, nothing would make him happier than to watch his daughters participate in the Olympic Games. There has been nothing more powerful and emotional for Terry than to watch his girls play and be successful in sports – be it at high school, college or club sports. The great joy he feels in his heart has brought tears to his eyes on many occasions. Supporting his and Lori's daughters is about giving them every opportunity to pursue and realize their dreams. On the other hand, if either Leanna or Sheridan were to become an Olympian, Terry and Lori know only too well that the lifestyle is a difficult one to balance due to the fast paced, often stressful and one-dimensional focus required to succeed at that level. This is not to say that this balance cannot be achieved. For now, Terry and Lori will continue to support Leanna and Sheridan in pursuing their own dreams, and if one of them were to make it to the Olympic Games, they would enjoy that adventure.

Some of Terry's best parenting memories are of simple drives down to Orange County, California for a club volleyball tournament on the weekend. The tournaments are usually on a Saturday or a Sunday, and the athletes need to be on the courts by 07h00. This necessitates a 05h30 departure from the Schroeder home in the dark with the girls sleeping in the car for the first half hour, and then they awake as the sun begins to rise in the east. On many of these day-breaking drives, Leanna and Sheridan have entered into the most in-depth father daughter conversations about some things that are important, and some things that definitely aren't. But it all paints a relationship tapestry that is as powerfully moving as God creating his own masterpiece in the sky with a stunning sunrise.

Fittingly, some priceless Schroeder family stories revolve around sports: Sheridan's competitiveness showed while playing American Youth Soccer Organization as a 6-year-old. There were no goalies, just empty nets, and Sheridan took advantage of that and scored 8 to10 goals per game.

The following year was frustrating for her because, suddenly, there were goalies and she was being shut out. After that, soccer lost its appealing luster for her. Instead, she turned her attention to other sports. Through the Olympic Games, Special Olympics and Reebok competitions, Terry and Lori had become good friends with Rafer Johnson and they had often shared with Sheridan what a great inspiration Rafer was in their lives; he was an Olympic champion in the decathlon and an amazingly humble giant in the sports world.

When Sheridan found out that there was a Rafer Johnson Award in the youth league of track and field, she decided that this was what she definitely wanted to do, and she set her determined mind on winning. In order to accomplish that, the potential-winning athlete had to compete and finish 6 events in one day. 8-year-old Sheridan was not the most gifted runner but she made it through the day, completed all the events, and Rafer himself would later present her with the trophy. She beamed with absolute delight.

Leanna proved how much of a natural athlete she was when she tried out

Sheridan about to win the
Rafer Johnson Award

for water polo in high school and made the team. In her first game she scored a beautiful backhand goal. She had never done it before but had methodically watched this magical shot by paying close attention at her dad's teams' games. The combination of water polo and volleyball caused a conflict in managing her time and resources, so she chose to stay with volleyball. The power and simplicity of witnessing Leanna make a giant "kill" in volleyball or watching Sheridan make a great "dig" brings a special kind of elation to Terry and Lori. Of course, all parents enjoy watching their children be successful.

A powerful de-stressing component in the Schroeder home is their unshakeable conviction in God's timing. When Terry looks back on the most stressful years of their lives, he realizes that the anxiety was entirely unnecessary because during all the uncertainty, God worked His plan despite all the medical procedures and the crashing disappointments of 13 in vitro attempts in order to have their first child. Leanna was brought into the world from the precarious odds of a Grade B frozen embryo that only had a 7% chance of implantation in the uterus. Today, Leanna is a tall, strong Amazonian beauty – and the wonder of how perfect she is – still brings her parents to grateful tears.

Leanna's strong and muscular body has definitely assisted Terry in feeling more comfortable now with her dating but this was not always the case. As a 16-year-old, his precious daughter was asked to go to a high school senior's prom. Terry and Lori had mixed emotions about it because Leanna was still so young. To complicate matters, the prom and the boy were up in Santa Barbara, California. So, Terry and Lori finally agreed to the date on the grounds that they would stay at Lance's and his wife Julie's home in Santa Barbara so as to be close at hand – and a strict curfew time was laid out to Leanna's suitor.

The evening turned out to be more tortuous for Terry than an Olympic gold medal game going south. Instead of just hanging out with Lori, Lance and Julie, he began to pace the house like a tormented bear in the woods. Since going to sleep was completely out of the question, the rest of the Schroeder family shouldered Terry's night of purgatory as he waited for 'the young man' to deliver his daughter home safely. As the curfew minutes approached, Terry stood guard at the front door like an overbearing patriarch. Finally, when Leanna appeared up the driveway a few minutes later than the curfew deadline, Terry thrust the door open, stared at her date with suspicion, and then finally exhaled like a man who had just completed a marathon. His daughter was home safely after one of the longest nights of his life – and he thudded off to bed – exhausted. His misery was finally over!

Terry's girls have brought a balance into his life that eclipses anything the Olympics could have done for him. So much of the first quarter of his life was one-dimensional - entirely focused on medaling at the podium. The Olympics consumed Terry, but as he held his daughters for the first time, he realized that being a dad brought him a sense of fulfillment that was intoxicating. He relishes any weekend where he is able to hang out with his girls and be a part of their exciting lives. Their humor reminds him about perspective, offering light reprieve from his world of serious tasks.

Terry vividly remembers when Leanna was just 4 years old. She sat down on a wall, called her dad over and said, "Sit down, dad; it's a free country." The comment struck Terry on two fronts: firstly, he realized what an absorbent sponge his young daughter was, and secondly, he recognized how brilliant she was at grounding him. Lesson understood!

Leanna seemed to be able to hold her own early on too. When she was two years old and attending swim lessons at the Daland Swim School, Ingrid, the wife of famous swimming coach Peter Daland, was giving her a lesson. At one point Leanna was struggling and the water works turned on. Ingrid, a voluptuously endowed, no-nonsense, tough German lady blurted at Leanna, "Be a big girl – don't cry". Leanna looked back at her through the film of tears and retorted, "Big boobies!"

Family vacations have been integral to the balance of work and play in the Schroeder family. Their trips together have provided much-needed quality time and the gravitational power of water has been one of the central themes. There have been numerous fishing trips with the girls including the entire Schroeder clan: Lance and his family, Tammy and her family, and Terry and Lori's clan with grandma all spending 5 days at the Klamath river - salmon fishing. It's a great environment for them to bond while creating and sharing indelible memories.

But the uniquely poignant trips have comprised of Terry taking either Leanna or Sheridan on a daddy/daughter Alaskan fishing trip. Both girls love

Leanna and Terry in Hawai'i 2016   Terry and Sheridan in Alaska

the great outdoors and have always thrived out in the wilds while displaying significant fishing skills.

Both of them have also showed their weight in gold when it has come to toughing it out in the bare elements. Terry's first trip to Alaska was inspired by his dad, and continuing that legacy is something he cherishes. Alaska was and always will remain one of his all-time favorite destinations.

After Bob passed away, Terry took Leanna to Sitka, a location that he, Lance and their dad had often enjoyed. The place turned out to be the perfect healing spot for Terry, who was still grieving the loss of his dad. The beautiful countryside of Alaska was the healing canvas but the essential beauty painted on it was having Leanna there to comfort him. She was the best fishing mate he could possibly have had. While on this fishing vacation, Terry was reading a book called 'Heaven' by Randy Alcorn, and Leanna's faith, combined with her perfectly-timed comments on Alaska resembling heaven, was a deeply restorative experience.

On Terry and Leanna's second trip to Sitka, Leanna proved just how tough she was. After downing a quick eggs benedict breakfast, they boarded their boat in the harbor across the way, but nature began pounding with waves that rocked the boat mercilessly. Unluckily for Leanna, her eggs benedict decided to take a leave of absence within 20 minutes of the blustering waves. After retching everything out of her system, Terry offered to have them return to shore, but Leanna adamantly stuck to the plan and insisted that they continue their epic adventure. That incident spoke volumes about her fortitude. After a few hours of lying inside the boat, she emerged smiling and took up the fishing challenge. That day she caught far more fish than Terry!

On Sheridan's trip with dad, they were fishing for silver salmon out of Seward, Alaska. The first day went smoothly, but mighty Neptune decided to cook up a storm on the second day. Just 18 minutes after the boat made it out, a scene reminiscent of 'The Deadliest Catch' brought giant waves crashing over the hull, forcing the captain to turn back.

The day could have been lost but Terry and Sheridan made a plan after breakfast to explore, and what an adventure they had as they found a quiet river in which to fish and enjoy the spectacular scenery. Like big sis, Sheridan also turned out to be a rock star fisherperson. To this day, she continues to be an expert at fishing for bass at their home on Lake Sherwood, California.

In 2008, Terry invited two of his most experienced fishermen on the USA Water Polo team, Jeff Powers and Tim Hutten, out for a day of fishing on Lake Sherwood. After around 90 minutes of fishing, Sheridan had caught 8 bass and Jeff and Tim had caught zero! Sheridan hooked into another and as she was reeling it in, she looked at Jeff and Tim and asked, "Do one of you want to reel it in for me?" The men were suitably embarrassed that a 7-year-old girl was out fishing them.

Other memorable family trips included some of the countries that Terry and his family were able to visit after water polo competitions. In 2007, the girls traveled with Terry to Rio de Janeiro, Brazil for the Pan American Games, and after the game, they notched out some special times. Terry and Lori were particularly appreciative of the sensitivity and compassion that their daughters displayed while exploring the country. While the beauty touched their senses enormously, they were also acutely moved by the blatantly existent poverty. Despite this, in some areas around the city, small children displayed absolute joy playing with their only toy – a homemade kite. It was a stark contrast to California – a land of excess - where children have more material stuff than they know what to do with. In this colorful environment, Leanna and Sheridan took an empathetic look at people who led uncomplicated, simple lives, and their accompanying poverty did not affect their capacity to be joy-filled. It was a valuable experience - helping the entire family appreciate all that they have.

Sheridan also made her mark in Brazil. Always the gregarious social butterfly who enjoys meeting people from others countries, at one dinner, she left the Schroeder family and went to a nearby table where she spent 45

Sheridan, Lori and Leanna - Thailand 2010

Sheridan and Leanna

Sheridan at the family's yearly
Hawaiian vacation

minutes conversing with a Brazilian couple whom she'd never met before. The amazing thing was that they were only speaking Portuguese while Sheridan was only speaking English but through their humanity, they managed to convey the essences of their stories to each other.

In 2009, after the World Championships in Rome, Italy, the Schroeder family spent another 10 days touring around Italy. The following year after the summer of water polo was concluded, they took a cruise through the Greek Islands with the clear blue Mediterranean Sea magnetically beckoning them. During their time on the water, Sheridan earned the name of the ship's ambassador because by the time the cruise ended, she had become firm friends with everyone on board the ship.

Leanna is vastly different. Shy and quiet by nature, she prefers to stay somewhat on her own until she comes to know someone thoroughly, so she is always blown away by Sheridan's boldness. On most of these trips, Leanna carries a volleyball so that she and Terry can practice in every port or beach that they find. Her favorite volleyball was aptly named *Wilson* (after the Tom Hanks movie) and he traveled all over the world with her until a tragedy struck: an employee at Thai Airlines decided that Wilson had to be confiscated and deflated for travel. His rough handling of poor Wilson resulted in an accidental puncture, and Leanna stood there horrified as she witnessed her friend, Wilson, deflating down to his death. It was enormously sad for Leanna to watch an insensitive person terminate Wilson's life.

After the World Championships in 2010, the family made their way to Thailand and spent an out-of-this-world 10 days on the pristine beaches of this exotic country. The food on these trips was always tantalizingly interesting and Terry, Lori and Leanna would usually try the local dishes. Not Sheridan! She stuck to the sensibility of ordering her staple Fettuccini Alfredo - no matter how enticing the options. Of course, she was always willing to try some of the local desserts.

Due to her August birthday, Sheridan has usually celebrated her birthday in several fascinating countries around the globe. Terry and Lori have also watched with pride the manner in which Sheridan has exerted her basic human rights. As she grew older, she soon recognized that Leanna, whom she revered, was acquiring the lazy habit of conveniently ordering her baby sister around. Finally, Sheridan stood up to her towering sister and said firmly, "I'm not your slave!" She was never ordered to do anything again. Sheridan's tough but gentle spirit is evident in so many facets. On many occasions she has jumped into an ice-cold swimming pool, and has not batted an eyelid - even though her lips were turning blue. She definitely inherited Bob Schroeder's DNA for toughness and stubbornness.

Of all the places that the Schroeders have traveled - Maui, Hawai'i has remained one of their favorite destinations. The consistency of the weather, the fresh food, and the hospitable people - have made it a spectacular experi-

The Schroeders in Hawai'i

Schroeder Hawaiian vacation

ence every time. There is no better place in the world like Hawai'i where the natural ambience of the islands promotes complete relaxation and peace.

On the Schroeders' 2016 New Year's vacation in Maui, Hawai'i, Leanna and Sheridan provided the entire resort with endless amusement as they swam around in mermaid suits and sunned themselves on the rocks of waterfalls with their long blue tails. Children ran up to them while declaring to their parents, "Look mom; here are two real mermaids. Look, I can see them!"

The Maui Mermaids exemplified everything about the Schroeder four: energy, imagination, humor and simple, clean fun. Even the underwater snorkelers took a double take as they swam underwater with their go-pro cameras. At first they thought they might have had one Mai Tai too many when they spotted the mermaids, and then they realized there were turtles, fish and – human mermaids; it was a completely sober sighting! The numbers of young male snorkelers soared the next day.

Humor can also mend broken hearts. On that same Maui trip, a family friend, who was vacationing with the Schroeders, was in the throes of a broken heart, and when Leanna witnessed the lady sobbing her way to the airport after an unwelcome text from the heartbreaker, Leanna put her imagination to work on how best to heal the friend. During the Maui vacation she had noticed how amused the friend was by a 6-foot-8-inch-tall off-season Samoan rugby player who acted as the hotel's security guard, jewelry salesperson and general-purpose utility man. That night, Leanna decided to find the Samoan rugby player. She pulled Sheridan into the plan, and together they followed him into the local grocery store, and took photographs of him filling up his trolley. At every corner, Leanna took a photograph of the giant, neck-less man with the exotic pony tail, and texted the pictures to her distraught friend. It was an instant elixir as she boarded the flight.

Recently, when Lori returned from a trip to Europe, Terry and his partner-in-humor, Sheridan, decided to fetch her at the airport dressed up as ultra-serious chauffeurs with smart suits, black caps and dark glasses. They even had a white board with 'Princess Schro" written on it. Inside their

Chauffeurs Sheridan and Terry
at LAX Airport Los Angeles

waiting limousine they had a bottle of champagne on ice, red roses, smoked salmon and a bucket of green spinach. It was a homecoming of note – augmented by their special family humor.

Leanna's levels of sensitivity have taught Terry and Lori some important lessons. Years back when she was a young child, they sat down with Leanna to have what they thought was a healthy, frank discussion about how she came into the world. Both Terry and Lori felt that Leanna should understand this important fact directly from her parents. They explained that she was an in vitro baby whom her Aunt Bobby carried because her own mommy's tummy was broken. They carefully tried to explain what a miracle it was that she had come from an egg that had been frozen. There had been two eggs remaining for this "final" in vitro attempt and one was not viable. The second egg was good except for the fact that frozen embryos have less chance of survival. This is the egg from which Leanna would eventually emanate. Leanna misinterpreted the facts and somehow deduced that she was from a broken egg. The logic she then calculated was that if the egg was broken, she must also be broken! She carried this burden for years and Terry and Lori were mortified when they discovered that this was her interpretation of their communication. It was a massive lesson about conveying words with more forethought – and then communicating regularly after the fact.

Leanna's deep sensitivity and perfectionism is none more evident than in her artwork and in her schoolwork. She pores over her art projects in particular, and spends the early morning hours achieving impossible standards of perfection. While her parents worry about her lack of sleep, they concede that she is at her most peaceful when she is immersed in creating a beautiful work of art. Leanna has often told her parents that when she is engulfed in her art - she feels closest to God.

Sheridan also shares that artistic talent with her sister, and this is definitely a case of the apple falling very, very far from the tree. While Terry and Lori have no artistic abilities, the girls' grandfather Bill Bell and grandmother Pat Schroeder must have passed on their genes to Leanna and Sheridan.

Musical gifting is another gene that has eluded most of the Schroeders. In fact, Bob Schroeder claims to be the only person ever kicked out of a church choir. So desperate was the choir director that he asked Bob to lip sync the words – instead of sing. Bob took the hint, and quit in embarrassment. Terry and Lance once took piano lessons from one of their father's famous patients. After 6 months they were ready for their first recital – or so they thought. The brothers were 7 and 5 years old respectively, and they were excited about their big day. Unfortunately, after listening to many of the 4 and 5-year-olds play their pieces – Terry and Lance were paralyzed by their lack of skill and both bombed their recital. Sheridan seems to have changed the trend and has progressed as far as advanced choir at school with a really pleasing voice.

At the time of writing this book, Lori and Terry had recently shouldered Leanna through a major heartbreak. Her first love of 4 years broke up with her – with reasons that made little sense. Making matters more complicated was the fact the she had also sustained a bad concussion during a beach volleyball match. For months, Leanna battled depression and cried herself to sleep at night, and even when she did sleep, she was besieged with the memories of a painful loss. It was heartbreaking for Terry to watch his daughter crumble from pain, and he and Lori spent many nights cradling and comforting Leanna with their love. But what made them so exceptionally proud of Leanna was the way she handled an emotionally-challenging year; her kindness and grace shone as she weathered the storm – and through her thoughts and actions, she taught her family how to come out of the furnace wiser, stronger and more beautiful. This was her journey and she wrote this blog on February 4, 2016:

"A year ago today I encountered a pretty serious concussion. And although that doesn't sound like a memory you'd like to think about and appreciate (and it's really not), it was an important day for me because this was the day that my life began spiraling out of my control. I've always believed that everything happens for a reason, especially when things don't make sense and don't seem right or fair, but I couldn't help but keep asking "why" each time another thing happened that seemed to make matters worse. I'm also a strong believer in God. And I've realized He has a way of making your life slow down when there's something you need to hear. Sometimes it only takes a whisper, sometimes a two-by-four... For me, it was an elbow to the head... along with a couple more two-by-fours to really stop me in my tracks. I didn't know it then, but I was lost, and I was stubbornly going in the wrong direction.

Today marks a year-long journey of getting through hardships and learning a lot of tough life lessons in a short amount of time. It marks a year of breaking down, of fighting and failing and falling, of getting back up again and again, of changing, of growing and healing, of letting go, and finally... of finding myself and becoming a better me. Today I am stronger. And I am exactly where I am meant to be."

Leanna is a special soul and Terry and Lori are so thankful that she has been at Pepperdine - close to the family during her difficult days. Terry has relished having Leanna close enough to carve out his once-a-week lunch with her in Malibu. Those lunches are a special time, where dad has learned to listen and enjoy Leanna's company while only giving advice when he is asked!

The Schroeder home itself is a luxury zoo where the animals outlive their natural life spans 3-fold because of the superlative treatment they receive. Bunnies receive organic spinach for breakfast while the Green-Cheek Conure brood enjoys healthy smoothies made of pineapple juice, blueberries and strawberries. Sheridan and Leanna are the zookeepers, and Sheridan is often spotted out in the local park taking bunnies and birds out on walks with harnesses and leads. When time permits from her full schedule, Leanna joins her with her Bengal cat, Leo, on a lead. The Schro zoo sports exotic chinchillas, a clever rat, leopard geckos and many other quirky members of the animal species.

The apple definitely fell close to the tree when it came to being animal lovers. Terry and Lori have always shared a deep love of animals. In their early-married life while they struggled to conceive, their "two children" were two little Shih Tzu dogs named Harry and Maxie. Harry was an amazing little creature. He would come to the office every day and make himself completely at home. He had an amazing knack for finding patients who were in severe pain, and he would naturally gravitate to their feet - and sit or lay with them quietly. Harry was a comforter and healer, and he was an integral part of the Schroeders' early practice.

Leanna - 2015

One of the vulnerabilities that Terry and Lori have shared as parents is not being able to say "no" to more pets – especially once they make eye contact with them. Chelsea, their miniature poodle, became a family member when an acquaintance left Chelsea for a few weeks while she was trying to find a home for this poor neglected dog. The friend wanted Chelsea to experience love in a good home and Lori, feeling the pain of this little dog coming from an abusive family, could not bear to see Chelsea leave. She and the family fell in love with her and helped to heal her brokenness. Chelsea is still a part of the Schroeder family.

But mom and dad Schroeders' acquiescence has often resulted in too many animals with the accompanying plethora of chores in cleaning cages and feeding the menagerie. Coincidentally, having so many dependent animals has also taught Leanna and Sheridan valuable lessons in empathy and caring about living creatures that require much more than mere food and warmth. The girls have also learned to grieve in a healthy way as their pets, who invariably become family members, eventually pass away way past their natural life spans. Their extended lives produce that much more attachment – making the final goodbyes harder. The Schroeder backyard is a vast pet cemetery where the little animals are buried in shoe-box caskets after a respectful ceremony in which all family members must be present.

But some of the pet experiments have gone radically wrong. The family has ended up with an unintended brood of guinea pigs and bunnies; there were the pet mice Java and Latte, who escaped into the walls of their home - never to be found again. The Australian tree frogs brought with them a restrictive maintenance issue: no one could touch them because touching them would remove the vital oils from their sensitive skins. When they escaped, Leanna was faced with the critical problem of having to catch them without touching them.

Then there was Daisy and Winston, the two baby ducklings whom Terry would bring home from the pond at Pepperdine. Apparently they had been abandoned at Pepperdine after Easter when the impulsive ether wore off on their fickle owners. The girls fell in love with Daisy and Winston, who felt right at home at the Schroeder Zoo, and showed their satisfaction by taking over the backyard. The downside to these adorable adolescent ducks was that they were making a huge mess in the pool and on the Arizona stone. They were eventually let loose into Lake Sherwood, where they now have their own families. The girls still visit with them when out on the family's electric boat on the lake.

Another unexpectedly crazy pet story happened one Christmas. Terry and Lori had gone to the pet store the night before Christmas and bought Sheridan a Chinchilla from Santa. The Chinchilla was put into a pet-safe box and the Schroeders were told that he would be fine there for a few hours. On their way home, they had to make another Santa pit stop. When they

The Schroeders with the Super Bowl Clydesdales on
Epona Farm, Hidden Valley, California

Sheridan and cheetah in Africa 2014

Baby tiger adjusting Terry

climbed back into the car to return home, everything seemed normal until Lori picked up the box and there was no chinchilla! "Chip" as he was later called – had escaped from his box and he was furtively loose in the SUV. When they arrived home, Leanna was commandeered to assist in the man-hunt for Chip. They eventually found him hiding way under the car seat – scared and hungry. The poor little guy recovered and is now one of Sheridan's favorite pets. The appreciation of animals is what made the Schroeder's trip to Africa a few years later so special.

One of the components that fuels love is passion, and Lori has been the consummate teacher, more than any super athlete Terry has known. Through the years he's watched in awe as she mustered more self-discipline and more determination than he could ever imagine – to create their family. He says, "she was so passionate about her team, her love, her dreams, that she carried us both for a period of time and taught me what it really meant to be a team player in a family. Lori has taught me so many lessons about the game of life that have helped to shape me as a man. She has always seen the bigger picture, and thanks to her, Robin and Chuck, and Stacy, we have two beautiful daughters. I needed to live my life intensely with purpose and balance, and Lori took me to that place."

The clichéd statement - behind every successful man, there's a great woman - is accurately true when it comes to Lori. In this case, 'behind' is replaced by 'along' – because Lori walks alongside Terry's side - professionally and personally.

While honesty, decency and humility have always been central to Terry's vast quotients of integrity, Lori has introduced an inestimably valuable dimension to his character. Through her, he has discovered the magnificent benefits of loving more deeply, living more contently and being more tender and kind. With those new gifts, he's been able to experience life in a much more compassionate way, and his capacity for sensitivity has enriched his life immensely. Most importantly, their love continues to take them to a place of such inner contentment that Terry knows – without the shadow of a doubt – that it far outweighs his original reason for waking up in the morning. Lori quite literally is his gold medal. In her he has found absolute peace in ways he never imagined. He rests in her arms knowing that this is where he's meant to be – that place where this strong woman with a heart the size of Africa – has him covered – completely and unreservedly. Through Lori, Terry's new depths continue to draw him closer to God's love. She is without question, the love of his life.

USA Men's Water Polo Team London 2012 Olympics

Photo by Curtis Dahl

CHAPTER 18

The Tide Turns

Failure should be our teacher, not our undertaker. Failure is delay, not defeat. It is a temporary detour, not a dead end
– Denis Waitley

On the morning of Thursday, 7 July 2005, 4 Al-Qaeda Islamist extremists - separately - detonated 3 bombs in quick succession aboard London underground trains across the city, and later, a 4th terrorist detonated a bomb on a double-decker bus in central London. 52 civilians were killed and over 700 more were injured in the attacks. It was the United Kingdom's worst terrorist incident since the 1988 Lockerbie bombing – and the country's first ever suicide attack.

The relationship between the terrorist attack and the London Olympics is this: On July 6, 2005, London was officially named the host city for the 2012 Olympics. In the Olympic bid, the city was touted as one that embraced diversity and multiple cultures. Clearly, Al-Qaeda was out to prove another point. They wrecked havoc in a series of coordinated suicide bomb attacks in the heart of London – and the targets were regular civilians using the public transport system during morning rush hour.

Right on the heels of those attacks and just two weeks later, a series of attempted attacks by Al-Qaeda were thwarted by Scotland Yard - the police responsible for safeguarding the London area. When it comes to dealing with terrorist activities, there are few forces as tactically adept as the British police. Years of attacks by the Irish Republican Army (IRA) gave them plenty of preventative and retaliatory practice.

The 2012 London Olympics evolved into one of the tightest and most advanced anti-terror security systems. Well aware that the Olympics was being targeted by Islamic extremists, the city made available 13,000 highly-trained police officers supported by 17,000 members of the armed forces.

Naval and air assets, including ships situated in the Thames, Eurofighter jets and surface-to-air missiles – were deployed as part of the massive security operation. 40,000 security personnel vigilantly watched everyone's movements in the city. All garbage disposal bins were removed from the railway stations. Air defenses were installed around the Olympic stadium to stop potential suicide airplane attacks.

There were 6 missile sites, 4 using Rapier missiles: these are surface-to-air missiles designed to shoot down airplanes using tracking and surveillance radar. Both south and north London were covered. In addition, two sites were selected for Starstreak anti-aircraft missiles. They were at the top of tall buildings closer to the Olympic Stadium.

The technology infrastructure surrounding the Olympics was designed so that the network perimeter was secured against electronic attacks. To everyone's relief, what transpired during the two weeks were a series of unsophisticated electronic hacking attempts, and in light of the fact that 25,000 journalists had access to network services, many of their computers infected with viruses and other malware became the only focus of concern.

After the 2008 Beijing success of USA Men's Water Polo, the team followed up with a strong performance at the 2009 World Championships in Rome, Italy. After making it into the semi-finals, the team lost close matches to Spain and Croatia to finish 4th. In 2010, at the FINA Cup, they came in 5th and in 2011 in Shanghai, China for the World Championships - 6th. Once again, the lack of full-time training in the non-Olympic years made it difficult for the team to compete with the elite teams. In August of 2011, the team qualified for the 2012 Olympic Games at the Pan American Games in Guadalajara, Mexico by beating Canada in the finals. It was a rough Pan Ams for Terry who was burdened by a severe case of Montezuma's revenge for the second week of the tournament. It was certainly not easy to maintain the focus necessary to prepare and coach high level games while running to the bathroom every 20 minutes.

The 2012 USA Men's Water Polo team was the same as 2008 – except for 3 changes.

Chay Lapin: won the spot behind Merrill Moses as second goalie. An all-American goalie from University of California Los Angeles (UCLA), Chay or "Lap Dog" as he was called by teammates, was mild mannered, quiet, and a great college goalie. He lacked international experience and was a bit inconsistent, but in the end he was a step behind Merrill and was probably not going to see much water time in London.

Shea Buckner: took the spot of Rick Merlo. Shea was a talented, tough, up-and-coming player. "Bucko" had a strong outside shot and could "bang" with anyone. His teammates liked him because he would not back down to any opponent. He was a versatile player who could play center defender or attacker. He had played at University of California (CAL) Berkeley and also at University of Southern California (USC). His weakness was that he was untested in really big games.

John Mann: was the final change but it was a big one because it divided Robert Lynn (assistant USA Men's Water Polo coach) and Terry. Ultimately, it was Terry's decision to put John Mann on the team but it was accompanied by a great deal of night sweats. The position was for second center behind Ryan Bailey. In 2008, JW Krumpholz had beaten out John Mann for this spot and JW had played a great Olympics in Beijing. Between 2008 and 2012, John had closed this gap and was actually outplaying JW going into the final weeks of preparation before the final cuts. JW had also suffered a setback with a major concussion a month before the final selections were to be made for the team. The concussion concerned Terry, because JW was not himself. He was forced to sit out weeks of practice and then had to ease back into training at a critical time. Robert was very close to JW and he believed in him - so when Terry made the decision to cut JW and bring in John Mann, Robert felt betrayed and hurt enough to even threaten to leave the team. The conflict proved to be an obstructive flaw going into the Olympics.

John or "Bear Mann" was physically bigger and stronger than JW, and in the months leading up to the 2012 Olympics, he was holding the position better than JW and generating more offense at the center position. There was no doubt that both players had worked very hard to make the team. In analyzing it more assiduously, perhaps John was fighting for the spot just a bit harder after being one of the last players cut in 2008. The factor that really made it a tough choice is that JW had played so well in Beijing, and he had that Olympic experience, which was invaluable. John was a University of California (CAL) graduate and since this was his first Olympics, the question was whether he could cope with the pressure. Nobody doubted that by the 2016

Rio Olympics, he had that big match temperament (and he was the starting center for the 2016 team) but London would be his Olympic baptism.

JW would be an alternate. The other alternate (last player cut) was Brain Alexander who found himself in the same position as 4 years earlier when he was also one of the final cuts. This was especially hard on Terry considering how Brian had put everything in his life on hold to come back and try to make the team in London. He was a great player and had improved a great deal between Beijing and London. It was a very tough decision and Terry felt tremendous pain on the day he had to tell Brian that he had not made the team.

The complexities that go into what makes a player excel at the Olympic level are extensive. The skill set that every player must have is a given – but navigating the tricky waters of psychological readiness makes the Olympics the riveting spectacle of human emotion that it is.

In the end – the best-skilled players in the world can turn on super-human effort that doesn't necessarily translate into winning. There are so many subtle influences like team chemistry on a particular day; the individual player's mood; a poor night's sleep; a bad meal; nervousness or simply – opponents for whom everything comes together at the right moment – making them invincible in their hour of supreme team cohesion.

The team that beats you on one day may well be the team that loses to you the very next day. It's a vast ocean of 'what ifs' on any day of the greatest two-week test that athletes will ever experience in their lives. The very complexity of the Olympics is what makes it so great to watch. Triumph and ecstasy can so easily be replaced with heartbreak, implosion and misery.

The birth of the Olympic Games on Greek soil is entirely fitting because spectators are drawn to the drama of a Greek Tragedy for the losers. That is the essential definition of a Greek tragedy: where the main character is brought to ruin – or suffers extreme sorrow as a consequence of a tragic flaw, moral weakness, or inability to cope with unfavorable circumstances. There is no greater stage in life where ecstasy and agony are so poignantly and brutally portrayed than at the Olympic Games.

Despite the USA 2012 London team being a virtual replica of the successful 2008 Beijing team, the group's fine-tuning was affected by multiple ancillary circumstances – which combined – took their toll. For starters, the players were all 4 years older. For those players in their 30s, their recovery time may have slowed, and their turbo-charged abilities were on the wane – no matter how dedicated the fitness training. Cruelly, many athletes in their third decade are past their prime. A few elite athletes have defied this notion

London Bridge - host city for the 2012 Summer Olympics

USA Men's Water Polo with Head Coach Terry Schroeder and Assistant Coach Robert Lynn

but they are the rare exceptions.

The cold dose of reality was that Team USA Men's Water Polo had 7 players in their 30s at London 2012. Ryan Bailey and Adam Wright were the oldest at 37, Layne Beaubien was 36, Merrill Moses and Jeff Powers were 35, Peter Hudnut was 32, and Tony Azevedo was 30.

Another dynamic that played into the team's prospects of success was that the individuals were at a different place in their lives. Since 2008, many players were now married, a few even had children, and their energies were more concentrated on their families. Those familial bonds appeared to take precedence over the team – and one cannot blame them for that natural shift. Terry himself was struggling to balance his time and energy between team and family. He felt his girls needed and deserved as much of his time as he could give them.

The team-building exercises that united the men before 2008 were no longer possible pre 2012 with the challenges of family priorities. One of the cohesive bonding evenings that was a staple fixture on the calendar pre 2008 – going out to dinner with the team once a week – fell by the wayside. While its exclusion might seem inconsequential, it wasn't. Spending time together outside of the water is a critical unity component, and that didn't happen come London time. While the players still held a deep love for each other, they were not as united as the team was 4 years earlier in Beijing.

Most critical of all were the expectations. It's always easier to arrive at the Olympics as the underdog where expectations are few – and the players feel non-pressurized with little to lose. Unlike 2008, expectations of the Americans were high in 2012, and the gold medal dangled in front of them like a taunting pendulum. The team put more pressure on themselves this time around, and the end result was not favorable.

In 2012, there were no surprises on Team USA. Each rival team, particularly the Eastern Europeans, scrutinized virtually every member of the USA team by watching hours of tape and scrimmages - and they devised a calculated response for each of the USA player's strengths. They knew exactly how to impede Tony Azevedo and company, and they were 100% prepared for whatever the American team did.

The Serbians, in particular, were still smarting from their loss to the USA in the semi-final match in Beijing 2008, and this was their opportunity to avenge their injured pride from the painful loss. Not a single Serbian saw that upset coming and it was payback time for them in London – against the Americans.

Despite all these circumstances and pressures, Terry still felt that the team had a solidly realistic chance at medaling in London. However, months prior to the Olympic Games, when the brackets were announced, Terry knew the road would be a difficult one, but he had no idea of just how difficult it would turn out to be. Bracket A consisted of Greece, Italy, Kazakhstan, Spain, Australia and Croatia. In with the USA in Bracket B were Hungary, Montenegro, Great Britain, Romania and Serbia.

Peter Varellas scores at the 2012 London Olympics

A private disappointment for Terry was the decision to disallow the coaching staff to march into the opening ceremonies with their teams. As minor as this new change may sound, it was another incongruent piece of a puzzle that was accumulating into a sense of disappointment from the inception. Opening ceremonies were a very different experience as Terry and his family watched it on TV from the USA house in London. It was anti-climactic and Terry felt torn from his athletes with whom he so wanted to share the experience.

Another factor that negatively impacted this USA team was that there was no 'Beijing Normal'. In 2008, this had been a second home for Terry's team as they had open pool times in which to train, and the food at Beijing Normal was vastly superior to anything supplied in the Village. The United States Olympic Committee had decided to cost save in London and the athletes lamented that decision.

Nevertheless, as the Games began, Terry felt his athletes were ready. Everyone was healthy and had just completed some hard and successful training with the Croatian team. Game one began with a huge game against Montenegro. The team played well and Peter Varellas led the offensive attack with a 3-goal game to help USA win this critical first game.

Ryan Bailey scores 3 goals against Romania at the London 2012 Olympics

Romania was up next and Terry considered this a must-win game. Once again, the team played a solid game and came away with a 10-8 win. Peter Varellas and Ryan Bailey each scored 3 goals.

Head Coach Terry Schroeder London 2012 Olympics

A promising start of 3 straight wins from Team USA at the London 2012 Olympics

Tony led the way in the 3rd game against Great Britain with 4 goals in a one-sided 13-7 win. However, despite beating them comprehensively, the chinks in the armor were beginning to appear. The team did not feel good about the manner in which they played - especially on defense. Allowing the weakest team in the tournament to score 7 goals was disappointing to Terry who knew that in order to beat the big teams his defense would have to improve.

By the 4th game against Serbia – the great avenge match seemed to chip at the core confidence fibers of Team USA. Losing 11-6 to Serbia, it was as if the tide turned irreversibly, and the comprehensive losses that followed seemed to amplify how much the tide had turned: Hungary beat Team USA 11-6. With a record of 3 wins and 2 losses the team finished 4th in bracket play which meant that they had made the top 8 and would make it to the quarterfinal round.

However, as the 4th place team in Bracket B, they would cross over against the number one team in Bracket A, which was Croatia. If the team was to make it to the medal round (top 4) they would have to knock off Croatia in the quarterfinal matchup. Although a daunting prospect, the team actually felt pretty good about their chances against the Croatians. Their previous meetings against the powerful Croatians had usually come out in favor of Team USA and they felt like they could pull off an upset.

Croatia would win this critical game 8-2 but the score only tells a portion of the story. Team USA actually outplayed the Croatians in many facets. Ryan Bailey played his heart out and drew 7 exclusions at center. As a team, they would draw 16 exclusions – giving Team USA 16 power play (6 on 5) opportunities. However, they would score only one time out of the sixteen 6 on 5 man advantage situations. Their abysmal 6% productivity on the power play displayed the team's disunity. If Tony and his teammates had scored 50% of these opportunities they would have won this pivotal quarter-final match. The reality is that the USA Junior team could probably have scored more than one time if given sixteen 6 on 5 opportunities against Croatia. On this day in London, the Cro-

The Schroeder family riding a tube
in London - 2012 Olympics

atian team was the better team. It seemed to Terry that his troops had no snap on their shots; their arms appeared fatigued and it was lack-luster in every sense.

USA's medaling chances had died with the Croatian defeat and it was one of the most painful days ever felt for Terry and his team. As the players emerged from their locker rooms, barely a word was exchanged, and for some – tears were streaming down their faces.

As Terry emerged to face the crowd, Lori, Leanna and Sheridan formed a circle of blonde protection around him, and they instinctively buried their heads into each other, absorbing the powerful comfort of the family's unconditional love. Terry's girls came through resoundingly – proving to him that their love – particularly during life's testing times – was the one great thing upon which he could always rely.

Even though the team's chances to advance were over, there were still two games of play to determine 5th - 8th place. Terry struggled to muster any spark in anyone for these consolation matches. They had trained with one goal in mind - to come back to London and play for a medal, and losing that dream devastated them. Despite Terry sharing with the men in the

The Schroeder 4 in union after the devastating loss against Croatia

locker room his biggest regret in his Olympic journey - which had been not finishing well in his final game in the Barcelona 1992 Olympic Games when the team had a chance to play for the bronze medal and ended up finishing a disappointing 4th place - his appeal fell on barren ground.

No matter how earnest Terry's words were, the team did not respond and instead played the final two games in a stupor, losing 8-7 to Spain and then 10-9 to Australia to finish in 8th place. Incredibly, after winning their first 3 games, the team had lost 5 games in a row.

Like the rest of the Olympic team, Terry would have to find his own unique way to heal from the devastation of their disappointment. The sadness was etched in everyone's faces as wives, girlfriends and families rallied. After closing ceremonies marked the end of these Olympic Games, the United Airlines flight that ferried the team from Heathrow Airport to Los Angeles International Airport - carried within its 12 hours flight time an ocean of exhaustion and mental analysis. What had gone so radically wrong in London 2012?

Terry's analysis of the London implosion is multi-faceted and summed up in his words:

"I had a sense that as a team we were not as hungry as we were 4 years earlier. We had enjoyed success in Beijing and the disease of success had set in a bit. Some may call it arrogance or complacency, but whatever it was, it diminished some of our hunger and this would show up in subtle ways throughout the quadrennial - especially in our training."

"I don't think we were as physically strong as in 2008. Many of our guys were now in their 30s and recovery from training or injury is slowed. Every time we amped up the training schedule before the Olympics, some of our veteran, key players would incur another nagging injury and this impacted our level of training and as a result our level of fitness."

"The team chemistry was not as strong in 2012. In March that year, we were having an intense scrimmage in practice and Tony Azevedo and Jesse Smith were on opposite teams. Tony was beginning to get the best of Jesse and Jesse broke. Tony fouled him outside of 7 meters, and instead of coming up to shoot the ball, Jesse legged up and fired the ball at 50 MPH directly into Tony's face - almost knocking him out."

"Practice ended and I pulled Jesse aside and told him that I didn't want him on the team any more; he was to pack his bags and go home. After about 5 days, Jesse asked for a meeting with me in which he apologized profusely and said he wanted another chance. My instincts told me to say no, but I met with the team and sought the opinion of the veteran players. They all agreed that we should give Jesse a chance and see if he could work hard and be a good teammate. With this offer came a "zero tolerance" policy – meaning that if he did anything else in training, he would be done. In hindsight, I should have had more in-depth conversations with Tony concerning Jesse, because I don't think that he could fully trust Jesse, and the chemistry between them was shattered. When Jesse came back to the team, he was the model citizen in practice. In the end, he made the team but I believe that the under-current of negative energy and mistrust impacted how Tony and some of the others played in London. The immense trust that existed between the players in 2008 had been damaged."

"There is a fine line of tapering and getting the team to be at its best during that two-week window of the Games. I think we missed that taper peak by a week. Two weeks before the London Games, we were training in Croatia and we were getting the best of them in scrimmages. In other words, we were beating the team that won the gold medal at the London Olympics. We played our first tough game against Montenegro well – and then we began to fade - like we were coming off of our peak. As the head coach, this is my responsibility to time this taper and I believe that I missed it."

"This next one is a big one because it lies on my shoulders: it was a difficult balance to be head coach, run a chiropractic office, be there for my patients, and also give my family the quality time they deserved. When all of these commitments were combined with the duties of a head coach, I was overwhelmed at times. Preparing for Beijing was different as that was a 14-month gig; it was short term and therefore easier to master because the sacrifice was only for a year. Preparing for London was a 4-year commitment and I knew that it would be a very different situation. After Beijing, the guys had asked me to stay around another 4 years to be their coach; I had warned them that it was not going to be easy because of my commitments. In reality, juggling it all effectively was near to impossible at certain times. As a result, I was not always at my best for the team."

"Underlying some of the problems was my choice to keep Robert Lynn on as an assistant coach. After Beijing, some of the older players and I had met and discussed what would be best for the team. I had interviewed other coaches and felt like a change might be best. I had no problem with Robert as a coach. He is absolutely one of the best water polo coaches in the world. The thing that concerned me was his loyalty towards me. Knowing that I needed someone surrounding me that was a strong coach, I gave Robert the benefit of the doubt and I gave him the opportunity to be the assistant coach again."

"Along the way, in my opinion, Robert could have stood up for me better with the team - instead of feeding into the problem. Believe me, I understand that being an assistant coach is not easy and I don't blame Robert. My commitment to the team was being questioned and some of the guys felt slighted that I was not at all the work-outs (I usually missed weights in the mornings); they felt like they were sacrificing more than I was. About 6 months before London, Tony Azevedo came to me while we were training in Serbia and said that many of the guys thought it would be better if I allowed Robert to do more and run the pre-game meetings. They still wanted me to be head coach but they thought it would be better to have Robert doing more. Although this was painful, I understood the why behind it and tried to keep in mind that sometimes the needs of the team outweigh the needs of any individual. I had to keep in mind what was best for the team. In my gut, I felt like this was not going to work out well - but I gave into it - probably because I was feeling overwhelmed. I met with many of the team members one-on-one and they all said that they needed my leadership and wanted me to be their head coach. Ultimately, this caused some division and created cracks in the seams of our team. "

"I was torn but I should have fought them on this. Robert is a gifted coach who knows the game of water polo extremely well; however, I knew that he had weaknesses, and those weaknesses were about to be exposed. Before our critical 4th game against Serbia, Robert ran the pre-game meeting and instead of the normal 30-minute pre-game meeting, we met for an hour and 15 minutes. The guys were all out of sorts over this and we did not play well. I am not saying it was because we had a longer-than-normal meeting, but as a coach, you try to create routine and the players and team get used to that routine. When you break routine, you tend to end up in trouble. I felt like I had been undercut to a point where I could not really be a successful leader. It was my fault for allowing this to happen. I knew then and there that the result would not be good but I still let it happen. In the end, I blame myself for letting the team down by not being the best leader I could have been."

Terry concludes with these words: "My biggest lesson learned from London was to trust my instincts and to be strong in what I know is right. I tend to be too tolerant at times, and when something big is on the line, I need to fight harder by doing what I believe and know to be right. I learned what it takes to be a stronger leader and coach; it's possible to still be humble and tolerant while standing up for the important things. I gave away some of my leadership power in 2012, and in the end, I was frustrated that I could not help the team finish better than we did."

"The Olympics are a once-in-a-lifetime opportunity for most people, and I let London slip away because I did not stay true to myself by asserting what needed to be done. I am not disappointed in the effort that I made with the team, however I am upset that I did not follow my gut. I dared greatly and failed. Deep down I am content – knowing that I had this amazing opportunity to work with this special group of guys. Also, I know that I learned some valuable life lessons that will guide me in the future."

Team Captain Tony Azevedo gives this candid summation of the painful London experience:

"For me London is a simpler response. As much as an athlete does not want to admit it, once you win something, there is a sense of entitlement. The hardest thing about athletes and teams is how to keep that desire, fire and passion burning year after year. After Beijing 2008, we did not sacrifice like the years before – and yet we still showed up at various games across the world and did well. As our results began to worsen, we didn't take it seriously or personally. 2012 was a much different form of preparation than 2008. I feel that we forgot how much we sacrificed, trained and suffered in 2008. We thought everything was sufficient instead of not enough! We beat a very good Montenegrin team in Game one because we were still the same guys who knew how to play an excellent game. The next two games were

Tony Azevedo

easier and we were heavily favored to win. Once we lost to Serbia in game 4, it was downhill. We didn't deserve to be on that podium in 2012. We deserved it in 2008, but you need to make your own destiny and not wait for it to be made, which is what we did in London. The price was failure."

There will never be a second chance to make right what went wrong with USA Men's Water Polo in London 2012, but in the end, the team that thoroughly deserved the gold medal, went home with the victory. Croatia was undoubtedly the strongest team at the Games. Ironically, USA's former head coach,

Ratko Rudić did the honors in taking Croatia to the top. Unquestionably one of the best coaches in the world, Ratko worked with his fellow countrymen who understood his style of tough love. The Croatians are raised to never break - even in the most adverse situations – and they certainly appeared to prove this point in London: they survived and thrived under Ratko's leadership.

The London 2012 Olympics was Terry's 6th journey down a familiar road that has become an endemic part of his life. Painful as it was, and as difficult as acknowledging his part in the disappointment has been, he is genuinely grateful for the opportunity he had to coach the team - and the lessons he's learned.

Win or lose, the Olympics challenge every athlete who partakes in the privilege of the experience – to an immeasurably edifying extent. Human potential, will and fortitude are tested like in no other place – and the victories and disappointments mold people into better human beings who come away with a greater understanding of life and their own complexities. Most assuredly there may be some for whom the experience is wasted – but the majority of Olympians share the benefit of a refining process that will ultimately take their game of life – up a significant notch.

The King of the African Beasts

1st Day on African Safari

Photos by Curtis Dahl

CHAPTER 19

African Waters

If I have ever seen magic, it has been in Africa
– John Hemingway

20 March 2013: The wounds of disappointment from the London Olympics were piercingly painful. Team USA touched down at Los Angeles International Airport in August 2012 to the antithesis of what they had experienced in 2008. Instead of congratulatory cheers and the rousing celebrations they had come home to upon their return from Beijing, the team dragged themselves off the airplane to a cheerless, hot city – relieved that they'd finally be able to start the journey of moving forward with their lives and healing in the arms of their family and friends.

Terry's pain was especially searing. As head coach he carried the burden of overall responsibility for the result – and for months his brain kept him awake at night with incessant mental gymnastics - dissecting all the variables that had collided instead of working smoothly together. The damage was irrefutable and done - with no way to fix it. The only solace was resolving to do a better job in the future. In times of deepest loss, tears and pain, there is usually always an opportunity to learn and grow from the experience.

A salmon fishing trip to Sitka, Alaska with Leanna later that month was the first palliative step towards closing up the wound. The serenity of staring out at the water while ensconced in nature's unfailing embrace – gave Terry's brain a welcome release from over-analysis. The inspirational healing embedded in Leanna's deep faith helped suture up the wounds of London as Terry turned to that most relaxing of past-times – watching and catching fish.

But providence had something waiting in the wings – a mammoth expeditionary plan that evolved out of a set of serendipitous coincidences that nobody could have fathomed coming together. Brent Wiltshire, a popular South African water polo player in Cape Town, invited Team USA to play in Cape Town, South Africa the following March. It was less than 6 months away. While some of the top players from the 2008 and 2012 Olympics – including Tony Azevedo - who was playing in Croatia - would be unable to make the trip, there was a core group of players from previous Olympics or World Championships who were available.

The major bargaining chip in convincing 30 busy Americans to embark on a 22-hour flight to Africa – was the lure of the Animal Safari portion - and Brent knew exactly how to package the deal with his inimitable panache. Physically-spent from the recent Olympics, most of the team's players had either retired from water polo after London, or they were taking the break they so desperately needed to recharge their batteries. But this was an irresistibly attractive proposition: one day's play in an international match and the rest of the trip – vacationing together in this beautiful part of Africa with wives, girlfriends and family in attendance.

Ryan Bailey, the veteran 4-time Olympian who was also a formidably strong and respected player, stepped up to the leadership plate and captained the team magnificently. This was the first time most of the players would be seeing each other since London – and so the endemic value of playing water polo together for the sheer love of the game and the camaraderie – would prove to be an invaluable healing mechanism. Included in this invitational team was Brad Schumacher, a former double USA Olympian in both water polo and swimming – and Wolf Wigo, former captain of the 2004 Olympic Water Polo team. Without any podium pressure, this group of talented athletes looked forward to a wild African expedition far away from home – with wild, ferocious lions in a beautiful environment - about to give them their first taste of a real African Safari.

This trip was poignant from another humanitarian perspective: Nelson Mandela, the greatest statesman of the twentieth century, was gravely ill in South Africa in 2013 during his 94th year. The Father of Africa led his people with magnanimity. He epitomized the very definition of humanity and resolutely stood for justice, equality and human dignity. After being locked away for 27 years of his life for opposing the injustices of apartheid South Africa, he emerged from prison without bitterness and he forgave the legions of people who wronged him. With humility and grace he became South Africa's first democratically-elected President in 1994 and said in his acceptance speech, "Never, never and never again shall it be that this beautiful land will again experience the oppression of one by another."

The power of Nelson Mandela's gifted leadership averted a potential civil war in the country. When angry people turned to violence as emotions

Nelson Mandela

soared after the long-held violation of their basic human rights, Nelson Mandela read and understood the pulse of his people. In his calm, measured way, he made a heartfelt plea to the simmering nation: "Let's surprise our opponents with compassion, restraint and generosity, and give them all the things they denied us." The magnitude of Mandela's grace touched all his people, and out of respect for him, they listened to the strength in his words and violence was averted.

Mandela's super-human qualities were evident in every facet of his life. Instead of feathering his own nest with money and material acquisitions, he took a fraction of the salary he could have earned, and led a simple life. Money and shiny, expensive objects had no relevance to his core values.

Every taxi driver and every South African that the USA team encountered – showed visible emotion and profound concern about their ailing leader's condition. There was a sense of massive dread surrounding this remarkable man's mortality. For so long he had been the nation's enlightened rudder, and the thought of losing him was an unbearable prospect. The acknowledgment of Nelson Mandela's contributions to the world made a deep impact on the team, and they felt that it was a privilege to have been in the country while his people were paying him the respect he so richly deserved.

Africa impacted the team in another sensorial way: It's a vast continent where the beat of life pulses more dramatically, more colorfully and less complicatedly. Within hours of arrival, the African sun blazed across the sky in vivid oranges and reds, and in the inimitable words of one of the Safari Guides, Brian Mullins, Africa irrevocably "got under their skins".

Terry's foray into Africa began with some interesting twists: while the team were enjoying their first sunset dinner at The Blues restaurant in Camp's Bay, Cape Town, Terry and Lori found themselves stuck in London because the officials at Heathrow Airport concluded that Terry's passport was overly full with international entry stamps; evidently there wasn't the requisite 3 blank pages required to place one stamp. This necessitated an overnight stay in London where the Schroeders celebrated their wedding anniversary, and

Terry ran to the U.S. Embassy the next morning to resolve the pesky matter. It was ironic that it was in London that Terry's dream had crashed just 7 months previously, and there he was again - overcoming another obstacle in cold, drizzly London. Undeterred, they made the most of their situation and enjoyed the luxury of having an extra night alone together.

The incremental healing began half a day later. As Terry and Lori touched down in Cape Town, a celebrity welcome awaited them. Generations of water polo players had watched Terry play and coach in the Olympics over the decades and there was palpable excitement when the real-life statue from the Los Angeles Coliseum made it off the airplane. South Africa has always excelled in water sports, particularly swimming – and the significance of Terry's arrival in this aquatic-loving nation resonated deeply.

There was some purposefully vague description around the role that Terry was playing in South Africa: Since the London Olympics were over, he was no longer head coach of Team USA – but he would be coaching South African coaches whilst in South Africa. But Brent Wiltshire and his fellow South Africans had other plans for their American visitors – particularly Terry - plans that were coated in prodigious humor and mischievous tricks.

The famous Masters Tournament quarry at Hillcrest Wine and Olive Estate in Cape Town was similar to one of those mysterious Hungarian rock-bottomed thermal spring waters. Players cannot see more than one

USA and South Africa line up for the anthems

Photo by Curtis Dahl

USA players jump off the quarry cliff

South Africa attacks the USA. Brad Schumacher, Merrill Moses and Ryan Bailey defend

South Africa defends as USA's Ryan Bailey scores

Photos by Curtis Dahl

foot below the water and since Americans are acquainted with crystal-clear, chlorinated pools, the South Africans knew that this was probably going to produce a few tertiary concerns amongst the visitors.

In fact, the jocular group, while downing a couple of beers beforehand, described to a certain anonymous school teacher in vivid details how the quarry was teeming with poisonous snakes and other amphibious relics from antiquity. While Brent tried to placate the Americans' concerns with promises of Navy SEALs going in there with aqualungs and sophisticated radar equipment to gauge the quarry's safety, his Queen's Park teammates destroyed all his efforts with their vivid stories of potential monsters in the deep dark depths of the mysterious quarry. They placed particular emphasis on how these unknown creatures especially relished Californian prey.

The South African hijinks didn't end there. On the day that the international game between the two countries was to be played, a formal invitation was issued to Team USA to visit famous golfer, Ernie Els' wine estate in nearby, picturesque Stellenbosch. The invite sounded fabulous except that it was a few hours before the soon-to-be televised game. Evidently the South Africans must have thought it would be hilarious if Team USA arrived at the game after an afternoon of wine tasting and alcohol-induced prohibitive coordination. The polite invitation was equally as politely declined – much to some of the die-hard, golf-loving team members' chagrin.

'Never a dull moment' would be a clichéd understatement of the first 24 hours in Africa. While Camp's Bay, Cape Town is generally exceptionally safe and well protected for the sake of all the international tourists, there are a few nefarious people who make their way into this sought-after area, knowing full well that there's money to be made from unsuspecting visitors who are relaxing on vacation. One of the water polo players, who was not directly involved in the incident, witnessed an American friend not associated with the team, become victim to a sophisticated extortionist. The price was high and the sheer malevolence of the extortion scheme was an abrupt wake-up call. It put new meaning to the relevance of a team sticking together – particularly at night – and having each other's backs. Elite athletes have targets on their backs wherever they travel in foreign countries and sociopathic people prey on money and reputations.

Yellow-socked Brent greeted the USA team at the quarry that afternoon. Determined to show the South Africans that they were as much jungle men as their competitors, Ryan Bailey led the USA team to the top of a cliff where they leapt off the 30-foot precipice into the mysterious quarry.

Brent Wiltshire's hospitality in Constantia, Cape Town

Shark Cage Diving off the Cape Coast

Laura, Merrill, Lori and Terry

Groot Constantia Wine Farm, Cape Town

Photos by Curtis Dahl

As they hit the chilly water below, the players felt their breaths taken away, and with a turbo-charged swimming response, they became resolved to keep their emotions firmly hidden as they began a match that was far from easy.

The game began and it was a friendly blast for both teams – the way that water polo should be played whenever possible. USA Olympic swimming gold medalist, Brad Schumacher, was a particular character of note. No doubt asked to come on the trip for many of his skills, notably his swimming speed, most people had forgotten that he'd been retired for almost 10 years and some of the good life had accumulated marginally around his waist. He asked to be substituted during the game so he could catch his breath if necessary. The problem was that the U.S. didn't have any subs and there were nervous jokes circulating about whom to throw in if a team member developed a cramp in the cold conditions. But Brad toughed it out and when asked if his fitness level had become a problem, he replied, "oh no; in fact it was perfect. I rested my stomach on my South African opponent wherever possible. It was very useful."

But the South African crowd wanted one thing really badly: after 21 years absence as a competitive player, they wanted the Rock of Gibraltar – Schroeder – to flex his muscles and play again. Unrelenting, the 2000-strong crowd started thumping their feet on the wooden stands shouting "Schroeder, Schroeder, Schroeder." Two minutes later they increased the crescendo to the beat of Queen's *We Will Rock You* with collective choruses of "Make him play". To the delight of the expectant crowd, on came the speedo, and in went Terry Schroeder. It was the best thing that could possibly happen to him. He was, is, and always will be – a legend in the game – and the South Africans reminded him of that fact in their unique and unpretentious way.

After the game, there was a congenial, good-humored celebration where all of the team members had a chance to let loose and party with their South African counterparts. From that moment on, Terry and his team would have a chance to really discover Africa.

The wild African animals were calling and the group of grown-up Americans responded like children. After Cape wine farm visits, shark-cage diving (during which the shark-cage guide asked the group if everyone in the team was able to swim) and delicious seafood dinners aplenty, Team USA headed to Shamwari Game Reserve on safari. 'Shamwari' means 'Friend' in the local Shona language, and the vast reserve is famous for its rehabilitation of the ecosystem that has been so vastly damaged on the continent. Between decades of destructive wars, famine and human encroachment, the African king of the beasts – the lion – has become extinct in 26 African countries. Their once vast terrain has been minimized to a small fraction of its former glory – and the South African reserves are critical in insuring that lions and other indigenous animals are protected so that they will still be around in our children's lifetime. It would be an unimaginable tragedy if leopards, cheetah, rhinoceroses, elephant and the teeming herds of antelope were no longer able to survive because of mankind's actions.

The first day's Safari began at 05h30 as the team clambered aboard the ultra sturdy game-viewing vehicles that demand substantial 4-wheel drive performance. Splashing and careening across partially-dried river beds and sword-sharp long grass that cuts mercilessly – the early-morning adventure promised to be enthralling and spectacularly unrehearsed. Out of their aquatic environment, the players and their families took on the challenge – not knowing what was around the corner.

Just then, an intense, partially audible radio call came in to the safari guides at the vehicles' helms – informing them to speed due north east in the direction of a kill that had just been made – by a pride of lions. With terrain-proof fortitude, the guides angled the all-wheel-drive jeeps across rocks, felled trees and holes while everyone onboard held onto their kidneys. Within 10 minutes, the arresting scene presented itself: A pack of huge male lions with bloodied manes were devouring the carcass of a kudu, which is a large African antelope 3 times the size of a deer. The larger more dominant males ferociously warded off less powerful lions in the pack with roars that were louder than anything the team had ever heard on a movie. As the pecking order fight for the spoils ensued, the wild African scene impacted the group in the intense, visceral way that Africa is supposed to impress. It is vastly more powerful than we ever give it credit – unless you are privileged enough to witness what the group had just observed.

As the rain fell off and on from the skies through the 3 days, the group refused to stay indoors. Being perennially soaking wet was a price they were willing to pay – and in any case – they were usually soaking wet in a pool. Splish-splashing through the mud, the trusty jeeps climbed up in first gear to terrain that was super dense and almost impenetrable – the kind of terrain that elephants like – and encountered another dramatic moment.

A herd of elephants were moving across the territory at speed – led by the large, protective matriarch. One of the instances elephants can be extremely aggressive is when there are babies amongst them. Their survival instincts - elicited from the constant poaching and killing they've endured in

First sight of wild lions in Africa - April 2013

2 young male lions approach at
Shamwari Game Reserve

Baby elephant tells USA Water Polo to
back off - Shamwari Game Reserve

African dancers and singers at Shamwari Game Reserve

Photography by Curtis Dahl

the last 120 years - have heightened these intelligent creatures' sensitivities towards man. Unlike zoos where elephants walk slowly, calmly and undeterred, wild African elephants are instantly wary at the sight of man and their body language has to be read if Safari-goers are to be kept safe.

In Team USA's case, the matriarch of the herd made herself perfectly clear: While she thundered the herd through the thick terrain, she turned and trumpeted at the chasing vehicles while flapping her ears frantically. Riskily and upon the orders of a persistent magazine editor who wanted photographer, Curtis Dahl, to take the quintessential National Geographic-type picture, Terry and Lori were asked to leave behind the safety of the jeep and walk on foot towards the herd.

Having had substantial experience with animals – both tame and wild – they kept a respectful distance from the matriarch but with their backs to her and her trumpeting sounds increasing in urgency – their adrenalin began to flow despite their fixed smiles. They felt marginally protected in that they had an experienced guide on the ground with them but Terry wasn't so confident that he'd be able to protect Lori on this one. His arm wasn't as big as the elephant's trunk and he wasn't confident that he could beat the elephant's pace back to the jeep. Unlike water polo where he had most of the answers, this was new, exhilarating territory and he loved it. The rest of the Schroeder family concurred unanimously: Lori, Leanna and Sheridan loved every aspect of the moment-to-moment adrenaline rush that the unpredictable African bush provided.

Africa got under everyone's skins in so many life-affirming ways. Not only did the wild animals and the perfection of nature's order impact everyone powerfully, but the soul of Africa was none more evident than in its people. Every day and evening, the African people enveloped the Americans with their hospitality and they shared their talents and skills generously. Included in their vast repertoire was their ability to sing in pitch-perfect 4-part harmony without any instrumentation. Their dancing was equally as arresting in its rhythmic cadence.

On the team's last night in the African bush, they were treated to a beautiful rendition of South Africa's national anthem, "N'Kosi Sikele Afrika", which means "God Bless Africa". Visibly moved and with equal spontaneity, Ryan Bailey commanded the team to stand on their dinner chairs and respond with the American anthem, "The Star Spangled Banner". With music and athleticism perfectly harmonized, the hooting night owls outside had some serious competition.

Schroeder family on African Safari

The healing powers of Africa were inestimable. For Terry, the continent's close proximity to a natural force more powerful and more beautiful than anything he had ever known, was a stark reminder of God's infinite power and life's bigger picture – beyond podiums and gold medals.

Most importantly, he was able to share that profound experience with the people who mattered most to him – Lori, Leanna and Sheridan – and some of the USA players whom he had mentored and coached for a substantial time. The people of Africa – particularly the ones in the Game Reserves - seemed to possess a quiet wisdom – one that worked in harmony with nature. They smiled with genuine joy and brought a refreshing new meaning to the word 'effort'. Nothing was too much trouble for them. They had servant hearts and they found joy in making others happy.

The continent drew Terry, Lori and Sheridan back a year later in 2014 – to go on another Safari and after that, Terry coached water polo in Johannesburg – joined by Olympic silver medalist, Ryan Bailey. This time, for the Safari portion, the Schroeder clan headed to Marataba Safari Lodge and Madikwe near the Botswanan border.

While at Marataba, Terry was anxious to locate 'Twitch', an approximately 13-year-old male lion with a magnificent black mane whom he'd photographed and encountered a year earlier. Both Twitch and Terry seemed to recognize something in each other during their 2013 stare-down. Lions, particularly the males, seldom make it past 12 years in the wild because of the ferocious territorial fighting that they do. Inevitably a bad fight usually leads to one of the two lions' deaths. Terry never did find Twitch and maybe Twitch had perished in the year that he had been away. Once again it was a reminder of nature's order and of the things that cannot be controlled.

Maybe that was the lesson that Terry needed to learn most of all while in Africa: that outcomes cannot be controlled, just as people cannot be controlled because they have the power of choice - and the free will to make honest, good choices or dishonest, damaging choices that deeply hurt the people who care about them.

What Terry learned is that there are forces that override everything that might make sense on paper - forces that defy effort and sacrifice. But if one keeps giving of one's best while exercising faith, patience and forti-tude – a bigger, more fulfilling picture will emerge – one that is part of God's perfect master plan.

'Twitch' at Marataba Safari Lodge

The bronze statue of Terry Schroeder outside the Los Angeles Coliseum

CHAPTER 20

Lessons from an Ocean of Life

To whom much is given much is required
– Luke 12:48

July 15, 2016: Recognizing that he was physically and emotionally spent from 2012, Terry did a stark reality check on the lifestyle he had been leading while coaching Team USA. The assessment had the same attention-grabbing impact on him as a bucket of iced water being poured on his head: his schedule had often comprised of two national team workouts each day, the second ending two hours before midnight. But that was just the tip of the crazy iceberg.

Squeezed into the intermediary hours, Terry tried to spend 6-7 hours per day in his chiropractic office while still answering all his emails before he crashed into bed for less than 5 hours of sleep per night. Somewhere in-between, he'd shove some carbohydrates down his esophagus as he stress-ate. With little quality family time, virtually no exercise, and no quiet time, his body and mind took a telling toll.

After 2012, the body of the statue that stood outside the Los Angeles Coliseum showed all the drastic signs of someone who was living radically out of alignment. Terry had packed on about 30 extra pounds - most of it belly fat. His body fat had spiraled from 15% to 25%. His blood pressure was perilously high, and he was on the pre-diabetic precipice. It was an abrupt wake-up shout that – if left unattended – would lead to serious health issues.

Now well into his 50s, Terry recognized that the 2012 pace would eventually destroy him. Those invincible, bygone days when the body's engine roars like a Ferrari on pristine fuel gradually dissipate as athletes reach their mid 30s. That irrepressible energy serves every young athlete fleetingly – but nature is kind enough to replace that loss over time with something supremely more valuable: accrued wisdom accompanied by emotional maturity. Those athletes who are sensible enough to allow wisdom to seep into their souls are rewarded profoundly in time.

The Olympic Games represent the ultimate in human potential: they demand incredible commitment, dedication and focus which amplifies the outcome: unimaginable triumphs, and for some – almost unbearable loss and disappointment. Men and women are tested on the world's stage as physical and mental limits are pushed to the brink. Only an elite few will rise above everyone else and win that most coveted of prizes – the gold medal – and return home with the knowledge that they were the best in the world in their event.

A small percentage of those gold medal winners will have their lives forever changed by becoming media stars where their fame will earn them a sizeable living. For most of the gold medal winners, though, they'll place their piece of gold on the wall, and go on with their regular, daily lives. Some will quickly come to realize that their moment of glory is very short-lived.

That transition phase after the Olympics is critical. Bitterness and lamentations of what could have been can adversely consume some of the athletes, or they can grow through the pain and achieve a level of maturity that makes them substantially better people. And for those who did achieve the ultimate prize of the gold – the test becomes one of how they handle their fame and whether or not they allow their egos to corrupt their value systems. Terry has learned to handle victory and defeat with the same grace and humility that continue to shape his life.

Bob Schroeder had always taught his son to use the gifts that God had given him; to give of his best at all times. Wasting potential and leaving those gifts to lie uncultivated – was a cardinal sin, in his opinion. Terry understood that principle and to this day firmly believes that not using one's gifts and talents is tantamount to squandering away something precious. Bob imbedded the message deeply into his son that resting on one's accomplishments is unacceptable. There is always room to improve, to strive for something better – to stretch oneself further. Essentially what Bob Schroeder was doing was reminding Terry of the Olympic motto every day of his life.

The Latin words in the Olympic motto "Citius, Altius, Fortius" mean "Swifter, Higher, Stronger". Beyond the very literal sense of the meaning, for Terry, the motto is about forward momentum; giving your best and strength of heart and mind as a human. It suggests constant growth and improvement – not just in sports – but in all aspects of life. In everything that we undertake, we should challenge ourselves to be better each day. This requires reaching within and digging deeply – to places that may be uncomfortable to visit.

One day, a wise friend advised Terry that in order to really be successful in life, we must learn to be comfortable with being uncomfortable. Stretching ourselves, while initially uncomfortable, eventually brings about a set of enriching, fulfilling discoveries. If all of us set goals and strove for excellence, we would push ourselves out of stifling inertia and develop ourselves into stronger humans – a better version of our previous selves.

Abraham Maslow once said, "The story of the human race is the story of men and women selling themselves short." The underlying meaning of his words was that most people never come close to reaching their potential. Terry believes that he can still create a better version of himself and he is committed to doing that. Humans are not meant to slump or stagnate in a quagmire of underachievement. Society would grind to a debilitating halt if we all did that. Rather, it's about waking up every today committed to excelling in the most positive ways so that we can discover the key components of life.

Terry now understands that creating a balanced life is central to living well. Being one-dimensionally obsessed with something is not the answer. Finding that inner harmony and contentment is largely about balance and in that place – health and happiness are much more likely to flourish.

Terry's first half century has been an invigorating and enlightening process of finding himself – and in so doing – recognizing that serving others has the edifying effect of bringing about true contentment within himself. His first concept of serving others within the context of his Olympic career came early on – when he recognized the immense value and joy in being a part of a team. Selfish individuals don't win in team sports. The corollary effect of selfishness is damage to the team. Constructive team effort where each person is supporting and helping one another – is how games are won in sport and in life. Society implodes with selfishness in the same way that teams lose with egocentric individuals. When teammates help one another to be successful by giving of themselves - everyone benefits and the team is stronger and has a far greater chance of being successful.

Terry's analysis of much of what he has seen in the past 50 years is partially summarized in these words: "Short-sightedness and instant gratification are two common American themes that will not serve us well in life. If true success is desired, then we must cultivate patterns through our choices and habits that will make us a champion throughout life - instead of a celebrity for a moment. Success takes sacrifice and oftentimes a great deal of patience and persistence. I believe that one of our society's greatest failures is that we no longer put a lot of focus on teaching our children how to form good habits while setting worthy goals. Instead, we've ushered in an age of instant gratification. It detracts from the edifying process of striving and waiting for something truly great. Perseverance and exercising patience are key components of our appreciation of the value of the end result."

Nothing could have been harder for a young boy like Terry – to have to leave behind the comfort and warmth of his soft bed in the early hours of the morning – to jump into a cold, uninviting pool to do lap training. There were no smiles in the car on the way there.

But what Terry learned is that big dreams and hopes require putting a lid on the instant gratification button. That impulsive magnet that beckons us to grab at the momentary glory is fleeting and it usually leaves behind damaging traces. He says, "It takes emotional maturity to put a pause on our impulse button; to stop and recognize that long-term fulfillment and gain requires a substantial, well-thought-out, disciplined plan." That momentary satisfaction doesn't hold a flicker next to the rewards of reaching for goals that require self-discipline and the ignition of our best character traits.

One of the USA's most respected Olympic Gold Medal winners, Scott Hamilton said, "The high road is always respected. Honesty and integrity are always rewarded." Scott became the ice-skating champion that he is by exercising veritable glaciers of self-discipline. Hauling his body off to a freezing cold ice rink every day at 05h00 – oftentimes when his trainer didn't even bother to show - wrought in him the steely determination he needed to reach the top.

Repeatedly as he was training for his Olympic debut, he would find himself working towards a goal completely alone, and in those isolated moments, he was faced with a choice: turn around and go back to a warm bed or get on the ice and practice solo. Scott chose to practice. He performed a self-assessment and committed to gaining the most out of each practice – and it paid off substantially.

Complacency has never had any place in Terry's life. He is constantly reminded of Coach Marv Dunphy's words: "Either you are getting better or you are getting worse." Sitting back on his laurels is a foreign concept. There are always new goals to set, new horizons to reach, and new challenges to conquer. Each morning he wakes up to the invigorating value proposition of what it is he wants to succeed in accomplishing. Constructive goals charge him, excite him, and give his life purpose and meaning. The difference between now and his younger years, though, is that he has a healthier balance to his life. A direct offshoot of that balance is an inner peace he has found from making time to relax, restore, rejuvenate and connect with loved ones.

The beach, nature and water, in particular, have always provided food for Terry's soul. Having grown up around the ocean in Santa Barbara, he never ceases to be anything but humbled by its magnitude. That vast liquid expanse is a comforting reminder of God's infinite power, the perfection of His creation, and His plan for people's lives. It reminds Terry that he is part of something much bigger than himself and it's there – while walking on the sand with Lori or just sitting in silence, listening to the ebb and flow of the waves – that he finds that reassuring inner peace. There are no cell phones, no deadlines and no pressure. He focuses on the present and allows the reinvigoration process to take shape – with no interruptions.

Swimming is another relaxing extension of the healing power of water. In his earlier competitive days, the pressure he felt from his parents to win stole much of the enjoyment of swimming from Terry. But as the years have progressed, and the competitive element has receded, swimming has become a spiritually centering place for the one-time second fastest back-stroker in the USA. The rhythm of his strokes and the tranquil sounds of the rippling water create a sacred zone where Terry's pace is in perfect harmony with the propulsions of his body and his surroundings. Fellow swimmers understand the meaning and importance of conditioning in that medium. It's the most consistently reassuring environment they know – and without it – they'd feel landlocked and potentially restless.

Terry's solid bedrock has always been his faith in a loving and caring God. While there have been periods in his life – especially in his younger days – when he floated out to space on an extensively long straying cord – he's always found his way back to that most assured place of God's infinite mercy and love which is always there for us. It is humans in their brokenness that drift away from Him.

The unhappiest days that Terry has experienced – after the 1992 Olympics – coincided with him being way out of alignment with his Maker. It was a period of depression, confusion and a destructive time in his life where he hurt himself and the people who loved him. Grace, forgiveness and the unconditional love of his wife were showered upon him when he chose to focus on his faith in an effort to become a better man, a better husband and a better father.

The rewards are massively evident in Terry's family today. There are few marriages where two people share a substantially greater love with each other 30 years later. The difficult periods together have taught them to love each other at a much deeper level. Through Lori, Terry has learned that humility, kindness, respect and love are the ultimate in human currency. That love-filled, inviolable bond has given them an unimaginable sense of peace. Leanna and Sheridan live in a home that may not always be perfect, but it is always filled with large quotients of love and a resolute commitment to supporting and upholding one another.

Terry is a strong proponent of the importance of making good choices in life. The power of choice that each of us has - brings with it a boatload of responsibility and that is the key to happiness in life. With each choice that we make, being willing to accept the responsibility of that choice, makes us far better people. Being responsible involves structuring a support system of trusted people who give each other regular feedback – so that each person is being held accountable for their actions. Blaming others for mistakes that we make is childish and self-defeating. In fact, it has been said that those that lead don't blame and those that blame don't lead. Terry firmly believes that "accepting the consequences when you're wrong; acknowledging the mistake, apologizing when we've hurt someone, having empathy for others, and learning to forgive others" – are all traits of someone who takes responsibility in life. It's important and necessary.

In Terry's chiropractic world, he is particularly aware of people who make unhealthy choices that ultimately tear the body down. Research shows us that only 5-10% of our health is due to our DNA (genetics). The other 90-95% is all about choices. We have the power to choose good or bad health. Oftentimes, people – instead of taking responsibility for their poor choices – prefer to immerse themselves in the victim role. By doing that they surrender all their power as they continue to decline in health because they're not willing to do the work to improve. It's exceptionally frustrating for a 'hands-on' fixer like Terry to do everything in his power to help improve a patient's health and mobility – only to have the progress eroded by the lack of partnership and effort in the patient. Simple choices made every day will either lead to good health or poor health. He thrives on helping people understand the power that they hold – and then watch them transform their own lives with healthy choices and chiropractic care.

Forming good habits includes making choices that take into account other people's wellbeing - as well as our own. Having watched his own dad's health decline because he wouldn't give up the rich food and indulgences he enjoyed – Terry is determined not be a walking contradiction to his talk. While giving sensible advice to his patients on health, exercise and diet, Bob simply did not walk the talk, and Terry wants to do things differently. It is much more sensible to prevent illness by making healthy choices than to fix what's broken – later. Being healthy is really just a daily commitment to making good choices.

Terry believes that habits are one of the biggest keys to success and health in life. He feels strongly that they are what delineate that fine line between winning and losing – between success and failure. This poem about habits is one he refers to and reads often.

YOU ARE WHAT YOU REPEATEDLY DO

**The beginning of a habit is like an invisible thread.
Every time you repeat the act you strengthen the strand.
You add to it another filament with each repetition,
until it becomes a great cable
and binds you irrevocably to each thought and act.**

**First you make your habits
and then they make you.**

**Your thoughts lead you to your purpose.
Your purpose always manifests into action.
Your actions form your habits.
Your habits determine your character,
and your character fixes your destiny.**

Your habits are either the best of servants or the worst of masters.

Orison Swett Marden

In the course of Terry's intensely full life, he recently formulated this checklist as a reminder to himself and others – of the habits that help us to climb life's metaphorical mountains:

Habits of a Champion

1. Self-Discipline – Self-discipline is the ability to make yourself do what needs to be done, when it should be done, whether you feel like it or not. It is very difficult to build any other good habits without this key element, for self-discipline is the key to self-mastery. Every act of self-discipline strengthens every other discipline and will help you to build the other habits that are important for becoming a champion.

2. Positive Self Talk – The things that you say to yourself will direct your life. If you wake up and say to yourself, "I don't feel well" or something equally limiting, you are probably not going to have a good day. If you wake up and tell yourself, "I feel great. It is going to be a great day," then your day will likely be much better. Listen to what you are saying to yourself. Are you building yourself up or are you tearing yourself down? Your inner voice is powerful in determining your health - and that positive attitude has shown to increase and strengthen the body's T cells – which are the key mechanisms in overcoming various factors that contribute to disease and illnesses of all kinds.

3. Attitude of Gratitude – Be thankful! One exercise for developing this habit is to take a piece of paper and on it, make 3 columns. Label the first column "Things," the second column "People," and the 3rd column "Other" (other = freedom, opportunity, friendship, love, intelligence, abilities, health, talents, peace, faith, God, experiences, kindness). Write the things that you are grateful for under each column as they fit. Read the list over at least three times a day. Being thankful and saying thank you are two habits of people who have discovered what it means to succeed in life. Gratitude becomes an affirming habit.

4. Be Goal Oriented – Before you make anything happen in your life, you have to have direction. Goals help you develop a vision for your life. Successful people write down their goals and they review that list regularly. For accountability purposes they also share their goals with others - making it that much more difficult to give up on. Create a vision for your life. When you are constantly thinking about where you want to go and what you want to achieve, you will have a much better chance of making that happen.

5. A Willingness to Take Action/Risk – Dreams and goals are important but without action they are empty. Having vision and executing action on those

goals will help you find success in all you do. Most of us fall short of ever reaching our potential because we wish our dreams would come true but don't actually "do" anything to help the process. Coupling goals with proper action will help you to close this gap. Are you afraid of failure? The champions are the ones who are willing to take the risk and put themselves in a position to take that winning shot. They are the ones who are willing to challenge themselves to get out of that comfort zone and see how much better they can be every day.

6. Have a Strong Desire to Learn and to Grow – The great coach and legend, John Wooden, who passed away recently, said during his 90s "I still like to read and I am going to continue to learn and grow for as long as I live. No matter what my capabilities are, I want to wake up each day and do the best I can. I cannot do that if I don't continue to grow and learn." We need to challenge ourselves to grow. If you are not getting better in life, you are getting worse; you never just stand still. Champions are always learning and growing.

7. A Willingness to Accept Responsibility – Accepting responsibility for your own mistakes allows you to grow. Those that play "the blame game" will never rise to the top and become true champions. Champions don't blame others but instead, they resolve to overcome their mistakes by personally improving.

8. Live by the Golden Rule – Treat others in the way that you would like to be treated. This really is "golden." It is a simple secret of life: what you give you will receive. If you are giving love, you will receive more love. If you are giving friendship, you will have more friends. If you are a better team player, you will be on a better team. A true champion understands the importance of living by the golden rule.

9. Good Time Management – Either you master your time or time becomes your master. Do you use your time wisely? Do you spend too much time with unimportant activities and then run out of time for the really important concerns in your life? Time management is about being able to prioritize and keep the big picture in mind. Spending your time wisely is a critical habit that will help you to improve and reach your true potential in life.

10. Live in the Moment – To become a champion in whatever you are doing, you need to stay in the moment. Present time consciousness is one of the

keys to be successful in all areas of your life. I have learned that when I am with a patient in my office I must block out all other thoughts and give my best to that patient. I try to make each and every adjustment the best adjustment that I possibly can make. My patients deserve my best. When I am coaching I must be 100% present to give my players my best. And when I come home from work at the end of the day I must be there in that moment for my family. I once had an athlete that I coached at Pepperdine who was one of the best pure athletes I have ever worked with, but he never really went as far as I believe he could have. The reason is that he could not let go of the last play. He would make a mistake and then he would be stuck thinking about the mistake (a bad pass, or a missed shot) and that negativity would dominate and adversely impact the rest of his game. He could not stay in the moment. When we carry baggage around from mistakes in the past, we impede our ability to enjoy the moment. Mistakes are learning opportunities that can be used in the present. On the flip side, when you worry too much about what might happen tomorrow you paralyze yourself. Staying in the moment will help you to become the champion that is inside you.

The 10 Habits of a Champion have proven to be important bedrocks for Terry's pursuit of excellence. "Excellence Orientation" is about waking up and focusing on being the best person you can be – every day. In time, excellence becomes a habit.

Terry Schroeder took American Water Polo out of a quagmire of irrelevance to sit-up-and-take-note relevance in their historically significant Olympic Gold Medal Final Games against powerhouse Yugoslavia in 1984 and 1988.

Having suffered from 12 long thirsty years of lack-luster performance, USA Men's Water Polo – under the captaincy of Terry Schroeder - finally proved to the world that they could win a gold medal again. The last time they had achieved this was in 1904, and their presence on the Olympic podium since then was a rarity until the Schroeder force came into effect in the 1980s.

After making the United States proud in 1984 and 1988, it would take another 20 years before the Schro effect would once again elevate USA Water Polo to an Olympic Gold Medal Final. In 2008, under Terry's astute head-coaching direction, USA shocked the Eastern European regulars by toppling Serbia to make it into the Gold Medal Final against Hungary. The common denominator in all three of these Gold Medal Final Games was the Schroeder leadership. Of course 1980 could have been the 4th moment of pride – given the fact that the USA was one of the favorites to take the Gold Medal that year - had the boycott not occurred.

It's not just the Olympics where Terry has excelled. His contribution as head coach at his alma mater, Pepperdine University in California, has been exemplary. In 1997 he guided the team to the pinnacle of the game at that level by winning the National Collegiate Athletic Association crown.

Fellow Olympic teammate, Gary Figueroa, said, "Terry holds a decade of United States Water Polo under his wing as a player, and another chapter as a coach. He has few equals in American Water Polo".

Having been one of the best water polo players in the world, the respect Terry garners as a coach is made exponentially stronger because his players know that he teaches from experience. It's not impractical theory he's meting out; he's relating skills and tactics that he has perfected in the water – and his ability to dive in with his charges and show them the brilliance of a maneuver – gives him immediate credibility.

But what is uniquely special about Terry's leadership is his willingness to lead from behind – to be last. It's about being of service to something greater than him. The most effective leaders, in Terry's opinion, always focus on others and not on themselves. To that end, he cleans up with the players after practice and arrives early to help set up. He's in the trenches with them – willing and able to do everything that he asks of them.

This style of leadership requires trust, respect and love from the top down and from the bottom up. While coaching the USA team in 2008 – it worked beautifully and the team performed above expectations - bringing home an Olympic silver medal.

For Terry, the Olympics uphold so many critical, valuable components of life. Every four years, a divisive world joins together in harmony and in peace. Opposing nationalities put down their weapons and their caustic vitriol. Instead of fighting and killing each other, they join in a miraculously unifying event that upholds the very best human ideals. That is why the United States 1980 Olympic boycott still hurts Terry so egregiously. The reasons for the boycott were about conflict and threats. Imagine the healing power that could have been affected if all the athletes from conflict-ridden nations could have come together in 1980 and shown the world a better version of their politicians. It was a missed opportunity of epic proportions.

For that reason, Terry is a staunch upholder of the principle of separating sports from politics. Back in 1986, he was part of the Ambassador Tour promoting the contention that politics has no place in the world of sports. That is why the Goodwill Games has that meaningful title. Sport has to have as its fundamental foundation the spirit of good will to all people and nations. It's not about land, politics, power and greed. It's about people who are enormously gifted – striving for excellence while displaying some of the best attributes of the human race.

Titanic German Olympic water polo player, Frank Otto, endorses Terry's opinion, but he's quick to point out how that lofty ideal will never happen in reality. He recently said, "Politics should never be the death of a sport, but the problem is that politics and governments finance sport. The rules are made by those who pay." It's a disappointing theory.

Adversity is a powerful phenomenon and it doesn't discriminate. At times we create our own adversity and then there are difficulties over which we have absolutely no control. Adversity affects the individual as well as the collective – regardless of race, nationality or station in life. When adversity hits a team or group, there is a sense of unity as everyone works together to overcome it. That is one of the aspects of "team" life that Terry truly came to love. When everybody is working for the same goal and committed to do his part, pulling together is a natural reaction. Collectively, when the team is unified, obstacles do not seem nearly as daunting, and can be overcome with shared effort.

Dealing with adversity individually is far more challenging because of the fear that emanates from the sense of isolation. Losing heart and becoming discouraged within that isolation is an understandable human reaction. The reality is that adversity is a part of life for all of us. Nobody is immune from suffering – but it is through the fire that we can become much stronger humans. Martin Luther King Jr. said, "The ultimate measure of a man is not where he stands in moments of comfort and convenience, but where he stands in times of challenge and controversy."

Terry adds to that: "During challenging times and adversity, there is immense opportunity for substantial growth. If we can climb that mountain or surmount the wall, there are great rewards waiting. In overcoming the challenges we face, we learn much about ourselves - and what we are really capable of accomplishing in life. We also gain valuable tools that will serve us for the rest of our lives."

Terry articulates his challenges: "I finally overcame the adversity I created in my life by making some positive choices and reconnecting with my goals. I had become stuck in a bad place and had allowed my feelings of loneliness and depression to dictate how I moved forward. When I started asking for help, I was creating a new team: a team of peers who could support me, push me and encourage me to be a better man. We were not designed to overcome adversity alone. By creating a new team and aligning with my goals, I reconnected with God and began to figure out who I was and who I really wanted to be. Obviously, Lori was crucial in that process. Her love and commitment to me and to our family saved me from destroying myself. I learned a great deal from her and watched how she overcame adversity within our own marriage. Adversity ultimately defines who we become as men and women. Every person will fall down at some time. Our destiny is not about the fall but about how we pick ourselves up; what we become once we are again standing. While I learned a lot as a water polo player, many of those lessons proved to be minuscule in the course of my lifetime. The Olympic boycott and losing big games is really not critical adversity when I put things into proper perspective. When I look back on the times of real adversity in my life - often the issues that I created by making poor choices - I realize what a vital part of my journey they were. They helped me to find my way back to being the man I wanted to become."

Between the messages Terry received from his parents, the lessons he's learned in his life, and the impact different coaches and mentors have had on him, he's evolved into one of life's great role models. He's made his mistakes, but regardless of the size of the infractions, he's owned them, and taken responsibility. Not afraid to hold himself accountable for each one of his mistakes, Terry has asked for forgiveness on every count, and done things differently thereafter. In so doing, he has found a grace that is deep within his soul, and that he feels can only come from a divine place.

Luke 12:48 says, "Much is required from the person to whom much is given." This is a challenge to all of us to step up our game. Terry Schroeder has led a full and blessed life – a life full of successful adventures and incredible experiences. He could have taken a radically different path if he'd succumbed to human weaknesses and instant self-gratification push buttons. Talented, handsome and smart, he could have fallen into the Californian vanity trap with red convertible sports cars and a vacuous playboy lifestyle. Instead, he steered himself away from the temporary sugary high of the candy, invested in a grueling training schedule, and reached for the Olympic dream with the

Igor Milanović

purest of intentions. Thereafter, he sought a life of meaningful purpose with a close, loving family, and a chiropractic business that is all about helping others who are in pain.

In complete compatibility with the "Swifter, Higher, Stronger" Olympic motto, Terry's humility has always propelled him towards a life of service to others – and choices that have fulfilled him immeasurably. It continues to be his fervent hope that elite athletes – through the opportunity of that most noble of pursuits – the Olympic Games – continue to show the world the best traits of the human race.

Fellow Olympic Head Coach Ratko Rudić – upon heading out to the Rio 2016 Olympics for his 11th participation in the Olympic Games (2 as a player and 9 as a coach) – says of the Games: "The magic of the Olympics is always the same. The whole world watches, and winning an Olympic medal is not comparable to any other competition. Every four years these athletes are ready to produce the best athletic show on earth."

While countries and politicians fight, and lost people wreak apocalyptic destruction, gifted athletes have the choice to shine a light where there is darkness. The Olympic flame represents harmony and goodwill to all people – a magnificent sentiment that is conveyed by every Olympic athlete.

Human relationships are sacrosanct and that value proposition has never been lost on Terry. The water polo fraternity, in particular, has brought into Terry's life people of immense substance whose qualities have enriched and supplemented his life. During his playing and coaching days, administrators, coaches, team managers, teammates, opponents and players have weaved an extraordinary and indelible impression on a man who has always been receptive to their gifts. It is through these human relationships that Terry has listened, absorbed and discovered the limitless potential of love.

In 2008, when Terry was the USA Water Polo head coach visiting Belgrade, Serbia with the USA team – he shared an illuminating evening with his old water polo friend, Igor Milanović who represented Yugoslavia with distinction in the 1984 and 1988 Olympic Games. Both men had shared the joy and the heartbreak of those electrifying two gold medal final games that changed and shaped their lives forever. Once they had finished jostling with each humorously, it became evident that the passing years had given them an enlightening perspective that was so much healthier than the perspective they had held in their Olympic playing days.

Under the light of the bright, silver moon, Igor and Terry talked well into the balmy night – appreciating the commonality and the inviolable bond they shared. Both these strong, passionately intense men had striven for the Olympic gold medal with all their hearts, minds and souls. They longed for it so badly that they could taste the desire: it consumed their young lives insatiably.

While Igor attained two gold medals in their playing days, Terry attained two silver medals, but what Igor shared with Terry that night resonated powerfully with him: Igor explained to Terry how desiring and longing for "more" – even though he had two gold medals – did not end with the Olympics. He had become so programmed to keep striving for "more" – that his programming engine didn't know how or when to turn off. It had taken Igor years to recognize that he had become so consumed in his journey that he had lost perspective of life in general.

For years, Igor struggled to find a sense of balance in his life. He shared with Terry how one day, true perspective smacked him in the face: "Happiness was right in front of my face, with my wife and kids!" he said. There was no longer any need to fight for more in his life. It was a watershed moment in which his life's big picture became patently clear.

From that moment on, Igor concentrated on allowing himself to flourish as a husband and a father - and for the first time – he experienced real contentment. Today, Igor is a happy, well-balanced man who leads a good and honorable life in Serbia. The nugget of gold elucidated from that experience was about training oneself to fully live in the moment – absorbing the value of the present. Sadly, those precious moments were cut short for Igor as he lost his wife to cancer recently. This was another painful lesson about the relevance of staying in the moment and enjoying each day with the people we love.

Terry relished those rare, enlightening evenings where different circumstances and the luxury of time allowed him to make those kinds of soul connections with his former water polo adversaries.

Frank Otto, the powerful German athlete whom Terry faced in the 1984, 1988 and 1992 Olympics, recounts finally being able to converse with his American adversary without being rushed off the platform after a game. "The special thing about water polo", he says, "is that even though we played really hard against each other in the water, we still held tons of respect for each other out of the water. The first time I was finally able to enjoy a long conversation with Terry was years after our Olympic playing days – in Italy when he was head coach of the USA team heading for Beijing 2008. I was assistant coach on the Australian team at the time. I had always remembered and respected Terry for being a tough, great player – but most importantly because he was a gentleman who played fairly. Those gentlemanly qualities came through again while we were talking. I asked Terry for a helping hand and some advice for my daughter who lives in the USA. He didn't hesitate to give me his support. Honestly, it didn't surprise me. That's the player I knew in the Olympics and he has remained a gentleman - always."

Frank went on to say, "Terry was an absolutely outstanding player in every Olympic U.S. team. He was respected big time because he was not only that great player who was impossible to stop, but in all our Olympic matches - even the most important ones - he always played fairly."

The friendship and mentorship that Ken Bastian offered Terry during his short lifetime influenced him markedly when it came to finding balance and a healthier perspective.

Through all of life's shifts, Ken maintained perspective; he knew what was important to him and he always moved forward with a clear determination of his priorities. When Terry was struggling with seeing the "big picture" after the 1992 Olympics, Ken's wisdom helped him to gain a clearer perspective; that he had an extraordinarily special wife, a daughter on the way, and his entire career as a chiropractor in front of him. It was a case of Terry discovering who he really wanted to be. Tragically and ironically, while driving his car and minding his own business, Ken's big picture was obliterated by the truck that hit him head-on. His

Frank Otto

death was a massive wake-up call to Terry - to appreciate each day more fully; to define his priorities and pursue the life he really wanted - for therein lay the key to a much more fulfilled life.

From his younger days where his entire world was fixated around achieving an Olympic Gold Medal, Terry has mercifully evolved into a multi-dimensional person who is much more fulfilled. While he still nurtures a healthy respect for the Olympics and all that it represents, he is no longer consumed by the one-dimensional addiction that was eating him alive. Today Terry completely appreciates the simplicity of relaxing with Lori and the girls in their backyard, having friends over for a BBQ, or just making time to sit quietly and pray.

Central to Terry's happiness is the quality of human relationships he has in his life, and his capacity to fully appreciate the gifts of friendship and love that those provide. He says with absolute conviction, "being loved and having meaningful relationships with my family and friends is by far the most important aspect of my life. I have been blessed with an amazing family and this nourishes my soul on a daily basis. Love will sustain us life-long."

It turns out that being on a relentless pursuit is exhausting and potentially fruitless, and it is Lori who has taught Terry to run less and savor the simple joys in life - more. That new perspective has given Terry a more measured sense of gratitude for his Olympic accomplishments, and an even greater appreciation of the deep bonds of friendship with his Olympic teammates and former game-time adversaries. This appreciation of relationships has guided him in his chiropractic practice as well. In his daily work as a healer he has found remarkable gratification in connecting with and inspiring many of his patients to live a healthier and more meaningful life.

Particularly pertinent to Terry as he continues to swim through life is the valuable opportunity he has to mentor future generations of water polo athletes. At Pepperdine University he has become a second father to many young men, and it's a responsibility that he thrives upon – to be able to positively impact them beyond the pool so that they are better equipped to take on the responsibility of being decent citizens. It is a person's integrity that will take them far in life, and if Terry can help nourish that growth, his life's work is made vastly more satisfying.

Terry's mentoring achievements are probably best encapsulated in the theme of actor Sidney Poitier's brilliant portrayal of a teacher who earns his students' respect in the movie *To Sir, With Love*. Poitier's quiet humility and the example he sets are the winning formulas that give him immense credibility from his students.

Extra dimensionally – the impact of one solidly decent person goes further than that. The most important ingredient in Terry's life is love – that capacity to open one's heart and to give love, without constraint. That gift is so much more powerful than anything else. The words from the movie *Goodbye, Mr. Chips*, resonate deeply. Put simply, they are:

"Did you fill the world with love?"

The answer is: Terry Schroeder sure has.

SWIMMING THROUGH LIFE

Terry Schroeder and the
USA Olympic Men's Water Polo Team

Diana Addison Lyle

IMPACT PUBLICATIONS

1 Corinthians 13:3-5

I may give away everything I have, and even give up my body to be burned
—but if I have no love, this does me no good. Love is patient and kind; it
is not jealous or conceited or proud; love is not ill-mannered or selfish or
irritable; love does not keep a record of wrongs.

Made in the USA
San Bernardino, CA
20 December 2019